HER UPSTAIRS

BY

SUSANNA WARDROP

Published by New Generation Publishing in 2024

ISBN: 9781835634080

New Generation Publishing
www.newgeneration-publishing.com

INTRODUCTION

Does it really matter anymore how much you or your family are worth? Does it really matter what your ancestors did for a living or what university they went to? Who really cares about all of that crap anyway? Are we meant to judge a person on the content of their character instead of the size of their wallet? Isn't it more important to focus on where you are going in your life, rather than where you have come from? Why do so many people think they are superior to others? Why does ones address make such a difference? Why does the make of one's car make you a better candidate in life?

We were taught in infant school that everyone is equal. It doesn't matter what you are or where you have come from. We are all human beings. Why are you then sneered upon and belittled when you are employed by someone who just happens to have more money than you do?

Why aren't we equal human beings then? Why does money turn some people who are educated, cultured, and who should know better, into nasty, bitter, selfish people? Of course, not all wealthy people are sneering snobs. I have worked for some lovely, kind, rich people, who have enough to last them for several lifetimes, but still down to earth people. There are those who have worked very hard to be successful, and as such, are pleasant to work for. They can talk to anyone and empathise with them and mean what they say. Some of them really are the salt of the earth, good people, who have and show proper class. Class as in respecting a person and their feelings, respecting what you do for them, and respecting you for being yourself. And then there are the others...

Selfish, uncaring, and utterly revolting humans who only see labels. Those who only focus on lineage and breeding. How Daddy made his money or what pile his family owned while growing up. What schools they attended or where they went for a holiday or what grocery store is suitable to order from. It makes you laugh really, people who think they are so important and better than us common, working-class people. What makes them such obnoxious snobs who should surely know better? Are they born horrible and smug, or does the money do it to them?

I believe that there are no excuses. People can come from awful families and situations and turn their life around, just as others can go in the opposite direction. They can become greedy and lazy—I refer to them as 'scumbag millionaires'.

I was eight years old when I immigrated to England in the 1970s. I came from one of the large Commonwealth countries and it was modern and sophisticated compared to the small rural town that I had been brought to. It felt as though it was still stuck in the 1950s and my school days were filled with ignorant comments and constant teasing. My mother always told me to ignore them and laugh, as they were only words, but they were hurtful and humiliating.

In the end I laughed at the small-town mindset. Today I reflect on that time, when bullying and taunts were seen as a rite of passage and disputes were settled with a punch up in the school yard and all was well afterwards. It helped to build my thick skin and I am glad I experienced that time in my childhood as it helped to prepare my way into adulthood and being able to handle the reality of living in the real world. Those days of tears and ridicule made me into the person I am today, a strong woman with a backbone, who is not afraid to stand up and say it as it is.

When I was ten years old, I had two part-time jobs. I

walked dogs after school and then cleaned a private office on Sunday morning for my Mum's friend. Kids wouldn't be able to do that nowadays and I think it's a shame as it builds character and a great work ethic, but I imagine that today most ten-year olds wouldn't want to know. As you can guess, I hated school and I couldn't wait to leave, leave the small town too and try and make my way on my own. Mum always encouraged me to be happy and to live my dreams; and the day after I left school at sixteen, I left home.

I had originally longed to become a nurse when I was younger, until the day my sister had come home with her knee cap hanging off after falling on a broken pop bottle. It flapped as she walked and was smeared in blood, and you could see the bone underneath. At school I had learned to type and had my heart set on being a secretary, however, that dream ended when I failed my shorthand course. I didn't fancy attending the awful polytechnic that became a dumping ground for most of the area's unemployable school leavers.

So, I moved to London and stayed with an old family friend for few days; then I got a full-time job at a well-known department store and moved into a flat with four other girls.

A year passed by, and I wanted to go travelling and soon found myself back in the country of my birth. I found work as a chauffeur, and then in an office working nine to five and it was great to be back amongst the familiar streets and old friends. But I was bored and feeling that I was missing out on life that I hadn't even found yet. The sedate new existence wasn't for me, and I wanted adventure, culture, and more spontaneity.

My Mum was living in London and died suddenly one day in the summer. I knew I had to return to the UK and this time, I knew I wanted to stay and learn to love this fascinating country, my ancestral home, and my home to this day. Once again, I stayed with an old family friend in London until I decided what to do with my life and I started to look around for work. In 1990 I started to work as a cook and housekeeper. It showed me what the other people are like.

"Make yourself an honest man, and then you may be sure there is one less rascal in the world." – Thomas Carlyle

"Try not to become a man of success but rather try to become a man of value." – Albert Einstein

"Be strong and courageous. Do not be afraid; do not be discouraged." – Joshua 1:9

LONDON
CHAPTER 1
THE DOCTOR

I had never been to Highbury before, and I was very intrigued and excited as I walked along the crooked pavement towards the elegant street of terraced Georgian houses. The area is now one of the most sought after and very expensive parts of London, with a number of posh shops and restaurants, but then it was still a bit shabby here and there. On the northern edge of the city near the Angel, there was a great street market and from there to my new abode was about a dozen lively and popular pubs. During the Elizabethan and Restoration periods the area was open fields and countryside where feuding nobles and aristocrats would meet to fight duels with pistols drawn at dawn. Now a great area for nightlife, it was awaiting the gentrification it deserved, and I would spend the next five years exploring and visiting as many of its famous public houses as I could. My favourites included the Hope and Anchor where many iconic bands had their first gigs and further along the High Street, The King's Head theatre, the Edward VIII and further afield, The George Robey and The Ten Bells. Fabulous!

I was so lucky to find and secure my first housekeeping job and flat so quickly and I immediately felt at home and bonded with my new boss, who made me feel very welcome. She was very kind and the only one of my employers who had sympathised with the recent loss of my mother, and she made a point of reaching out to me with a shoulder of comfort if I needed it. She was very high up in the NHS and had spent years working very hard and striving to try to make a difference in the institution. She would leave for work at the crack of dawn and not get home until very late for most of the week. Her two sons were at boarding school in the Midlands and her husband worked in the city, so I only ever saw them when they entertained on Friday nights. Back then I wasn't an experienced cook, but I was trusted on menu creations and party ideas, and there was never any interference in the kitchen. Only God knows how I ever pulled it off, but the dinners were always a great success and very much appreciated by my new boss, who was the only person ever in my entire career to bring me into the dining room and make a point of telling the guests that I had made the food that they were eating. It was the first and last time that I would get to work for such a selfless and loving woman, someone who liked to help others and nurture their aspirations rather than take the usual route of being smug and selfish and loathe to helping anyone without reward.

Part of the package of my new job was a basement flat and a little car to use for shopping and errands and I was allowed to use it on weekends and while off on holiday. I could drive an automatic, but I had never driven a manual; I had no money to take lessons, and I was scared to tell my boss. I was really scared to tell her that I had never even driven in England before and I was having sleepless nights about it. However, one morning as I unloaded the dishwasher there was a knock on the front door. I opened it to find a cheery older man who introduced himself as my new driving instructor and behind him, parked outside of the house, was a brand-new Renault with the little plastic BSM dome sitting on its roof. My boss had booked me full lessons to learn to drive in London and had also paid for the driving test when I was ready to take it. Wow! How nice of her! How thoughtful of her to think of my safety – can you imagine that happening these days? I doubt that an employer would hire you if you couldn't drive, even if you were the best candidate and they liked you. Usually, they will favour the one who will cost them the least amount of money. I passed my driving test a few weeks later and I was given the keys to a brand new Micra. I felt so pleased with myself and happy to have found such a fantastic new boss and I started to imagine all the new skills that I could learn and master while I gained experience and had fun in my new surroundings. I started to love my life again. It was a world away from where I had come from, and the recent driving lessons made me look back and reflect on how far I had already advanced.

I had been classed as a professional driver in the country of my birth and I had taught myself to drive and passed the test when I was eighteen years old. A year after that I passed an advanced driving test and found employment driving limousines and I spent the next few years driving anxious brides to their weddings and intoxicated teenagers to their high school proms. I have lost count of how many times I watched the bride in the back of the car produce a flask from beneath the bouquet or a joint from the cleavage of her dress and proceed to get as high as a kite, then witness a total transformation when arriving at the church and the awaiting ceremony. One started to cry and become hysterical, and I had to pull over just before we got to the church and help her to fix her hair and makeup and I never forgot her as she added a huge tip to my wages as a thank you. I hope her marriage worked out. If I had had my way, I would have talked her out of it and driven her far, far away to save herself from the misery she must have known was coming her way.

The children were the same, all smiles and best manners when you first picked them up and then within minutes they were effing and blinding and chugging the booze straight from the open neck of the bottle. You would find all sorts of things when cleaning out the car at the end of a shift, like various types of narcotics, discarded knickers and under garments and once I found a really expensive ladies clutch bag that was all white leather and crystals but full of vomit, so not worth my time trying to return it to the animal who owned it. I could feel and hear the contents sloshing around as I threw it in the garbage and wondered what sort of female would do that.

The groups of rowdy men that I drove to some of the large sporting venues were almost as bad in terms of drunkenness and their lewd talk, describing their girlfriends or wives and man about town encounters hardened my heart and made it easy to accept their tips, each trying to outdo one another at throwing the cash at the novelty of a woman driver. If I ever found a lost wallet stuffed with cash after a long shift of testosterone filled bullshit, they most certainly would not have got it back. Payback!

A few months of driving the ultra-stretch limousines – which were just large taxis with bars and ashtrays – I was promoted to a nicer car, which meant having a nicer clientele to deal with. The car cost more to hire and could only fit three in the back seat so it was usually rented by more affluent people for more exclusive and glamorous events. The class of car and venue may have moved up the ladder a notch or two, but the antics and debauched bonhomie of a typical wealthy party goer had not.

One night I was sent to an address in the oldest and most exclusive part of town and picked up a couple and took them to a private marina, about thirty minutes' drive along the coast. They seemed like respectable people and not much conversation was had between us during the drive, but when we arrived and there, amongst the deluxe yachts and other pleasure boats, was the biggest vessel with a lively party on board and in full swing. I had been hired to wait and bring back the same couple to the original address, so I had brought a book with me to read while I waited for them. A few hours went by, and I was approached by one of the party guests, a young woman who was near my age and she asked me if I would like a drink or to use the facilities and would I like to accompany her onto the boat.

We were not meant to gatecrash any of the customers' frivolities but if they insisted on offering their hospitality to the driver and invited us to partake in the lavish merrymaking, then we had our own discretion to use and to join in and party if we wanted to. I quite fancied a trip to the buffet and a long cool drink of something, so I jumped at the chance and made my way along the jetty and up the ramp to what was the most beautiful and luxurious floating palace I had ever seen. The gleaming teak decks were littered with massive multicoloured silk pillows and numerous quests were lounging about on them and each had their own ice bucket and bottle of champagne. Paper lanterns enclosed the twinkling lights that swayed with the breeze and cool jazz music flowed from the loud speakers that were strategically placed around the decks. Down inside the cabin were the buffet tables, laden with steaming trays of dim sum and other delicious Chinese dishes and a whole table had been dedicated to a lavish spread of desserts and cakes. It was a gorgeous warm summer evening, and the moon was almost full. You could not have had a more perfect setting for a twilight soiree.

I collected a tray and filled it with little heaps of the tasty looking dishes and although I was invited to stay on board and eat at one of the tables, I decided not to and made my way back to the car. I took off my jacket and sat down on the grass and ate the food, the solitude and approaching darkness making the impromptu picnic seem all the more intimate and exceptional even though I was all alone. I moved back into the car when it started to cool off and settled in the back seat with the book that I had brought with me. The book was very easy to read and from time to time the peals of laughter and raised voices of the party could be heard in the night air. I eventually started to struggle to read the words in the poor light of the car's interior and felt myself starting to doze off and gradually, drifted away into a deep and tranquil sleep.

I woke up in the morning with a pounding headache and noticed that the lights were still on in the car. At that moment

I began to feel that strange feeling you get in your ass when you know you are in grave danger, or you know something terrible is about to happen. It's like a cramp but in your bum hole and it starts to shoot up into your belly. I prayed for the car to start and turned the key in the ignition and a sweet feeling of relief rolled over me as I heard the engine roar into life. I let it idle for a few moments before I dusted off my wrinkled jacket and put it on and I slowly made my way along the path to the boat, hoping to see some signs of life and wondering what the proper time was.

At first sight of the boat, I thought that I had taken the wrong path and was on the wrong jetty, or I had somehow overslept, and it had sailed off. And then I saw that I was in the right place and the boat was in a total state of disarray. A few lifeless bodies lay on the grass beside the water, broken bottles and glasses and half-eaten plates of food that was now swarming with flies were dotted about. The bunting that had adorned the railings of the boat had been torn off and was now sadly floating in the water and I could see strange splashes of brown paint running down its side, which on closer inspection turned out to be vomit. In fact, vomit seemed to be everywhere and a few of the guests had the unfortunate fate of waking up in it and having to wear it home.

I walked up the gang plank onto the boat and was met with more carnage and depravity. Several more guests were out cold and, in the nude, or in various stages of undress, and the whole cabin that had been used for the buffet had been smashed to pieces and food and broken crockery had been strewn throughout the decks. There were large piles of empty bottles and more large piles of vomit and clothing. The smell was horrendous, and my head was still pounding, and for a minute I felt the swirly and frothy contents of my own stomach start to hit the back of my throat. It didn't help when at that moment, one of the guests rose up zombie style and proceeded to be sick over the side of the boat. The tide was coming in fast, and everything was swaying and bobbing, and the motion of the waves lapped the boat in time with the zombie purging itself. I felt ill at that moment, and it didn't help that I was worried about falling asleep and not driving the clients home and what sort of trouble was I going to be in with my boss at the limousine company? What excuse could I come up with and how would I be able to stop myself from throwing up all over the nice silk cushions that had survived the nocturnal destruction? I was bound to lose my job, but right then I didn't really care, and then the woman who I had driven to the marina appeared before me.

She was immaculate and her fresh set of clothing and her sleek hairdo shone in the morning sun. I expected to be chastised and ridiculed on my ability to provide the services which I was hired for, and to my surprise, she smiled at me and invited me to join her and her husband for some breakfast. I was still trying to appear normal while fighting off the effects of seasickness and I accepted her offer immediately as I knew I could relieve my symptoms with some caffeine and be able to use the facilities to discretely puke my guts up if I had to.

I made it through the meal and thanked my lucky stars that I had kept everything together as the opposite was happening right before our eyes. We could see a few of the guests stagger from the boat to begin their journey home, some arguing, some covered in food and we all nervously laughed as we watched from the cabin windows. We pretended that it was all right, just an ordinary morning and standard behaviour from your average VIP. The people I had driven there last night and now having breakfast with were the owners of the boat and had been hosting their annual party for their exclusive friends and associates. They took the events in their stride and explained that it was cheaper to host the party on the boat and less of a risk in case the party got out of hand, less risk of a scandal exposing itself, and easier to clean up afterwards. The party could be written off as expenses and then the boat could be redecorated.

They had booked the car and my services for the whole time and gave me a massive tip after I had dropped them back at their home. It's funny when the people who you think should behave a certain way, turn out to do the worst things imaginable, especially when they appear to be elite and upper class. It made me wonder what it would be like to chauffeur around the rich people in London. I assume it would be the same.

A few years had flown by, and I loved my boss and the historical neighbourhood that I was living in. The family were very tidy and orderly, and it took me no time at all to complete my daily routine of household duties. They had a pet dog who I was very fond of and the only thing that could piss me off and related to the job was this dog who sometimes liked to ransack the kitchen bin and run riot with it all over the house. I had to make sure that the bin was empty before he was allowed in the kitchen, and the bins in the bathrooms were not left all week as he would have them spread everywhere too. The area at night was alive and exciting and I explored every pub, club and cafe. Friends would come over to my little basement flat on Friday and Saturday evenings and we would drink wine before hitting the town. We would go to Camden or Angel and sometimes we would head up west and go to the clubs in the West End or slum it in King's Cross or a squat party or biker bar. We had such a fantastic time, but I am sorry to say that a lot of it has been forgotten due to the copious amounts of alcohol and various medicines that were ingested at the time. Looking back, thirty-odd years ago, I think the people and the times and what was deemed acceptable was a lot more relaxed and tolerated, and fun! Folks nowadays are very uptight and rigid and a bit boring compared to those carefree days of my youth. I am so glad that I am not young now in this world of Botox, iPhones, and PCs – the new normal. But is it? Why would you want to have stuff injected into your lips or speed date or try to influence other people on the internet? Is that what is considered to be fun these days? I want to meet people and talk to them in the flesh. If I want to meet a man, I want our eyes to meet across a crowded room full of people. I want those pheromones to kick in. I want to do it the old-fashioned way, animal attraction, sweat, hedonism. How the times have changed!

I really looked forward to the weekends. Fridays were magical in the house, and I would have had it cleaned the day before so I could spend all day shopping and then preparing the Friday night dinner. It was always special and there were always guests and the last one I did in that house stays in my mind and always makes me smile. By then I had chosen to move on as the kids would be off to university and there wouldn't be that much to do during the week. The next door's nanny had agreed to take on the extra hours as she wanted to save for her Australian adventure, and it worked out better for my boss as there were now only two of them and they were at work most of the time. That last Friday dinner almost didn't happen.

I got back late from shopping due to a security breach at Pentonville prison, which was just a few miles down the road. Traffic was heavy and had been diverted through the side streets and had caused a massive hour-long tail back; the congestion had taken me over an hour to drive two miles. Whoever had escaped from prison that day sure had no problem getting as far away from the area as possible, particularly if they were on foot. I started cooking as soon as I got in and I emptied the shopping bags and put all the ingredients out on the countertop before I ran to the loo, having held my pee in for over two hours trying not to wet the seat. I finished and went back into the kitchen and the bloody dog had not only knocked the bin over, scattering food and garbage all over the floor, he had also eaten all the lovely fresh haddock I had bought for the starter and was now having a go at the fillet of beef on the floor amongst the garbage and chewed up paper fish wrappers. I screamed at him, and he scooted to the other side of the kitchen, wagging his tail furiously and looking very pleased with himself. I started to clean up and couldn't believe it when the little bastard jumped up on to a chair and then the counter top and then made a beeline for the new pack of butter that I had put out on a clean dish. He must have known I was really mad at him, and he ran to the back door, hoping that I had left it open for him, but I hadn't. I don't know if it was sheer terror or his gastroenteritis, but he literally exploded from both ends. Doggy Diarrhoea and puke everywhere. Nice.

It took about forty minutes to clear it up and fumigate the house and then twenty minutes to get near him to calm him down. You know how a dog acts when he knows he has done something he shouldn't have; he had been hiding in the bushes and when he emerged, he was covered in his own sick and his fluffy shorts had poo on them.

I looked at the time and freaked as I had an hour to prepare three courses and no money left. Even if I dashed out to the shops again it would take me hours to get everything and back on time as my boss and her colleagues would be waltzing through the door not long after. I opened the fridge and prayed that I would find some stuff to cobble together for their dinner and I went into the dining room to the drinks cabinet and chugged down a few gulps of brandy to steady my nerves. I went back to the freezer and grabbed a packet of fish fingers and an almost out of date and freezer burnt tray of grey and ice encrusted pork chops.

Foraging in the back of the cupboards I found a bag of cake mix, quite ancient as the dry mixture had started to harden and half of the words on the packet were fading. The star of the hunt was a tin of fruit salad, and I was glad I wouldn't have to eat any of it. Knowing that this was the last time I would cook a Friday dinner, I was also shitting myself thinking that it would be awful, and my boss would think that I didn't care or think enough of them to put in a good effort. They had been so thoughtful and kind to me and I really did respect her. *Maybe I should just give up and tell her the truth?* I thought. *Maybe she would not mind and opt to take her guests out to dine instead?* Then, I thought of all the things she had done for me when she didn't have to but had done so because she had wanted to and that was the type of person she was. A few more gulps of brandy and I had made up my mind. This was going to be the best dinner I had ever made, and they would all eat it and then praise me. I also hoped that they would all be drunk by the time the food was on the table, and they wouldn't notice it anyway. The whole point of a dinner party is sharing it with friends and loved ones and if the food is good, it is even more of a bonus.

I laid the dining room table and ran down to the cellar and brought up twice as much champagne and wine as usual. I knew I would be able to delay the dinner a good thirty minutes or so, just enough time for another bottle to be opened and drank. I opened the tin of fruit salad and put it in a loaf pan and then poured golden syrup all over it. The cake mix was one of those cheap ones that don't require eggs or butter, just water and oil and I mixed it up with olive oil in the hope that it would give it a more exotic flavour. I poured it over the fruit and syrup and put it in the oven and then racked my brains about what to do with the fish fingers which would have to do as some sort of starter.

The original menu was meant to be smoked haddock terrine, beef medallions and then an elegant layer cake iced with Italian buttercream. Now it was going to be fish finger terrine, pork medallions and a cheap loaf cake covered in cheap fruit cocktail and syrup. The awful pork chops had to be good enough to substitute for the lovely beef that was, and I came up with making a thick madeira sauce to hide it with. For the terrine, I scraped as much of the orange breadcrumbs off the fish fingers as I could and mashed them with extra quantities of herbs and seasonings. I had a bag of watercress to use as a bed for the upturned terrine and some cherry tomatoes for extra garnish and camouflage. I nuked the pork chops in the microwave and cut the bones off them and then used a mug to cut around a shape from the middle of each of them. I made the madeira sauce and wondered if the candle lit table and ambient light of the dining room would help the appearance of the food. The cake was cooked and cooling, and the terrine was going to be ready in ten minutes, so I had another swig of brandy and smiled to myself knowing that my secret was safe, and nobody would know what had happened to the expensive fish and cut of beef that was inside the dog's stomach and hiding in the bottom of the kitchen bin. I put the meat on a fancy dish and poured the sauce over, covered it in foil, and popped it in the warming drawer of the oven along with the dinner plates.

The sounds of chatter and corks being pulled could be heard from where I was standing in the kitchen. As I had hoped, the numbers of bottles that I had brought up from the cellar had proved to be very appreciated and an hour had passed before the starter made its way into the dining room. As I was assembling the dishes of potatoes and assorted vegetables that would accompany the main course, one of the guests had brought the dirty plates into the kitchen for me and proceeded to tell me how delicious it was. "Divine, darling," she slurred, with what sounded like a tiny and dainty ladylike burp. I anticipated the same result in about half an hour after they had eaten the main course as I took the food into the dining room. It was quite dark, and I could see by the count of the empty bottles on the table that everyone must have been absolutely pissed. Seven guests, four empty champagne bottles and six empty bottles of Chateauneuf du Pape. The carafes of Evian water were full. Thank God they were all well and truly intoxicated!

The second round of plates were brought into the kitchen along with the serving dishes and only a few petit pois remained stuck in the remnants of the thick sauce along with a few pieces of roasted garlic. The cake looked exquisite when it was inverted on to a silver plate and the bits of fruit glistened under the twinkling candelabra. It didn't matter in the end as the diners were beyond eating anything else and instead requested Spanish coffee and glasses of port.

I looked at the truckle of Stilton cheese which sat intact on the cheeseboard and relived the events of the afternoon when the dog was on the kitchen counter and attacking the groceries. It was the only thing I had bought that he didn't destroy, and I felt like laughing. At the end of the evening and the guests were leaving, I helped them with their coats and one of them asked me for the recipe for the fish finger terrine. Could the day become anymore absurd?

I tidied up the kitchen and washed the floor and then I went down to my flat. As I stepped down the dozen or so iron stairs, I could hear noises coming from the old coal bunker, which in the old days was filled up at street level through a coal hole in the pavement. I descended the last few steps and thought that I was looking at a man who was having a piss beside my front door, but it turned out to be, on closer inspection, some old tart giving a man a blowjob. What an end to a rather hectic day at work I thought to myself. At least I did have a good old laugh. That was my last weekend at my first housekeeping job in London. I already had a new position lined up, although only a temporary one it was in a different part of the city, and I was looking forward to it. I hoped the new lady boss would be as nice and kind as the one I was leaving, and as I packed up my meagre possessions, I decided that I would miss Islington and that it would set the bar as far as job satisfaction and happiness would go. It is definitely in my top three of best and most memorable jobs.

CHAPTER 2

DUCHESS

During the last few months in Highbury, I had signed up with a few agencies that specialised in private staff. I had found my first assignment in the best and oldest magazine *The Lady*, a service I have always favoured when seeking employment, as you can select your own potential employers rather than be sent out by an agency. If you are new to an agent, they will try to talk you into their more difficult placements, and by difficult, I mean the ones that more experienced housekeepers will avoid. You can spot those by noting how long or often they advertise for staff and a high turnover usually means they are very fussy or mean, and staff won't stay long. This is something the agent is aware of, however, they will want their commission so they will send as many people as they can out for interviews, along with several other agents who will have the same troublesome clients on their books.

Today we have the internet, and you can look online at the jobs board, but back in the day it didn't exist and all you had was *The Lady* magazine, the *London Evening Standard*, private staff agencies or word of mouth. Gumtree and the like are great to look for jobs but do look out for the types of employers you don't want to work for, as many try to cut costs by not offering a proper contract or a desirable wage. There are some gems out there too, however, so just use your discretion when looking for your dream job when searching online. A proper employer will always make sure that everything is above board and transparent and your tax and national insurance contributions will be paid monthly as well as your workplace pension, and you will receive paid holidays and be subject to workers' rights.

Cash in hand jobs seem great at first but should also be avoided as you can lose everything and have no right to complain or have any compensation if the employer decides to sack you on a whim, and it is easier to have any T&Cs reneged onto their advantage. These types of employers will promise everything and deliver nothing, and you can expect to work over your agreed hours with no reimbursement and little appreciation. As you gain experience you will be able to spot the obvious and know what to look for. Don't let anyone try to bully you into a job either as it's always connected to the money and an agent will want the commission and an employer will want value for money and will, more often than not, be trying to save a buck. Go with your gut feeling and trust your instinct and rule with your head and not your heart unless you are like me and go for less stressful conditions that come with a smaller wage packet.

When you are being interviewed, try to look beyond the employer and study the housekeeper if they are present. Sometimes they are hovering around the house or doing their chores and you can tell instantly by the look on their faces if they seem happy or they can't wait to get out of there. Make a note of the state of the house and property. If you have a keen and experienced eye you can see the dirt and dust and you can smell anything that shouldn't be. A potential employer may show you the whole house to let you see how much work will be involved and if not, it could mean that it is a filthy tip, which you may not find out until your first day on the job, by which time it is too late. If their children act sullen or look at you like you have two heads it means you will be treated like a lackey by them and usually by any guest or friend of the family who comes to visit, and they will all be very well practised in the art of deception and in keeping up appearances. Lying is as natural to them as having breakfast in the morning and children learn this sort of behaviour from their parents.

Try to avoid jobs that say they want an "all-rounder", as this means you will be doing the job of four people, and all for just one wage. It's good to be flexible but don't be pressured to have to bend over backwards on a regular basis, as you will be expected to all the time. The straight forward housekeeping job will become a cook, a nanny, a chauffeur, a gardener, a PA job... and generally anything else they feel you should be doing for your wages. If you are willing to accept these positions, please make sure you know your worth before your interview and try to negotiate a wage that reflects it as you will be run ragged, and no doubt regret your choice of position.

My new situation was through an old and established agent, and I was fortunate that they did not take advantage of the fact that I was new to them, and I still only had a few years of hands-on experience. The client was an elderly lady who lived in an old mews house and had recently lost her husband who had been high up in the armed forces. She had been born in the Victorian era and had all the class and manners ingrained in her from that generations gentry. She came from old money and knew how to treat her household staff with fairness and compassion. It truly is a rare treat these days to find such a wonderful employer and she was very nice although there is a very fine line when it comes to employers and their staff. You are not their family, but you must be treated with respect and empathy and the same goes the other way.

I have found in my years of service that the people who always tell you that you are part of the family are the ones who will take out their personal crap out on you when it suits them. They tend to think that you will take any of the abuse as they are paying your wages, and it is their right to, and part of the job. I would rather work for the elderly, old money clients over the younger clients any day, as they are less maintenance, kinder, and always better educated.

My new boss, the Duchess, had been the wife of a well-known and much respected Knight of the Realm. Although her official title was Lady, I remember her and use the name Duchess as a term of endearment. She was a sweet old lady, very regal and imperious, but also kind and generous. She was living her life as though it was still 1930, and I very much admired her and enjoyed being there and in her company. After a few weeks the veil of mystery and aloofness was lifted, and she gradually warmed to me. I felt comfortable and able to be more of myself and I made her very happy by conforming to her vision and expectations of an employee circa 1930. We would spend hours chatting and sharing heartfelt stories and I looked forward to her wonderful memories of her glory days and of a lost generation and the sublime carefree days, the period between the wars and of a country quite unimaginable to what it has become. It must have been beautiful.

She lived in a very stable and secure environment and became a widow in the early 1960s. She had known all the glittering opulence until then and now she was old and frail and confined to a tiny mews house in a grand old part of London. The mews was a little shabby and forlorn, a relic from another era and waiting to be restored and modernised. It wasn't difficult to imagine it full and bustling with horses and carriages and their drivers, the original chauffeurs before the motor car. They were dirty and crowded alleyways and now they sell for millions and the mansions to which they were once tenured sell for tens of millions.

She had several staff and employed a driver when she went out once a week to get her hair done or to go to the seasonal events like the Chelsea flower show and the men's final day at Wimbledon. She had an old Rolls Royce from the seventies that was well used but pristine and it lived in a space which was next to the bedroom that I slept in. She also had a daily housekeeper who would come in twice a week to clean and then there was me who was only there to cook for her and to make sure she was safe and secure.

She had an impressive collection of art and various antiques and I loved to read the books that were in the kitchen. Apart from the cook books that were Victorian and Edwardian there were books on how to hire staff and what to look for when buying a side of beef, and how to cook during the war when there was rationing and nothing much to choose from in the shops. I read them all and to this day I can still make a tasty meal out of any leftovers or produce a nice spread for very little money.

All I had to do was cook her breakfast, lunch, and dinner, and provide elevenses and tea at four in the afternoon. I learned how to bake the perfect cake and how to make sauces and gravy that could accompany a mundane plate of food and turn it into a dish fit for a restaurant menu. I still use what I learned then when I cook today. Once you master the basic methods and practice it and then start to experiment with your own ideas, you can create anything, and anyone can be a cook. If you can follow a recipe and with your added enthusiasm, and imagination, you can achieve good or better results than you would find in your average restaurant, pub or cafe. Of course, it does help if you are interested in food and cooking in the first place. I can never understand people who say they used to be great in the kitchen but then never set foot in one again. I hate it when people will scarf down any meal you put in front of them and then have the gall to criticize your cooking afterwards, as if it was awful and disgusting in the first place. Why the hell do they eat all of it if it tastes like shit? Why do they have to be so ungrateful and rude while they are shoving it down their throats like there is no tomorrow? When this happens, you know that the food was great and that the person moaning about it usually moans about everything and they certainly could not have done better.

The Duchess always appreciated whatever was prepared and put on her plate, even if she didn't like it; she was brought up in an era when you didn't complain as it was considered fussy and petty. I wish people today were as kind and genuine as she had been as many of the younger ones are too shallow and absorbed in themselves to stop and think about what another person has taken time to create for their lazy and feckless arses.

Once a week I would walk to the supermarket to buy groceries and then load them into a taxi to bring it all back. The area was another part of London that I was not familiar with, and it turned out to be an excellent place to walk around and discover new things. During the seventeenth century when the city was thriving, this area was still countryside and wild and full of robbers and highwaymen. It gradually became more populated and small villages grew and spread together and the rural area now became one of the affluent parts of the western end of the city. There are loads of lovely walks throughout the area and the famous parks, Hyde and Green can be easily reached. I used to love finding my way to see the houses with the blue plaques, which are found on historical buildings and places of interest that notable figures of the past and present have resided in or have had a connection to, and they give the name of the person and the dates to when they would have been there. My favourite was the house that both Mama Cass and Keith Moon died in and the house that Jimi Hendrix and Handel had. I absolutely love the wild and crazy antics of all the Mitford sisters so the house where Nancy Mitford lived was also great to visit on a regular basis. Florence Nightingale and Lord Horatio Nelson lived nearby, and Somerset Maugham and PG Wodehouse's former homes would round off the walk and inspire me to seek out the blue plaques in other parts of London. A few miles further and I was spoiled for choice and the homes of Mozart and Mendelssohn, TE Lawrence, Vivian Leigh, Sir Isaac Newton and Lord Kitchener of Khartoum vied for my attention. Another great walk was down the road and up to Buckingham Palace and the Mall. Further along was Westminster and the Abbey, St James's Park and Big Ben. If I went a different way I could easily get to Piccadilly and spend hours window shopping.

The Duchess had some beautiful and rare art, along with unique and traditional heirlooms on display around the tiny house. A Constable graced the wall next to her favourite armchair in the sitting room and a pair of bronze art deco statues shared tables with different Lalique creations of coloured glass. Off the kitchen, the old larder was home to her silver canteens of antique cutlery and her collection of Clarice Cliff tea and coffee sets and downstairs near the entrance was a little gilt table, covered with greeting cards and ornate formal invitations and various tokens and small framed photographs of senior royals. An adjacent cabinet held her dead husband's collection of World War Two medals that he had earned and several old and framed sepia photographs of her childhood almost a century ago, a little girl dressed in a white smock and holding her beloved pet cat. It is enthralling to see a person's life pass by in the form of their cherished possessions and memories, their prized personal objects and old and faded photo albums. Mementos, a gift from a long dead, paintings of ancestors, and houses long ago demolished and forgotten – a vignette across the passages of time. Much more meaningful and sincere treasure to admire and exhibit, an array of a life well lived and loved, and personal items far more valuable than anything money can buy.

Today the designer label is king. If it is expensive and comes from Harrods or some other high end department store, then it is automatically considered the epitome of taste and ultra chic as not everyone will be able to afford it. It is as if nothing is as good as how smug feels. It's all about the brand and the price tag rather than if it is practical or functional and the old saying is so true and that is "a fool and their money is easily parted". Give me the minimalist look any day over a house full of overpriced crap that people think impresses other people who have no taste or clue, just like themselves. Sad people who buy *Country Life* and *Modern Interior* just to put out for display on the ugly coffee table, trying hard to create some sort of impression for other idiots who have nothing in common with the countryside or know anything about interiors or design. The type of snob who has never done anything in their life, yet born into money and privilege, and says they have an eye for design or is an expert on art or is some sort of consultant. I suppose the arrogant twats have to come up with something to make themselves relevant and more interesting and intelligent than they really are. And it makes for good conversation while attending their various and pretentious luncheons and dinner parties, each one of them trying to outdo one another with their boring accounts of amazing-isms. Everything is amazing; amazing experiences of travelling really means that they stayed in a five-star resort and never left it as outside of it would be too dirty and disgusting, and waffling on about how one's amazing life experiences has made one so grateful for everything they have in life really means "look at me", furiously trying to virtue signal and pat my own back because I threw a few worthless coins at the homeless person while taking selfies with them for my Instagram facade.

It is usually the meanest spirited and selfish people who feel the need to have to big themselves up and often remind you that they are righteous and such upstanding members of society. Duchess was nothing like this. Her true class and breeding meant she didn't have to act like that, the sort of person who would never mention money or wealth or status, the type of person who never had a bad word to say about anyone and kept her opinions to herself. She was very dignified, sublime and true. Unlike her grandson.

One morning about three weeks before my contract ended, the grandson showed up at the front door, all bolshie and arrogant and rude. His sneering attitude and withering glance said it all, that he was an over indulged and uptight bore. His creepy limp handshake and overly exaggerated clipped accent matched perfectly with his condescending and patronising persona. I noticed he had already started to go bald, and his teeth were crooked and heavily stained with nicotine. He reeked of tobacco and BO and seemed very dishevelled; the morning hangover had left him glassy eyed and slightly disorientated. He pushed past me and slowly ascended the stairs to where Duchess was seated in the lounge and proceeded to air kiss her cheeks and prattle on about the party that he had attended last night. As I closed the front door, I noticed his car parked outside with the boot fully open. It seemed a bit odd.

I prepared a tray of tea and biscuits that I had made myself and carried it into the lounge to where they were both sitting and pretended not to listen to the conversation. The grandson was droning on about the fabulous party he had been to and mentioned to Duchess the list of D grade actresses and other insignificant faces who had shown up and she looked bored and overwhelmed and about to doze off. Must have been a room full of nobodies then and no doubt far from fabulous.

I went into the kitchen and started to prep the meat and vegetables for lunch, and as I was slicing the carrots, I heard footsteps running downstairs. I carried on stuffing the chicken and wrapping it in bacon and then I heard the grandson behind me, asking me in his lisp voice if I could pop to the shop and buy Duchess her weekly magazine that he had failed to bring with him after promising her that he would. I said of course and I slipped into my coat and headed off to the nearest newsagent. It only took twenty-five minutes and when I got back, I could see that his car was gone. *Thank God*, I thought, *at least I won't have to listen to any more of the bullshit flowing from his buck toothed freak show of a face.* After lunch was served and eaten and all the remnants were cleared away, I put the television on so that Duchess could watch her favourite afternoon chat show that she looked forward to most days.

I made my way downstairs and along the hall to my room and I immediately noticed an empty space on the wall where one of the naval oil paintings had hung for years. The wallpaper was a few shades lighter and a smaller and more modern looking framed print of the seaside was in its place. The cabinet looked as if it had been ransacked and I suddenly thought that a thief had broken into the house while I was out at the shops buying the magazine. A few of the dead husband's medals were missing from their stands and one of the little drawers on the side had been left open. I went back upstairs to the kitchen and opened the door to the larder and the Clarice Cliff tea and coffee sets were both gone, and an empty box was on the floor with a tea towel half wrapped around a set of silver teaspoons. The grandson had taken the time while I was out at the shop to select some expensive items that he could quickly bundle out to his car while pretending to visit his Granny. What a shitbag. I thought his greeting had been artificial and forced, over the top gaiety and highly animated gestures of respect, however, the whole time he was there he was calculating how much booty he could abscond with, and she was totally unaware what his true intensions were. He ripped her off and blatantly stole from her and I was right when I sussed him out when I first laid eyes on him, a real creep, who as it turned out was also a filthy opportunist thief praying on his own family. A weak willed and lazy bastard who felt that he was entitled to take what he would have argued was his inheritance anyways.

I was outraged and immediately called my agent. I knew this was abuse of the elderly and vulnerable and there was no way I was going to be somehow blamed for letting it happen when it had been carried out by a member of the family. I was sickened when the agent told me to say or do nothing and to not get involved in any of it. It turned out that Duchess's granddaughter had done the same thing a few weeks prior to when I started working there and the family had stepped in and defended her actions. I guess they all thought that her possessions were already theirs and that it was just a matter of time until she died, and they could have whatever they wanted.

It really made me feel sick to my stomach and I hated the thought that the Duchess was being taken advantage of by her own family. What utter and complete bastards. Why couldn't they wait until she was gone? They all had their own money and mansions and all they wanted was more. They didn't give a shit about her or her life. They couldn't even be bothered to make it over to her house once a week to visit her even though they all lived within a half hour drive away. What lame excuses for human beings, too interested in themselves and their pompous lifestyle to care about an old lady who didn't have a lot of time left. How can you do that and still be able to sleep at night?

This was the first time in my life that I had witnessed such disregard and neglect of an elder and I had been brought up to believe that any normal and caring family would do their utmost to prevent any of this behaviour. Was this normal for wealthy and privileged people to behave? Was this how the elite acted when a life was near its end? Why, with all that money and property and numerous staff could they not have had her living with them anyways? Why were possessions being plundered and why was I told not to get involved? Was this how the super-rich treated one another? Was this normal? Yes, it was, and it still is, and this was my first encounter but certainly not my last with rich dirtbags who should know better. It was appalling and it was only the beginning.

THE HOME COUNTIES
CHAPTER 3
THE NOVEAU RICHE

A change was in order, and I wanted to leave London and venture out into the beautiful English countryside. Most of my friends had either moved away from the city or had got married and as people do, moved on and had lost touch. After eight years, I longed for greener pastures; although I loved London and my time in it, I also felt that there was more to life than city living. My agent had a job lined up for me in a lovely part of the country and not too far from London in case I wanted to come in for a weekend or a shop or to see a show or what have you.

The new job was in the Cotswolds, which is one of the nicest areas of outstanding natural beauty and a haven for celebrities and very wealthy folk, who flock to it on the weekends and throughout the summer. Many have weekend homes there and it is a much sought after place to raise a family and enjoy country living. The day I arrived at my new job it was freezing cold, and the roads were icy, and it was sort of half snowing and half raining. I found the village quite easily having studied the map the previous evening and found the property at the end of a sleepy village. As I drove by the property and its stone wall I could see a massive horsebox, the kind that the top racehorse trainers have and cost in the region of a quarter of a million pounds; there was one of those clock towers that you also see in big racing yards

– although it did look a bit silly in this small village – with old timbered cottages and an ancient churchyard.

I drove through the large gates of the property and was greeted by some nice-looking horses who all seemed to simultaneously poke their heads over the stable doors to say hello. A pair of old greyhounds walked out of the tack room and a dirty feral cat looked on with suspicion while hiding underneath a loaded wheelbarrow and I parked the car and made my way up the path to the front door.

I knocked on the door and was let in by a huge bear of a man who would be my new boss and he led me into a hideously decorated sitting room and I sat next to the fire. As I sat down on the sofa an empty bottle of wine came rolling out from underneath and I noticed a box in the corner of the room filled with more empty bottles.

Now I do like a bottle of wine myself and I don't begrudge anyone a drink, but I did think it a bit strange that someone would store empty bottles in their sitting room. My new boss had interviewed me the week before at the head office of the company he owned, and it made me start to think what his wife must be like. If the man of the house interviews you for the housekeeping job it will mean one of four things: the woman has her own career and is too busy to see you; she has loads of kids and is busy doing stuff with them; she is off visiting or on holiday, or worse still, a lazy shit who can't be bothered to even chat to you or meet you. The new boss's wife was that lazy shit and that was putting it kindly. I wasn't offered any refreshment, and I wasn't shown the flat that I would be living in which was across the stable yard and up some stairs below the over the top and brand-new clock that I had driven by on my way in. The flat had two bedrooms, but it hadn't been cleaned for a long time and it was very dusty and smelled mouldy, and there were hundreds of dead flies all over the place. It felt like it had never been lived in, but it was neglected and dirty and cold. I dropped off my bags and made a quick note of what I would tackle first by way of cleaning and then I made my way back over to the big house to start my first day.

I was shown a tiny dark box room which was lit by a single bulb that hung down on a thin cord and was encrusted with cobwebs, which was the laundry room, and I started to iron a huge pile of clothes that had been dumped on the floor beside the washer. While I spent the day ironing and folding about three months' worth of laundry, I could hear the occasional sounds of a woman's voice, shrill and slightly hysterical and coming from another part of the house. It is the norm for the lady of the house to make a show of greeting the new staff and welcoming them with a cup of tea or something similar and having a general chat about what your duties will be and then showing them the layout of the house and what she would like doing for the week. Not this one. I could hear her coming closer and still bitching and moaning about nothing, but she didn't bother to say hello and all I got was a waft of her sickly perfume and a clinking sound of the bottles she was carrying.

I heard a door slam, and I went into the kitchen and waited a while to see if she would come in and suggest I rustle up some dinner, but nobody came, and it was now after five o'clock. I left a note explaining that as it was my first day and I had done seven hours of ironing with no break, I was going to go over to the flat to clean it and put my clothes away and I would be back at nine in the morning and to please feel free to call or pop over for a chat. By nine that evening I had cleaned the whole flat and had had a nice hot bath and dinner, and still nobody had called.

The next morning, I went across the yard to the big house and knocked on the door as they had not provided me with a set of keys the day before and I thought it very odd and rude to leave me waiting outside in the rain. I was just about to return to the flat when the kitchen door opened, and the pair of old greyhounds came bounding out and my boss apologised for being late and for oversleeping. I went into the kitchen and the floor was covered in dog pee and turds and plates of crusty food were piled in the sink and had been left overnight. A note had been left for me on the kitchen table and I was asked not to make any noise as it was still very early, and the wife was still asleep. I cleaned the shit up off the floor and proceeded to load the dishwasher and wipe down the counter tops.

While I was familiarising myself with the new and strange kitchen layout, finding what drawers the cutlery and glasses lived in and locating the fridge that had been built into the cheap pink woodwork, I noticed there was no fresh produce or eggs or anything fresh. The cupboards were full but only tins of things and nasty tins of fruit and veg. There were nasty tins of processed meats and UHT milk. A whole kitchen length of cupboards was home to biscuits and crisps and cans of fizzy pop and pot noodles and chocolate. I opened the fridge to put the opened UHT milk carton away and there were more processed and cheap packets of sliced meats and cheese and half-full tins of soup and a block of stork margarine. I couldn't believe my eyes and had to check out the freezer while nobody was around. It was packed full of cheap pizzas and breaded chicken and the cheapest sausages that come in bags of a hundred and gross no name oven chips and large tubs of the cheapest supermarket brand ice cream. Oh my God. It truly was a chef's hell. I looked out of the kitchen window that overlooked the stable yard and saw the custom painted horsebox that cost the same as a large family house and I shook my head in disgust. Now I know some people do eat like this out of preference or out of necessity and I realise that many do not have disposable incomes and must live on very little money, but I am sure that if they did have the money to eat well, they would do so.

I found my way to the sitting room and opened the door, and the reek of stale cigarette smoke made me feel ill and I noticed that the stack of empty wine bottles in the corner had grown bigger. I tidied the room, swept out and laid the fire, and as I did so, I could hear movement above my head in the room upstairs. I checked behind the sofa and the cushions for empty bottles and then turned towards the door and then came face to face with the woman of the house.

I think she was about ten years older than me but the first thing I noticed was, in her sad attempt to roll back the years, was her overdone orange face of tan and makeup, which was at least five shades darker than her own skin on her neck. She looked as though she had already had a few face lifts and procedures, hair extensions, fake nails, and a way too large boob job. This was when lip filler and Botox hadn't been invented and she would have had that done to herself too if she could and I would put money on that she has had all of it by now. Her clothes were expensive but uncoordinated and hastily thrown together. She was teetering on six-inch stiletto heels, the type you would see on young dollops in nightclubs or on hookers and it was still only a few hours after breakfast. She lit a match and puffed on a cigarette and then threw it in the fireplace, then reached behind the curtain and grabbed a half bottle of wine from the windowsill along with a glass and filled it. She asked me if I could leave her without even introducing herself and I left the room and made my way back to the kitchen. The boss was in there and asked me to tidy the games room and pool area. Pool?

I followed him through a door off the kitchen into a room that looked like it was a set in a film studio. Not all posh and grand and filled with fine antique furniture and old masters hanging on the walls. No. It was awful. A huge billiards table was right in the middle of the room with a cheap plastic imitation tiffany lamp hanging over it and the carpet was a sickly green shag, which looked grim and as ugly as it did when it was fashionable in the 1970s. There were more cheap lamps placed on horrid pine side tables like the kind you would find at Ikea and have to assemble yourself and none of the armchairs or sofas matched and were made of faux leather and smelled of plastic in the hot room. The assorted house plants and flower displays were all plastic and the wall art read "live-love-laugh" in bold gold letters alongside groups of framed prints of clowns holding balloons and crying. There were no bookcases or any reading material but there was an enormous satellite television that was so big it looked as if it was an item of furniture. There was a bar in the corner with optics and beer mats on the counter. Tankards hung from hooks on top of the frame of a plastic and diamond shaped padded structure. A fine layer of ashy dust covered everything and there was a discarded crust of pizza and an empty crisp packet thrown in the corner of the room.

He opened a second door and held it open for me and I could suddenly smell chlorine and feel the humidity of an enclosed swimming pool. I stepped inside the room and looked at a vast and almost Olympic sized pool, which had a slide built up around it to slide into and an island in the middle of it that had a large plastic pirates' chest and plastic palm trees living on it. It really was huge, and it must have cost a fortune to heat and maintain and you could tell that it wasn't used very often. The water in the pool was murky and green with algae and cheap plastic lilos with cup holders and others shaped like doughnuts and comical sea life bobbed about on the surface. A few traditional deckchairs were placed here and there, and plastic beanbags and cushions lay beside them. There was another bar festooned with fairy lights in one corner and more large, framed prints of crying clowns holding balloons. I went behind the bar and noticed a coil of old and dried dog shit laying on the rubber mat and it looked like it had been there for weeks. I laughed to myself and thought that it somehow had cheered the place up a bit.

I spent the rest of the week in the downstairs part of the house as there was a party being thrown and the place needed a good clean. The original old part of the house was very small, and the rooms were pokey and crooked, but the larger ones made from the modern extension were vast and it took ages to get them cleaned properly and up to my standard. I still hadn't been asked to go upstairs and clean and I hadn't been asked to do any shopping or prep any meals either. I was so glad that I had the weekends off and I spent the first one deep cleaning the flat and driving to the supermarket to stock up on food. I drove to the nearest large town and was pleased to see a wide variety of specialty shops which included a delicatessen and an independent butcher and bakery. There was also a traditional costermonger and a wet fish shop and a fabulous looking florist that had a window display worthy of a magazine cover. There was a good choice of restaurants, Indian, Chinese, French, Greek and the like. The delicatessen was huge and one side of it was for cakes and sweets and the other side was for the savouries and meats and a queue had formed at the sandwich counter where great slabs of salt beef and piles of fresh bagels waited. I felt that I was in heaven with such a lovely selection of anything you could think of, and I parked the car and slowly strolled along the street, browsing through shop windows and ending up having a coffee and a snack in one of the cafes. It would have been nice to buy everything I needed on the one street and return to the flat, and although all the items were so tempting and delicious looking, it was way too expensive and just one shop would have eaten into most of my monthly wage. I finished my cup of coffee and made my way back to the car and drove towards the giant supermarket that was on the outskirts of the town.

Monday morning came again, and I was back at knocking on the kitchen door to get in to work. I still hadn't been issued with any keys, which was odd as they are usually the first thing given to you when you get your flat keys. I was let in by my boss again and was told again not to make any noise and the kitchen looked like a rubbish tip with two days' worth of mess and dirty cooking pans, and there was another note left for me with a list of tasks to do. The bin had been left to overflow in the corner and the dogs had ripped it open and spread its contents all over the floor. The dirty dinner plates had been put down for them to lick clean and they had shit on the floor again. Animal poo doesn't bother me. I would rather clean up after an animal than flush someone else's toilet that they have left full of poo or clean toilets that are covered in human skid marks. I agree that it is wasteful to flush a toilet every time you pee, and gallons of water are wasted just to make more water disappear, but I cannot understand why someone would leave their poo for someone else to find. Maybe the person who does this has a bit of a poo fetish or just likes to show off their poo? To me it just screams of a poor upbringing and sheer ignorance and even worse when there is no paper present with the poo. It wouldn't surprise me if some people do this on purpose as they know that someone will be along soon to discover it and it is a kind of extra little degrading thing to do to a person, most likely the housekeeper, as it is seen to be their job to clean up.

Years ago, while working at a large and popular pub in north London, the barmaids took it in rota to check the toilets at the end of an evening to make sure none of the customers had passed out in any of the cubicles and to pick up any glasses that had been left there. One night it had been my turn and as I went in, I had to hold my breath as some dirty bastard had taken a huge shit into a pint glass and had left it for all to see on top of the electric hand dryer. To this day I wonder if that could have been a woman who had done it or had one of the disgusting excuses for a man done it and then put it in the ladies toilets? Looking back and remembering some of the clientele – and personally knowing some of them – still leaves me undecided if it was male or female who was responsible.

Peeing all over the toilet is just as bad as leaving poo in it and the ultimate stomach-churning thing is leaving a used sanitary pad or tampon on the floor or on top of a bin, unwrapped in paper and left out with no attempt made to try to hide it. There are no excuses for any of this behaviour; even if you are drunk and out of your mind you should still make sure to clean up after yourself and have a bit of dignity. The same goes for vomit. Lying in bed and then hanging your head over the side of it and throwing up on your own bedroom carpet is no different than squatting in the corner and plopping out a poo. It is dirty and scummy! Don't do it!

The day of the much-anticipated party had arrived. The

tasteless games room and pool area had been cleaned and I did an extra check around both of them for any dog poo and then began to stack the fridges in the bar with bottles of beer and wine and cans of pop. The booze had been delivered that morning and I noticed that there were also a few boxes of Dom Perignon champagne. I placed several ashtrays around each room and was told that a few bartenders had been hired and the company who was sending them was also supplying the glasses and the butler. The butler? I thought it was strange, but I didn't say anything and was relieved that I wouldn't be expected to walk up and down with a tray of hors d'oeuvres, pretending to smile and being patronized by a huge room full of unfamiliar people.

In the kitchen a load of shopping had just been delivered from Tesco and I was looking forward to making some canapes and tasty dips and other titbits for the buffet table; but as I unpacked the bags, I began to accept this wasn't to be. Yesterday I had been told that I was in charge of the catering, and I had planned to make some nice homemade hummus and a tray of stuffed mushrooms. I asked for some nice camembert to bake and some fresh crab to make up a batch of mini quiches. Nigella Lawson's fabulous honey roasted cocktail sausages are always the first things to go and I wanted to do those too. I was going to make grilled bacon wrapped dates and bake some mini chocolate cheesecakes for anyone who fancied something sweet. I couldn't disguise my disappointment when all I saw in the bags were four loaves of cheap sliced white bread, some cheap supermarket brand margarine, and several packets of wafer-thin ham and bags of generic grated mild cheddar cheese. To round off the party buffet table there was a giant bag of assorted crisps and a carton of twiglets and another of salted peanuts. My thoughts turned to the poor man who had been hired as the butler and whose job it would be to tote the sarnies on a silver platter while having to don a dinner jacket and I really felt for him.

As I started to prepare the sandwiches, the boss came into the kitchen and began to rummage in the cupboards and then turned to me and handed over a large tin of pineapple chunks. He smiled as he asked me to make him his favourite party snack which was cheese and pineapple on a stick. He left the kitchen and then came back with a tube of toothpicks and suggested that I cut the crusts off the sandwiches as they looked nicer on the plate.

I made the platters of sandwiches and covered them in clingfilm and then I decanted the twiglets and nuts into the prettiest bowls I could find and arranged them on the trestle table in the games' room. There were no large serving bowls, so I had to put the crisps into several plastic containers and there were no napkins or smaller plates for the guests to use. I tidied the kitchen and then I got out of there as fast as I could go as I didn't want to be there when the guests arrived and have them think that I was the one responsible for the dismal spread.

Thank God that I hadn't been asked to attend and help with all the coats and be on hand to prepare more food as there was nothing else to make anyways.

A few hours later the people started to arrive, and I have never seen so many supercars in one place at one time. It was like a car show and a few of the guests had decided to have a drag race through the village and do handbrake turns and smoke their tyres. It was dark outside and from the top of the stable block I noticed a few of the neighbouring houses twitching their curtains to see what was going on. I closed mine and turned on the television. I poured myself a large glass of wine and got comfy on the sofa and started to flick through the channels looking for a film to watch.

I woke up hours later with a start. I had dozed off while watching some rubbish and I glanced at the clock, which read three in the morning. I could hear two women screaming and shouting at each other and they were eventually joined by a man who also started to scream and shout with them. From what I could make out, one of the women had been flirting with the other woman's boyfriend or husband and the abusive language was straight from the gutter, but it made me laugh my head off. Shouts of "whore" and "effing slag" were hurled back and forth, and a few death threats were repeated between sounds that sounded like slaps and punches, and one of them had fallen or had been pushed over. More of the partygoers started to come out of the house and make their way home and there was more engine revving and tyres squealing, and one of them, either pissed or going too fast, lost control of the car and smashed into the gates. It didn't stop, and the noise was loud, and it must have caused a lot of damage. I never did find out which car it was, and I wouldn't have been surprised if it had been written off. The sound of the super-charged engines could be heard a few miles off in the distance and the night air carried more sounds of people fighting and objects being thrown, and bottles being smashed. As I got into bed, I was so glad that it was the weekend, and I wouldn't have to feel awkward going into work until Monday morning.

On Monday I went in and was greeted by the usual state of the kitchen and leftovers from the weekend, but this time it was times twenty. Someone had been kind enough to attempt a bottle collection and there were a few black bin bags overflowing with them in a corner. I found a bucket and filled it with a roll of bin bags, a duster and polish, and an extra duster and bottle of flash. I hooked it over my arm and carried the hoover in my other hand and pushed the door open to the games' room that the party had been held in. It looked like hell on earth. It looked like a brawl had taken place inside it and from all the noise from the guests leaving on Friday night this must have been the epicentre of it. There were broken sticks that were once chairs strewn about and amongst upturned ashtrays and cigarette ends. Bits of sandwich and crushed crisps and empty bottles were thrown everywhere and the fairy lights from around the bar had been pulled down and stepped on and someone had left a huge pool of urine on one of the plastic sofas which had dried and had started to stink. There was a rip on the green felt on the billiards table along with a shattered pile of peanuts and one of the plastic tiffany lampshades had a big chip out of it and was badly cracked.

I gingerly stepped through the carnage and looked into the pool room. It was much the same and there was discarded items of women's clothes floating in the water and a deckchair had sunk to the bottom in the deep end. To my horror I noticed a metal pole that had been erected, the sort that strippers in strip clubs use, and in the end, it took me three days to tidy both rooms and get them back to how they were before the party. A foul smell persistently lingered and I thought it may be that the dogs had found their way into the room, but when I went behind the bar to empty out the ice buckets, I found the sink full and blocked with thick yellow puke. I must have poured a whole bottle of bleach down and around it and as I turned on the taps to swill it all down the drain, I noticed a small, framed photo that was on the wall near to the sink of a family trip to Disneyland. The one next to it was a photo of my boss holding a large cardboard mock-up of a cheque, the ones you see the people posing with when they win a big lottery and it really had been a big lottery. Twenty-six million pounds worth of lottery.

It all made perfect sense now. New and sudden money and a new lifestyle to go with it. A few days previous while I was cleaning the dining room, I was taking my time and had a chance to study some of the photographs that had been hung on the walls, a big variety that included some of the lovely horses and the boss's wife when she was a lot younger. I love looking at other people's photographs as you can fashion an image in your mind of how and what they came into this life with and how they came to be the sort of person they are today. According to the photos, the wife had worked for an airline in her earlier days, not one of the exclusive ones, but one of the ordinary everyday short haul household name brands. She stood there grinning in the photo in her air stewardess uniform surrounded by other stewardesses and looking young, fresh and happy, and in stark contrast to what she had become.

Earlier days of a normal working-class upbringing. She had probably been like most of us were at that age and looking forward to starting her life in a career that was in line with her level of education and social class. Working class. The salt of the earth. What you see is what you get. My favourite kind of people who are real and honest and uncomplicated. If you find yourself in whatever setting or situation especially at the bottom, I am all for the underdog climbing up the ladder to success or someone from a different social class finding love and luck and getting a leg up that way. What I don't like is people who rise by whatever means to a loftier position and then treat the people underneath them with the exact same coldness and indifference as the people who have treated them like crap before they rose up. If you have recently started to act like an entitled spoilt brat, you should be ashamed as you should know better. People expect the snobs to act entitled and spoilt so when the underdog who has made good does it – it is twice as bad. When I see people doing this it always makes me howl with laughter because it reminds me of the classic comedy of Harry Enfield when he does the brilliant sketch with the magnificent Kathy Burke as "Wayne and Waynetta Slob" when they win the lottery. The same thing was happening right now in front of my eyes.

I refused to let them irritate me and force me to look for a new job just yet as I was starting to save money and it was a nice area and flat to be in. I became an automaton going through the motions of everyday household tasks and human interactions. I was as pleasant as I had to be and nothing more and as the weeks and years passed by, I prided myself that I had survived so long on the job without them ever having to know me, which might sound awful, but when people want to treat you in the same way the options have very little appeal.

I was always taught that you should treat those as you would like to be treated yourself, but I figured that it only applied to nice people as I would discover years into my career. There are good and bad people in every country, religion, and race, and in every stratum of society and in every place of work. Many like to bang on about how great unions are when they quite elitist, as they are only there for a few of the professions, and you can only be a part of them and enjoy the benefits of being a member if you pay into it. How can they be of benefit or use to the average worker (meaning that unless you pay them, you will be excluded from its protection and help) when you should have protection and help from your workplace health and safety and the charter of human rights? When you have no safety net and only basic employment rights and you are privately employed in a private home, then you make up your own rights as in you switch off and just do what is required of you and keep going until payday… and keep doing it every month until the day comes that you leave.

I also don't understand how those with wealth can think that because they have lots of it, then it automatically elevates them above everyone else, particularly in modern-day society, where every aspect of it reminds us that we are equal as human beings wherever you are or wherever you have come from. This simply is not true when you take the whole world into consideration and it is mainly the western countries and their societies where this is practised and much of it is overlooked, depending on race, wealth, and status. It is all very well and good sympathising with a group of people, whether the sympathy is aimed at poverty or religion or supposed suppression, but it is all meaningless when you exclude other human beings who are suffering the same said prejudices because they are the majority. Why are some groups of people provided with and given material and mental help more than others who are suffering with the same material and mental disabilities? Why is a certain group of people more deserving of help and sympathy and support than all groups of people who need help? Surely everyone should be getting the same level of concern no matter who or what they are or will become? No one is being treated fairly, especially right now if you are an average taxpaying citizen anywhere in the world.

It has been just over one hundred years since women were given the right to vote in England, which is fantastic although a lot of people still don't realise that it was only for the elite land owning and financially well-off women. It was only in 1928, after the equal franchise act was passed, that ordinary working-class women could vote too and, when you look at today's class differences over a hundred-year period, then not much has changed. I don't think we can imagine how it must have felt to be treated like an animal. Segregation is still very much alive, and there are people smugglers, traffickers and scumbags, exploiting and living off others' misery and it will keep on happening because some like to capitalize on fear and desperation and will use it to their advantage when a profit can be had. These days the segregation is in the form of wealth and class, although the colour of one's skin does cause a problem with some people, and it will sadly never end anytime soon.

When I was growing up, class always meant us group of kids being taught at school or a period of time when we were taught a particular subject. Then as I became older and moved out into the wide world of work and socialising it took on a new meaning as being stylish, chic, and fashionable. It meant someone had manners and graciousness and mutual respect and empathy for everyone. A group of people within the same economic and social position and rank and order in which goods, services, and people are put in accordance with their standard. In the twenty-first century, class means a tolerable form of apartheid; but now because of political correctness, the system divides people depending on wealth and status. Politically correct class. It is a class war that we are still losing.

The start of working week, and I was told to work upstairs which was surprising as it was the first time I had ever been to the top floor, which was as equally depressing and stale and drab as the rest of the house. It was a shame as the house was originally a small and traditional farmhouse, but it had been ruined by modernisation and the life had been sucked out of it. It was cold and dead. I worked my way through the dreary and over decorated rooms and noticed more cheap furnishings and artificial flowers. The master bedroom had a canopy bed draped with net curtain that would not have looked out of place in an old lady's front room window. A vanity table was in one of the corners and was piled high with cheap makeup with the odd expensive brand here and there and an additional side table held about forty different brands of perfume bottles and more vases of synthetic blooms. There was a bin next to it and it was three quarters full of old and used makeup remover pads and cotton balls, all stained a deep terracotta and black and a plastic transparent box full of fake eyelashes was being used as a coaster for a half drank glass of wine. On the floor and surrounding the vanity table were dozens and dozens of bags from very expensive designer clothes shops: Gucci, Chanel and Lacroix. Bags full of brand-new clothes that had been bought and then forgotten and just chucked on the floor. One of the receipts was lying on the floor and I gasped when I saw that it was for £6096 just from Harrods alone. For that price you would have thought that they would have been hung up and put in the closet.

I changed the bed sheets and moved into the bathroom which was just a plain old bathroom that you would find in any average home. No frills just functionability, and I thought that the one that was in my flat was a lot nicer with its black granite floor and countertops. Their bathroom didn't appear to be too bad when compared to the rest of the rooms which were dusty with cobwebs in the windows and ancient food crumbs stuck to the carpets. The towels were clean and fluffy, and they weren't damp to the touch. The boss and his wife had both left the house for the day and I wondered if they may have used a different bathroom; maybe there was another larger and more modern one that I hadn't discovered yet. The shower hadn't been used and it was bone dry just like the towels and there was no trace of water in the hand basin and the bars of soap looked brand new.

My suspicions had come true and there was no denying

that the pair of them were not fond of bathing and personal hygiene, and I estimated they probably only had a weekly shower or bath. I didn't know the layout of the top floor and it was a fraction of the size of the downstairs, and as I opened a door at the farthest end of the top of the staircase, I discovered a child's bedroom. I didn't even know they had any children. The room was unlived in, and I made a point of not inquiring about any children as there might be a sad story attached and I knew some parents kept a room closed and left in the same state as when someone had inhabited it.

I didn't meet the kid until he came home one afternoon at half-term, and he didn't acknowledge me, and he spent most of the time in his bedroom. I wouldn't see him again until I watched him get into the boss's car, which would take him back to school two weeks later. Children are moulded into thinking and acting like their parents. Looking back, I can see myself as two people: Mum and Dad. Good and bad.

When I was little and through to my mid-twenties I was like my Mum, kind and carefree, and it wasn't until my thirties and beyond that bad Dad took over and I became cynical and cautious, and I questioned everything. At an early age I was allowed to make up my own mind and to make my own decisions and it's really sad that these days most kids aren't allowed to do this and are never trusted to be themselves. I grew up in the sixties and seventies. Generation X. My Mum let me do what I wanted within reason and if I stepped out of line, Dad would be there with his belt to remind me I couldn't go too far and take the piss. I was a toddler during the flower power era. Hippies and free love and anything went, but my parents were born during the Second World War and, although very modern and free thinking, they taught my sister and me all the old and traditional values of respect, right from wrong, manners and integrity. It makes me sick to see how some parents are bringing their kids up these days and it feels like they are from some new and alien generation, very self-interested, lazy, and inept. They lack spirit and personality and have been dumbed down by our over the top and hand wringing liberal society. Even the kids are segregated by their intelligence and the slow learners are abandoned while the clever ones get pushed through another tier of conditioning and meaningless courses and useless degrees. The lucky ones who have been privately educated or have been awarded grants and bursaries, will attend the elite and greatest of the universities and then find themselves with nothing in common. Many will go home to their family estate or gated community, and the others will go home to the average working-class family.

Towards the end of my employment for this family, I saw how they were treating their animals, the dogs and horses. They were there only for show along with the brand-new stable block and the ostentatious clock tower and the extravagant horse box that cost the same as your average family home. On further inspection of the stables, I found that they were not just for the horses, as many were being used as storage for quad bikes and mini tractors, bags of feed, and tack. There were five brand new saddles on the floor with their £900 price tags still attached and assorted new rugs and bridles dumped and collecting dust. The beautiful horses were out in a dusty paddock with no water or shelter and not enough room for them, and they seemed to be waiting for anybody to come and groom them or ride them, or just come visit them with a kind word and a pat on the neck. Nothing. They were put in their stables at night and fed and let out into the paddock during the day and that was their life. Once every six weeks a farrier would come to trim their hooves and fit them with new shoes but that was it. They were being used as props. Showpieces for friends and neighbours or whoever came to the property. I never found out their names and I never saw anyone ride them and a few times I saw a little old man come into the stable yard and fill haynets and I guessed that he was the person who was taking care of them.

The dogs like the horses never seemed to leave the area and they lived in the yard during the day and in the big house at night. I didn't see them being walked the whole time of working there and nor was I asked to, although I would have leapt at the chance to do so. Like the horses they were never groomed or petted or spoken to, and they too were there only for show. The animals were being used to make their horrible owners look like the landed gentry when in fact they were the complete opposite. The poor things were being used as fashion accessories and I don't know why some people bother to have pets when they can't even be bothered to give them any attention or comfort or basic care. These are the same types of people who think they are superior human beings to the rest of us and most of them don't give a shit about the environment either. Exploiting animals for some warped perception of country life. It was so false and disgusting and it helped me to distance myself from them and the job I was doing for them. I started buying the *Lady* magazine every week and hoping and praying that my life would change soon…

And then it did.

CHAPTER 4

HIGH SOCIETY

Although the new job was the same as in the usual aspects one can expect to do as a housekeeper, it really was a rung up the ladder in terms of learning the fine arts of a traditional, yet higher calibre of private domestic employee. I will not say servant as only the pretenders will use this outdated and derogatory term in this day and age. The people who still like to use this word are always the ones who like to humiliate and condescend to others who they feel, in their tiny minds, are beneath them. These people sneer and scoff and label people like "common" and "of low status". My new boss had descended from a Lord from southern Europe and had married into our own home-grown establishment. Most readers would assume that they would be the epitome of what not to look for in an employer, that they would surely treat you like a stupid lackey who was put on this earth to fetch and carry and to take any order or harsh word on the chin and to know your place or piss off. No. They really knew how to treat their staff with respect and reward and compliment when warranted. They would look you in the eye and always talk to you in a calm and encouraging manner and made you feel respected and that you were an asset to their home and well-being. There was no hierarchy, superiority, or feeling of division when you were in their presence and most of their guests were the same. Sometimes, however, the odd idiot would come to stay and would behave like a fool and pretend they were of the same status, but the pompous ego would show them up and their attempt to talk down to the staff would raise a few eyebrows.

You can always spot these types in all levels of society, and it has become worse with the advent of social media and all the new technology. It is like D list so-called celebrities trying to attach themselves to an Oscar winning actor. They don't realise that they stick out like a sore gangrenous thumb and think that they are clever and have blended in naturally, but their lack of real talent clings the First World War the whole concept of the serving classes changed forever. The working-class women could now have an unrestrained life with a fair income without having to rely on domestic positions, and men, if not in the armed forces, who were in demand for the work that kept the country going. The men and women who kept the factories and manufacturing alive were now serving the country instead of the wealthy and aristocratic, and after the Second World War domestic service was almost antiquated.

Old money had been lost along with the bombing and destruction of many of the grand houses that had relied on a small army of staff to function. The price of living in large houses with numerous staff had become very expensive and the old system of social class was changing. Or so we thought. It never really went away but instead became somewhat unfashionable for a few decades as the destruction brought on austerity and the ones who still had their wealth were reluctant to flaunt it although many carried on as normal. As the 1980s emerged the new wealth ushered in the new self-indulged smugness of the yuppies who grasped it with everything they had. Now I have no ill will towards people who have started with nothing and through hard work and determination rose up and became successful, just like people who have been brought up with a silver spoon in their mouths and don't know anything else, but I do object very strongly to people who then use that power and wealth to knowingly wield it and use it as an excuse to belittle and look down on others and project an image of superiority because of the size and location of their property or model of their car or size of their wallet. Men who do this are lacking in the downstairs department and women who do this are odious bitches who are never satisfied with anything and never will be.

The first year of my new job was spent learning the finer elements of what was expected from those who had had the good fortune of coming from a life of privilege. I was shown the differences of what and how the everyday tasks in the household should be performed and the different methods and tools used in each task to cater for say, an ordinary day for family and friends, or for a formal gathering of diplomatic dignitaries for an evening of cocktails and several courses of dinner. The best time for the big spring cleaning of the house is May, as the weather usually changes for the better so you can take furniture and rugs outside to clean and the children will be back at school. Additional staff can be brought in for the duration and exact products to use when cleaning certain surfaces and fine Objet d'art. Only ever just dust a bronze. Clean wicker and rattan with warm water and lemon juice. Soak a decanter in salted water. Wash mahogany with vinegar and then polish with a soft cloth dipped in linseed oil. Only use beeswax on fine wood furniture. Clean ivory with a paste made of sawdust and lemon juice. Clean vintage wallpaper with white bread. Although we have a modern product for every type of household item known to man sometimes in an emergency or unable to obtain the modern and convenient product these old school remedies and solutions really do work.

If you are working in a very old property and there is a lot of very old fixtures and fittings and furniture, then some of the new products out there on the market will damage or ruin things that have had little or no modern chemical applied to them. It was interesting to be caring for and learning about a Tudor era building, and its furniture, and it is astounding to see some things can last for hundreds of years and still be functioning and working with a little love and attention. It is so different to today where things are mass produced so cheaply and shoddily that you have no choice but to throw it away after a few months use when it is broken. I learned how to make the perfect bed and to use the proper blanket or quilt and sheets for the changing seasons. How to set the perfect table for breakfast, buffet style, as one is not waited on during the first meal of the day; what style of napkin should be chosen for the luncheon table – which is usually a seasonal design or themed to match an occasion or holiday – and how a dinner table should be formally set with proper cutlery and glasses to accompany the various courses. Knives should always be sharp, bread should be sliced in identical thickness, and vegetable dishes to be placed on the sideboard and not on the table after serving. Always serve food from the left-hand side and wine and beverages from the right. The most important or elderly guests should be served first before women, and then men. Silver service is fantastic if you are good at it and have practiced the art of correctly holding and manoeuvring a spoon and fork in one hand, but you can get away with allowing the guests to help themselves while you hold the platter or bowl of food for them.

The art of flower arranging is very useful and appreciated although effective combinations of cut flowers and their suitable receptacles should reflect the circumstance or time of year. If the house is old and has mature furnishings you should choose traditional blooms like lavender, sweet briar, honeysuckle and rosemary. If it has large and high ceilings you should go for large displays and flowers like sunflowers, hollyhocks, lupins and any tall free growing or wild weeds such as cow parsley and hemlock to add to the display. Smaller and more exotic flowers look better in a modern house or those with a minimalist decor.

I learnt how to distinguish manmade lace from the real thing and how to identify a Canaletto from a Caravaggio. What to look for when recognising an authentic hallmark and the difference of silver and silver plate. I also learned the finer aspects of cooking and using fresh and seasonal produce using every bit of leftover meat from an expensive joint and how to make a tasty and satisfying meal from very little ingredients. I always go by the old saying that "less is more" when it comes to food and its preparation and presentation and people tend to think that wealthier folks always have some sort of elaborate and expensive meal every time they dine, but this simply isn't true. Of course, there are people who do and good on them but how boring! It's sad to think that some will turn their nose up at fresh but simple dishes and think that is what a person would have on a lower income, but they really are missing out. Give me a plate of Welsh rarebit or some chipolatas from the butcher or some freshly laid eggs, soft boiled with buttered soldiers any day, rather than some stodgy meat and potatoes coated in cream sauce or dull and tedious pasta any day. It makes me laugh when people think that buying food from more upscale supermarkets and shops are somehow better for you (which can be if you are buying one hundred per cent organic) but there is no point if you are only buying a few select items. It is what you do with those ingredients that really matters, and most of the meals I made were quite simple and tasty. Most of the fruit and vegetables came from their own gardens and orchards, and all the meat came from the local butcher.

During the holidays a hamper from Fortnum's would arrive, usually a gift from friends, filled with sweets and savouries and maybe a truckle of stilton, but most of the food was everyday fare, which was cooked with love and care.

I do hate it when a large portion of food or meat is destined for the bin because it is not deemed worthy of eating anymore. At least treat the dog or cat if you are going to dispose of it. It is hugely disrespectful to the animal which was slaughtered, and I think that meat has become so mass produced and in turn cheapened that it can easily be thrown away. It is good that food is cheaper and poorer families can enjoy meat more often, but I hate the whole idea of factory farming and if I had my way it would become again what it used to be, an expensive treat to be had on high days and holidays and the utmost respect would be given back to the animal by way of how it is raised and kept. I have seen so much waste over the years cooking for people and the other thing I really hate are those awful metal capsules of coffee that go into a machine and out pops a cafe style cup of java that you can easily make in a cafetiere or old-style hob top percolator. Those metal capsules are polluting the planet, and no one ever wants to recycle them and they are more than often tossed into the bin. It's so lazy and thoughtless to use them and what a waste of money too. So gauche! And unnecessary.

Food is also an illusion. You can make a cheap cut of meat into a delicious and Michelin Star standard dish and you can also make an expensive cut of meat and ruin it either with improper cooking or serving it with ingredients that don't go along with it or serve it with an atrocious sauce that masks the delicate flavours. Food can also be ruined by choosing and cooking the same old recipe or same ingredient day after day and becoming so bored of it that it tastes bland and uninspiring. Your tastebuds become immune to it and food can also be ruined by thinking that the more elaborate the name of the dish and ingredients are, the better it is going to be. This is how a food snob thinks; a true cook knows that variety is the spice of life, and older and simpler recipes will usually impress and be tasty rather than an over fussy recipe with complex stages and way too many components. A food snob will eat what you cook for them and after they have eaten most of it, they will tell you how grim it was and describe to you how they could have done better. It's always from women who can't or won't cook as it is either too much work for them or they are too thick to follow a recipe. The sort that does this are the first to wolf down a cake you have made and then complain and tell you what a gifted and talented baker they used to be and how their friends would compare them to Nigella Lawson. Don't try to bamboozle us, love! You are as much a domestic goddess as I am Queen Elizabeth. These food snobs are all about appearances and image and will order their groceries from

Waitrose so the neighbours will see their delivery van pulling into the driveway.

Years ago, I had a friend who drove a catering truck for a very well-known and popular airline. He would drive to a factory in north-west London and pick up food that was destined for the airlines first-class passengers and its expensive cafe in the airport departure lounge. The factory was a sandwich factory which made sandwiches for all the big supermarkets and other brands that were sold in the standard plastic sandwich boxes. They made a variety and used all the usual sandwich ingredients and different types of bread, some very plain and some were a little more sophisticated, but all were packaged the same except for the shop brand label. Some of the more upscale and decadently filled sarnies were made for the exclusive food retailers and some to the top Condon department stores and well-known high street chains and coffee shops and cafes. The more plain and everyday traditional filled sandwiches were made in the same location beside the posh ones and double the amount of these would be made to supply the corner shops and popular supermarkets and the emphasis would be on quantity not quality as these were the top sellers. Your average sandwich that you see in Asda or Sainsburys is the same one you will find in a posh shop except with a different label and a different price. You are paying different prices for the same item made in a factory by poorly paid workers and some of those sandwiches cost more than the worker is making in an hour.

The sandwiches that were made for the airlines and airports were a bit different but only in the presentation and the same sandwiches bought by the masses would be put on an extra conveyor belt to have their crusts cut off and then placed on a china plate with a sprig of watercress and covered in cling film instead of its usual plastic box. Sometimes hygiene standards were not always adhered to and on one occasion there was a sewer malfunction, and the workers were all at their stations on the conveyor belts working away, assembling the sandwiches while standing in four inches of north-west London's raw sewage. Yum!

My new Boss was a joy to work for and there were no pretensions or facade associated with the true upper echelons of society. Neither they nor their friends ever bragged about their possessions or property portfolios. They never wore ostentatious jewellery or clothes or drove the ubiquitous top of the range cars. They didn't have to display their wealth like the young pretenders do and they never moaned about how much things cost or dropped names of their famous and connected friends. They had impeccable manners and they had true effortless class. They thought of and treated everyone with kindness and the very image or display of self-importance and greed repelled them. One member of the family is a very well-educated and known celebrity and has been a regular face on the television for the past twenty years. She is very experienced in what she does, and she still makes me laugh with her wit and dry realist humour when I see her on her programme. When I see her instruct her clients to embrace change and let go of old habits, I remember her and her mother teaching me the finer points of hospitality and paying attention to the smallest of detail, doing things properly and diligently, and how to achieve the best level of luxury for any scenario and at any level. She has worked all around the world and in the most prestigious and opulent establishments – both private and accessible to the general public.

Some of the women I have worked for have had the nerve to bang on about being interior designers and how they have transformed their houses and second or third properties. They would pay an established and professional designer to help them look through various magazines and endless swatches of fabrics and wallpaper and take weeks to decide what seemed to be the same colours and similar shapes on outdated materials and furnishings, how to upgrade a look they already had but had grown tired of. They needed to have the same look of the many similar and trendy and tedious images of what they thought was chic and clever and modern, when it was very mainstream and sedate. No individual flair or style and if they had to think about non-conformity they were lost. They had once picked out a matching duvet and curtain set for their snivelling brats' bedroom and now thought they knew it all. When I go into a house now and see any hideous swag curtains, I always smile and hear her voice asking why the hell would anybody still have them?

I had been working away for a few years now and all was well but as always there was a little problem starting to brew in the background. The problem was another member of staff who lived in the cottage next to mine on the estate and it became clear that he absolutely hated me because I was happy at my job and with life in general. Why does this always happen when I work with other people? Some can't stand it when you have something that they will never get and, instead of working on it themselves, they like to project their hatred toward others because it is the easier option. If you are being praised and rewarded for a job well done, they become the green-eyed monster and when it is their turn for the rewards and glory, they act all smug and indifferent and still hate you.

This hateful staff member was the gardener who in reality was only a common labourer and was masquerading as a tradesman and had somehow blagged his way into the role and remained bitter and older than his years. His morbidly obese wife and delinquent son lived with him and helped to contribute to his explosive temper and downtrodden demeanour. He had no interest or pride in his work, and it showed in the haphazard fashion of the raggedy looking flowerbeds and the amateurish way in which he mowed the lawns, leaving them cut unevenly and not bothering to collect all the grass cuttings and leaving them to die on the lawn. He had a creepy penchant of letting himself into the big house when he knew you would be alone and coming up very quietly behind you and scaring the shit out of you and then laughing about it in a sinister way.

When the boss and family were away in London during the week he would be inside their house having a good old snoop around in the bedrooms and sitting rooms while he did his laundry in their washer and dryer. He was the sort of useless worker who never seemed to be around or contactable if there was an emergency and was needed but he was always popping up everywhere in and around the house at odd times and inopportune moments. He was always looking and watching. His wife never left their cottage and never spoke to me, and the feral son was never at school but was always dressed in his school uniform. I tried my best to avoid him at all costs and thought him repulsive when he would use the staff Land Rover to take his wife shopping when he knew I needed it to get the weekend groceries in for the boss and it would make me late. He tried to prevent me taking any firewood that had been allotted to the staff and would take most of it for himself or ruin it by hosing it down and making it wet. Another one of his favourites was to take a massive shit in one of the twelve toilets in the big house and not flush it and hope I wouldn't find it in time for when family and guests would arrive for the weekend. He would occasionally take the wire out of the aga during the week or turn it down to its lowest setting, knowing it would take a few days to reach optimum cooking temperature; he would let himself into the house after I had left for the day and do things to cost me extra time to fix, like start the fires so they had to be swept out and re-laid; he would switch off the mains electricity and lock the cellar so I had to spend time trying to get hold of him, so he could come and switch it on again. He even went so far as to open a locked door in the middle of the night, so the alarm went off, and as he was taking a few days off as holiday, I had to go over and switch it off.

One summer I had a few days off and was away at a friend's house a few miles away. When I returned, the chickens hadn't been fed and hadn't been put away at night and a fox had been in and killed a few of them. It was his turn to take care of them while I was away, and they had no water, and he hadn't bothered to take the dead ones away. He had known that I was very fond of them, and laughed when I became upset. I noticed that there were no eggs anywhere to be collected so he had been around for that but didn't give a shit about their food or safety. What a mockery of a man.

Apart from having to live next door to this asshole and forcing myself to be cordial I did enjoy being there and I really looked forward to when the house would be full and guests from around the world would come to stay. When the guests came the large house transformed into a hotel and I became the chambermaid in the morning, making beds and tidying rooms and bathrooms, and then spent the rest of the day cooking. They were always very kind and clean, and they would acknowledge and speak to me and genuinely take interest and be grateful for my help. They would leave me lovely large tips when they left, usually in the form of cash but sometimes they would leave an expensive box of chocolates or bar of soap, and once a lady left me a pair of tickets to Glyndebourne that she didn't have time to attend.

It was nice that they knew how to treat staff who had provided a pleasant service and it is such a shame that twenty-odd years later there are some people who come to stay where you are working and cannot even manage to say hello or even smile at you, which demonstrates that equality doesn't apply to everyone, and it's fine to be a stuck up bastard and a cheap stuck up bastard at that.

During the summer a lovely Spanish businessman would come and rent the whole house for a few months to escape the heat of Madrid. He would bring a team of staff with him: cooks, cleaners, chauffeurs, chefs and the like, and bring crates of lovely foods and wines and sets of beautiful dining and silver table settings. He and his guests would have long three-hour lunches on the terrace and late dinner parties in the large, cavernous dining room, which would then turn into rather raucous but highly anticipated revelry. The guests would be out in the gardens and on the patios swaying to classical flamenco guitars and drinking red wine, and from where I was in the old coach house I could hear the tempo of the hot night and ballads being sung in foreign but familiar accents. The businessman would make a point of greeting the staff every morning and take particular interest in the extra effort I was making towards the comfort of his friends and in the large floral displays that were in all the rooms throughout his stay. One of his friends who had arrived from Seville offered me a job on the spot in her flower shop and loved my English style of arrangement. I was so flattered and in awe when she handed me her business card; I felt giddy and was thrilled to have been spoken to in such a gracious way. She had taken the time to walk from room to room and look at all my arrangements and to tell me in her lovely accent how they made her feel and how I had evoked a spirit for the artisan, and I should feel proud to have the gift. Wow! I hadn't heard such words of praise and encouragement for years, since my mother was alive. and it made me so happy.

Sometimes I think of that moment and the florist in Saville and wonder what might have been if I had gone for it and it always makes me smile. When it was time for them all to go the visiting staff would pack everything up and spring clean the house from top to bottom leaving it all polished and fresh and ready for my boss to return for the weekends. On the last day all the staff would be lined up to shake hands and say farewell and the businessman would be there with envelopes of cash as tips to distribute to me and the creepy gardener who had surprised us all by appearing at the last minute with his incessant silly grin and his grubby hand out. He had talked the young chauffeur into mowing the lawns with the ride on mower so had done the least amount of work and was the last person to deserve such a nice gift.

At New Year the house was rented out while my boss was away in America on holiday. I was looking forward again to new guests arriving and hoped they would be as nice and easy going as the Spanish people were. They turned out to be English and had children and they were staying for a short two-week break, so I imagined it would be a quiet break for them and myself, but it turned out to be the total opposite. It turned out to be two weeks of hell and it came along with a large helping of utter disbelief and outrage.

You would like to think that the sort of people who think nothing of paying ten grand for a two-week stay in an Elizabethan mansion would be respectful and aware of its age, history, and contents, and that they would be the type of people whose children would have courteous and impeccable manners. Wrong! It was like something I could never imagine, and it made me want to leave and never come back. Now I know that every mother is different, and they have different methods as how to raise their children, but this family was something else and proved that all the money and privilege in the world and at your fingertips meant absolutely nothing.

What is the point of having it when the harm has set in and it has made you so self-centred, oblivious, and feckless that you can't even be bothered to communicate or engage with your own children? I was aware that they had brought a nanny with them to care for the kids, but I did not know she would be off her head, pissed up for two weeks and letting the kids run wild and that the so-called parents would be fine with it as long as they didn't have to deal with them. The kids managed to run riot and wreck just about everything they could get their mucky little hands on. The parents didn't give a shit and had the attitude that as they were paying a lot of money to stay then the kids could do as they pleased, and they were justified to leave it with thousands of pounds of damage as it was just a holiday rental. There are a lot of people out there with the same mentality. So arrogant and devoid of any responsibility that they really do think they are untouchable, and God like, an icon of affluence, a self-assured and stellar peer of the realm who can do anything and treat everything like it was put there on earth to be a plaything just for them.

I was on my holiday break after working most of the Christmas holidays and was on the estate for the guests as a daily to come in and change the beds every few days and do a quick tidy up in the mornings and light clean and maybe the odd trip to the shops if they needed anything. Things like newspapers or a bottle of wine or collecting a takeaway meal from the next town as the estate was remote and there wasn't much around it. Every morning when I went into the big house, I could not believe what I was seeing. The parents would be nowhere to be seen and would still be in bed or in another part of the house hiding from their offspring. The kids would never have any clothes on, and I thought it was strange that they were both still in nappies even though they were of school age. They didn't appear to be able to talk and could only yell or scream and neither had been taught any basic table manners and they would eat while sat on the floor with their plates of food, using their hands and throwing it around and playing with it like infants do when they are bored with it. The nanny would be sat in a chair watching them and she would never attempt to rein them in or say anything or even look like she cared what they were doing.

As I went through the rooms, I would spot the broken and smashed toys that had been thrown around amongst soiled clothes and dirty shoes and revolting full nappies that had been left, sitting on the Axminster carpet or perched on top of a Tudor oak table. One morning I discovered several of them resting against an ancient and faded wall tapestry and more in the dining hall placed on the Georgian silver salver. Half-eaten lollies and sweet wrappers were strewn about the great hall that had been built in the 1500s; an upturned potty that had been full of urine had stained the old flagstones; and I looked up at the oil paintings of the old ancestors with their snooty and dour expressions, and felt that their stern disapproval was totally justified. The ultimate of disrespect came when I went upstairs with fresh laundered towels and an overwhelming stench of putridness had permeated throughout the top two floors of the house. At first, I thought an animal had got in or that someone may have tracked dog shit into the house, but there were no animals and no dogs around. I located the offending odour and the room it was occupying and discovered to my horror that it was in the bedroom that the kids were sleeping in. The bedroom was the one that my boss used for her grandkids when they came to visit, and it was a sweet little room with hand painted walls featuring a traditional country garden with woodland creatures and fairies and toadstools and the carpet matched the pastel shades of the lampshades and quilts.

The entire room was in disarray and one of the filthy brats had shit in the corner and then trod in it and it was all over the carpet and the floors of the adjoining bathroom and hallway. The bathroom looked like hell on earth; the kids had squeezed the toothpaste all over the surfaces and smeared it on the windows. They had filled the bath and dumped the whole supply of toilet rolls into it along with about half a dozen clean bath towels. I was so shocked I didn't say anything and was completely dumbfounded. My God, are people really bringing their kids up in this way and considering it to be acceptable behaviour? I have owned animals that were better trained and in control and I felt like going to see the nanny and the parents and slapping their faces. I had no words to express, and I was so sickened by it that I left the house without saying goodbye and I remember promising myself that I would not step foot in there until they were gone. I didn't care if I got the sack or not, but there was absolutely no way I was going to spend any of my time cleaning up after their scummy brats.

I rang my sister and made her come and pick me up and I spent the last few days at her house waiting for the pigs to leave. I was dreading going back and to have to clean up the crap they ultimately would be leaving behind. But I did. And to my surprise, they had actually tidied up and had put all of their rubbish and filth into the bin. So, it turned out to be a relatively normal clean up, although they had broken a bed and failed to clean the shit off the carpet adequately, so I had to hire a carpet cleaner and waste half a day cleaning it. They hadn't even had the courtesy to leave a note and when my boss saw the damage and I told her what sort of people they were, she went ballistic. I didn't blame her, though; can you imagine someone doing that to your private home?

I have worked for and have come across many scumbags, but I have never witnessed such brazen and wilful neglect of basic human decency as I did with these guests who were so hubristic and deranged to call themselves parents.

I bet those kids who are now older teenagers have not changed much and their parents will be similar. Kids learn from their parents and as I would find out in future jobs, all this abnormal behaviour becomes normal in some cases, especially the wealthier and more prosperous the family are. You would think I was working in some deprived third world country with no morals, decency or values, but I was in a very affluent area in the south of England. This scenario is always associated with poverty, ignorance or substance, abuse and neglect, but no, this was in the fifth richest country in the world. What you would expect to find in the underclass and lowest echelons of society is very much alive and thriving amongst some of the richest people too, along with some of the nouveau riche and pretenders who were never brought up with class and manners and who are now so rich that protocol and etiquette doesn't matter to them.

It is amusing to think how things have changed. It used to be the poor people who ate the brown bread, and the rich would only eat the white; and now, the brown bread is fashionable and expensive, and the white bread is cheap and frowned upon. If you had a tan in the old days, it showed that you were poor and had one because you were outside toiling in the fields or streets all day. Today, a tan is a status symbol to show you have been abroad or can afford to have a perma-tan sprayed upon you all year at your local salon. The use of tobacco, sugar and opiate based drugs have all the look of being out of fashion within the elite circles who were the first to be able to afford them and use them, but now are a mainstay in the world and with poor groups of everyday people.

When I was a child in the 1970s, we had family values

instilled in us at school and we were brought up to respect elders, policemen and authority, just like the kids who went to the private schools; we were taught the same manners and esteem. Now it looks like all children have become the same and total disregard for most things is the order of the day. Now it is all about "me" and how to get everything to benefit and work for "me". Respect must be earned. I can still feel what my father's belt felt like if I stepped out of line; how it felt when a teacher screamed at you in your face in frustration and dragged you out in front of the class to the headmaster's office to get a ruler slapped across your hand. That would be classified as abuse these days, but it never hurt my generation and although I was a cheeky shit when I was a schoolgirl, I knew my place and my limit, and I like to think that I have turned out okay and that I am decent person. I think a lot of kids nowadays need a bit of a kick up the arse when warranted, not necessarily physically, but in a lot of cases that wouldn't hurt either and most could use a dose of reality along with whoever is in charge of them.

After the fiasco of the unusual guests, I settled back into my routine and carried on as normal, working and enjoying life and then the summer arrived. I had gone above and beyond in my duties and went the extra mile, and my boss rewarded me with a week's holiday and the keys to one of her homes in Cornwall which included the services of her live-in housekeeper. It was so nice of her to do this, and it was a very special treat for me because now I was being made to feel pampered and cared for and this warm-hearted gesture made my spirits soar. When I visit Cornwall now, I always think of her and that beautiful house and how lucky I was to have experienced it. The holiday had been glorious and like most holidays I didn't want to come back to my daily life and now I wished I hadn't as misery was waiting there for me in the guise of the creepy and spiteful gardener. The hideous gardener was so incensed that I had been given something that he hadn't and made it his mission to destroy my career; however, I was determined not stoop to his level and kept pretending that I was happy. I would leave on my own terms and would not let him think he could intimidate and coerce me, and I started to buy the *Lady* magazine again to start looking for something new. The creep was having time off at Christmas and I knew that if I could get the timing right, I would have my revenge and I knew that if the housekeeper was to leave suddenly, then he would have to be on the estate until a new housekeeper was hired and had moved in. I know it sounds mean of me, but this man was so devious and calculating that he deserved it. There was no way I was going to let him walk all over me. He was going to take everything I could throw back at him and I didn't care about his family either, who showed utter contempt for me by never attempting to communicate or even say hello. I'm sure they knew how he was treating me as they were doing the same thing as he was.

I ended up enduring weeks of torment but his sophomoric plan of mental torture towards me wasn't working and I could easily outsmart him while I continued to pray for a job to come along at the right time. He tried everything to stir up trouble and cause as much conflict as possible, but he failed. He didn't seem to realise in his tiny mind that for me, changing jobs was no big deal and I had no fear of doing so as I had experience under my belt, and I was willing to travel anywhere in the country.

I was in a good position to be able to pick and choose whatever job appealed to me and that it was the luck of the draw which one I would end up with, which is always the fun part. This terrifies some people, unknown territory and new faces. Some people are frightened of change and will happily plod along in life doing the same job and living in the same street and talking to the same mug. That is fine for them but for me it is what I ultimately run from. I love to explore different surroundings and all forms of life and changing my world on a regular basis is what has made me who I am and has also given me a bit of an advantage in everything I do. Some employers will often comment on the number of jobs

I have had and don't like the fact that I have moved around and had both live in and out jobs. It is a myth that employers want you to be tied to one job with one employer for most of your life and that it shows stability and reliability, which it does, but it can also show lack of vision and ambition and flexibility and creativeness. Especially in the last decade or so when jobs were scarce and the recession dragged on and there were more people trying to get them; even now, employers aren't looking to keep someone on for years, so don't be scared to have an assortment of jobs on your CV as it shows you have heart and are up for trying new things.

On the scale of things life is short. Take a chance. Take a risk. Try as many new things and ideas as possible and create adventures as you never know when your life will end. Be the underdog. Bet on the outsider. Don't let anyone tell you or make you think that you can't achieve your wildest dreams, and if they do, just ignore them and be glad that you aren't a bitter and jealous individual who has failed in life as a human being. Don't let others oppress your unique qualities by making you feel beneath them. You can take yourself as far and as high as you want to go. Grasp it with both hands and never look back. No regrets. You can always try again. If you fall off get back in the saddle and take back control. Try to avoid negative personalities and don't feel you have to put up with certain situations that you know are wrong and make you feel uncomfortable. Always do what is right for you because that is what everybody else is doing. You are number one and always look out for you. You deserve no less.

I went out on a few interviews and ended up having to choose between four potential new employers in four different areas of the country. I had done the hard work and now it was down to luck, which as you know has a certain element surrounding any choice you make in all aspects of life. As luck had it, the one job that stood out from the others didn't start until mid-December, and although it coincided with my plans for revenge, it appealed to me the most as the people who interviewed me seemed very laid back and welcoming. They were so lovely it felt like I was talking to people who were actually interested in me as a person and who respected what I did rather than making everything about them. I accepted the job a week later and then started to plan my escape from the cretin gardener and the job that had turned sour due to his relentless and unfair sabotage of my every movement.

The silly games continued, and he carried on with a vengeance, dismantling appliances that I had to use and draining the diesel out of the vehicle used for errands and hiding the linens that would be returned from the laundry. All the while my boss was starting to think that I was becoming incompetent and taking the job for granted and it became so bad that one day I told her what was really happening.

She was very cool and calm about it as if she believed me and I know she did, but she seemed to dismiss it as well and instead acted as though she didn't want to become involved in our standoff with each other. It was sad to realise that she didn't want to step in and end it all, but in my head I didn't care anymore. The goings on in the house didn't really impact her life anyway, and what was happening to me was not going to be considered a problem.

That December she would be on the other side of the world, and I would be moving out under the cover of darkness to start my life again. She would be unaware for weeks. Why should I give her my notice if she wasn't interested in my wellbeing anymore? The creepy gardener would have to cover for me until she came back from holiday after the New Year. No holiday for him and I didn't feel one bit of remorse or pity for it.

CHAPTER 5

THE LOVELY COUPLE

The "lovely couple" job has to be one of my favourite and more pleasurable experiences in the role of housekeeper, and to this day I remember them with much fondness and, with a bit of sadness, as I would like to think I would still be working for them if it wasn't for the interference and nasty tactics of ruthless and cowardly people who they had the misfortune to be related to.

I had now prepared myself to look out for rivals in the form of so-called colleagues, but I had no idea that some of the most hateful and cruel treatment could ever come from an employer's family and especially, associated with such nice and genuine people who had now become my new employers. They truly were kind and supportive and had impeccable manners that came from the greatest generation. He was a very intelligent and successful engineer and inventor, and she was the daughter of high-ranking military and her beauty and elegance reflected in everything she did, right down to her passion which was her love for animals. She devoted much of her time to their welfare by creating a sanctuary for waifs and strays within the grounds of their estate. She devoted most of the day tending to them and seeking out other creatures who needed rescuing and she would never give up on them, even if their death was imminent.

Anyone who can show so much love and empathy towards an animal, giving time and money for little in return, is a sublime and honourable being. What a shame that there are not more people like her in the world today, especially a wealthy one, who does good things with their money instead of being a smug and greedy cretin who hoards it or uses it as a shallow fashion accessory.

You can always tell the very rich from the middle classes. The ultra rich will never mention their wealth or talk about money, and they will always give it generously when needed and not waste it on bourgeois crap either. The middle classes constantly moan about it; the fact that they haven't enough of it but like to think that they deserve so much more. The super rich don't have to brag or pretend they are something they are not and the aforementioned behaviour would be thought of as being crass and vulgar. My working-class background, which was neither poor nor deprived, came with the same morals. Do not discuss anything personal including your financial business and do not discuss religion or politics when amongst an unfamiliar crowd or group of people in an unfamiliar place. Same with behaviour. Do not scream and shout and then expect to have any respect. The pretenders will always give themselves away when they do this.

I was so glad and lucky that my new boss was kind and conventional and a pleasure to be around, and she was always grateful and full of praise in everything I did. She would thank me every afternoon after I had finished for the day and she trusted in me and never tried to interfere in any of the housekeeping chores, just as it should be. Her husband was also very kind and full of integrity and affable and whenever there was a problem, or a matter needed resolving you could approach him with no fuss or drama. He always treated me with much courtesy and fairness. He was the salt of the earth, and it made me so angry that some of the people that were the closest to him, who he had put his confidence in and supported financially, would ridicule him and his wife, hoping for the day he died so they could move in and help themselves to his legacy.

I had a beautiful cottage to myself on the massive estate which once belonged to a prominent racehorse owner and breeder in the 1970s and the property was still intact with its many acres and gates and secluded position. It had fabulous views, and the large house was modern and very tastefully appointed.

The actual job was very easy as the house was a newly built and therefore it was never dusty or musty, or full of bugs and insects, which is usually the case with older houses and especially old timbered houses. I like old and new houses equally if the owner gets it right and furnishes it in relation to its age and size. Nothing screams amateur or looks more hideous than modern furniture and fixtures and fittings in a Georgian house or a Victorian one stuffed full of heavy old oak furniture. Antiques are cool and vintage bric-à-brac can be charming and everyone has their own idea of how their home should look and feel, but most get it wrong. They may have hired an interior designer and stuffed it full of expensive crap, while some like to think that because something is old it is worth a lot of money, when it is usually quite the opposite.

I loved the new house I was working in. It was a complete contrast to the Tudor mansion I had come from. I now found myself in a light, totally white and airy sophisticated new house which was like something you would see on a cliff top on the Californian coast or in the Hollywood hills. The extensive gardens and rhododendron bushes when in bloom added to the aura and when coupled with the warm wind that would blow in during the summer and surround the estate, it would feel like being in the perfect utopia for the soul. It felt like innocent paradise. In the winter just before Christmas it would be transformed into a wonderland and the trees would be lit with twinkling lights and the interior of the house would be decorated in seasonal colours and trimmings. The annual lavish party would be held with at least a hundred guests in attendance.

It was great that my new employers were very young at heart and their friends and guests were all friendly and they treated me as an equal. They never made me feel like the hired help as a lot of people tend to do nowadays when visiting. Some people think you are so beneath them that they don't even look at you, let alone say hello and will even make a point of letting you know you will not be acknowledged again once you have opened the door to them and let them into the house. When this happens to me now, I treat them in the same way. I don't say anything to them or offer them anything. I carry on with my work without a glance in their direction and then leave the room which they are in, finish up, and then leave the house with the shitty vibe that they have brought with them. If you start trying to seem gracious and caring don't bother as they just want you to kowtow and grovel to them, to stroke their ego, and they don't deserve any special treatment if they are rude bastards anyways.

The guests at these Christmas parties were all very proper and old school and I soon discovered that the ones with the attitudes were, of course, the pretentious caterers who would come every year and a few of the in-laws who were unfortunately connected to my new boss. You can expect shitty treatment from extra staff that are brought in at certain times and they will hate it that you are new, and they will think that they are justified to bully and exploit you. I was amused when they commenced with their pathetic display of their culinary genius, heating up the cheese on toast which had been renamed "petit fondue", I felt embarrassed for them when they gushed to the guests to try the "southern gumbo", which they made from a pre-made packet of Spanish style rice, a spoon of it plopped into a cup and a sad and anaemic prawn placed on top. Voila! It's amazing how some people are in such denial. I guess they are raking the money in, though, with the below average quality of food sold at extortionate prices… but hey, what does an uneducated and glorified cleaner like me know about anything? It's always the same when people know they have been sussed out. Even more contempt and scorn will come your way. Most of these fools don't realise that what they do isn't rocket science and that the difference between you or I doing the same job is that they are getting paid a fortune for the same thing you can do. But, because they have a mediocre certificate saying they have passed a basic test, they believe that only they can do a good job and they are then authorized to tyrannize and dominate others when all they have done is put a frickin meatball on a stick and made a dip out of ketchup to go with it. Anyone who loves food and can cook can be a caterer and start a business doing it. Some of these caterers are on the same level as some arsey interior designers and party planners, unfit to represent their chosen profession and uncertain of its true interpretation. Anyone with an ounce of common sense can do these types of jobs. Gardening, painting and basic car maintenance are all easily doable by anyone who has a little common sense.

My tied cottage was situated on the estate and roughly two hundred yards from the boss's house, and another larger cottage was situated a further hundred yards along from there. Her cousin lived in it and if you were to meet them both it would be like comparing chalk and cheese. As the months went by, I was very happy, and I gradually got to know this female cousin better. It started out with the occasional invite to pop over for an evening drink and then over the years it became invitations to lunches and dinners and sometimes to just come over to hang out with her and her boyfriend. At first it was all very pleasant and friendly, and I looked forward to going. Sometimes they would come over to my cottage and we would have the most lively and jovial dinner parties, the mood would be very light and gay, and I really thought they enjoyed my company as I did theirs and that we were all quite good friends.

On holidays and other special events other family members of my boss would come to the big house, and I was always invited – as a guest – being wined and dined, but also to help out with the food and to set and clear the tables and so forth. The immediate and closest family members were very nice and polite and had welcomed me like my boss had, but a few of the in-laws who were connected by marriage did make it clear to me that they didn't appreciate my company. It didn't bother me at first as I knew they had married above their status and that their common manners and etiquette had given them away. The older children were all successful and good-natured and had been brought up to respect everyone but, as usual, one or two of the spouses had let all the trappings of wealth go to their heads and now were playing a charade or as I like to call it, having their Marie Antionette moment. Precious and precocious.

Look at me, because, ME. I did as I always do, laugh in my head and let it all slide. I liked my job and my boss so much and back then the snotty attitudes didn't bother me as much.

One day after an Easter weekend which was ruined by one of the women getting drunk and causing a scene and an argument with another family member, my boss pulled me aside and warned me that one day this conceited trouble maker would do the same to me and to be on my guard. She was talking about her cousin, my neighbour, who lived next to me and as the years went by, I regret that I didn't heed her warning. It always happens if you are of a sound and kind nature. Someone somewhere will seize on this and take it as a sign of weakness and then use it against you for whatever reason. It is very sad and common for a lot of people who are trying to be a good person and just get on and enjoy their life. It is always the bitter and ugly people who will twist this virtue around and use it to hurt you and then think themselves very clever and righteous to have got one over you and basically swindled you.

Psychopaths will do this to you all the time and it is a form of perceived elitism and oppression and twisted nastiness. It makes me very angry when it happens to the elderly and vulnerable, especially when it is coming from the set of people who should know better due to their upbringing and level of education. The nerve of them, with their airs and graces and undeserved advantages and privilege, deciding you are stupid and gullible, all because you happen to be a genuinely nice person.

As time went on, I naturally spent more time in the family members presence, and I got to know each of them a lot better. I started to like some of them very much and looked forward to their visits, but I also started to see the dark side of some of their natures and incentives and I did not like the look of it or the feeling I got when I knew I would have to be near them. I remembered how I felt when I worked for Duchess and I started to resent and fear them for I knew they were of the same ilk as her grandson and they only cared for themselves and what they could gain and acquire through stealth and deception, just like a horrible and painful disease beginning to course through the body of its victim. Leaching and destroying every ounce of life out of its host so it can overwhelm and thrive and obliterate, all for its own survival. I worked out that these awful and ruthless people were plotting and scheming who was going to get their hands on my boss's wealth after they had died and they didn't care who knew about it, including me, the person who should have been left out of it completely. What an absolute bastard you must be, not only being a family member only related by marriage, but wishing people dead who are decent and kind, all for your own advantage. It's not like these bastards were hard up and destitute, they all had comfortable lives and lived in countryside homes with all the symbols of status that went with it. How the hell can people who do this sleep at night? If they have children, what affect are they having on them and what are these kids going to become when they are older? Surely, they must realise that one day, when they are older and wealthier that their kids will do the same things to them. How can this be okay?

Or is it just okay among the wealthy in society? How can people do this to their own families? Why is it always about money and possessions, and having more? Why are some people so greedy and thoughtless and disgusting? Why can't people be happy with what they have and if they don't like it then change their situation on their own? It made me start to feel that I was very lucky. I was lucky to have had an average upbringing and an average life and that money, although an essential resource, was not the meaning or way to happiness and that it really is the root of most evils. It started to show me how it could really make some who had it seem even more miserable and a cycle of excess and avarice led to nothing but torment and anguish. To those of us that have been brought up modestly – the thought of a nice little house to own or living a comfortable life – without worry of debt or having a legacy to pass on after our demise sounds wonderful. But at the end of the day, when I have the blues and am feeling down, I always turn it around and count my blessings, knowing that I too am rich when compared to the true poor and unfortunates living in many other countries around the world.

As a mature woman living in a western society, I am lucky. I am working class, and I am very grateful to be so. If I ever win the lottery or become financially successful through my writing, I vow I will never become one of these bitter and twisted women who crave more on top of what their birthright has already given them. It is so true of the old saying and I wholeheartedly agree that money does not make you happy. Trouble was starting to brew, and it was already the fifth Christmas that I was helping with, and the time just seemed to be flying by. I still loved my job, my boss, and living in the area, but I could feel undercurrents of change coming in fast. The cheery dinner parties I was sharing with the cousin and her boyfriend started to become less stimulating and jolly and gradually became more alcohol fuelled and reasons to vent anger and complain and unburden resentful feelings. One evening ended up with them arguing and revealing to me their true and frightening natures and she flipped out just as my boss had warned me years ago and she really laid into me and did a good job at making me feel like nothing. She hated the fact that I was on such good terms with my boss and that I earned good money and was living a nice and comfortable existence. She couldn't handle the fact that I, a lowly housekeeper, was treated like a family member and that the perks and fair treatment I received was out of order. She twisted it around in her head and was now accusing me of taking advantage of my position and using the family and manipulating them into giving me her share of the inheritance. What! I couldn't believe my ears. This woman who was living there for nothing and who had a yearly allowance given to her was accusing a housekeeper for just doing a job. She hated it because my boss valued me as an employee and as a person. Once again it was all about money, money that wasn't even hers and shouldn't have been mentioned to me in the first place. She had poked her nose in, and it wasn't even her business. How petty and corrupt her mind was and why should she concern herself with what I was being paid? To make matters worse she continued to argue again with her drunken boyfriend and what I heard made me shudder and recoil from them further as the horrid tale unfolded.

The boyfriend had just sold the house that had belonged to his father who had recently died, and the proceeds were to be shared with his only sister who was, unfortunately, suffering with mental health issues and was partly disabled and confined to a wheelchair. She needed a daily carer and had lived in the house her whole life and the death of her father had greatly affected her. Her brother had chosen to approach the local council and dump his sister in a warden assisted flat and told them that he himself was mentally and physically unable to care for her and when the flat became available, he sold the house and didn't tell his sister and then ripped her off for her share of it. He then took all the money and bought himself a house in a different county away from his sister so she could never find out. He stole his sister's inheritance with the full approval and support from his bitch of a girlfriend, my boss's cousin, and now they were stood in front of me arguing about the length of time it took him to find a buyer for the house and how much more money he could have got for it if only he would have sold it earlier and dumped his sister quicker.

After hearing this I was glad that the sister had been able to get away and at least was now safe in her council flat and would always receive the care she needed and have a roof over her head that she was meant to have all along. What a shitty thing to have happen to you and what a creep of a brother to not only deeply disrespect his sister but also his poor father, who had wanted everything shared equally between his two children. I hope the creep will always have sleepless nights over this and I hope that one day his conscience will get the better of him and he lives out the rest of his tawdry life in purgatory and shame. He, along with his psychopathic, sick girlfriend, are probably still alive and no doubt doing the same thing to the poor housekeeper who is working there now. It is likely they are arguing about money that isn't theirs along with the other horrible family members and hangers on and they will be counting down the days when that inheritance will come a little closer. I hope that my old boss lives to be one hundred years old and keeps them all in misery for a lot longer. I hope she is well and happy and still giving lots of love and hope to all the rescued animals who need her help. I hope she is still pissing off her nasty relatives with her unconditional kindness and concern for others and that she is continuing to give the much-needed warning to the new staff about the withered, ugly crone who lives in the cottage next to them and has the world's most devious and cretinous boyfriend who has ever lived. I had not encountered such an awful and deplorable woman as this one was until years later (who you will read about later) and was the one who helped me to make up my mind to write this outrageous memoir.

Awful women seem to be very common these days, and I am afraid to say that they are here to stay and will become even more selfish and abhorrent. It astounds me that I was so unfortunate to have to encounter and become involved with such lowly specimens as these two, and the most surprising one was the woman who had been brought up properly and who really should have known better. She was what you would recognise as the epitome of everything that is wrong when describing the phenomena of a rich bitch. Privileged upbringing, who wasn't that smart at school but became an expert in deception and illusion. Married several men for their money and then spent the rest of her life being envious and nasty to anyone who was happy, successful, or independent. Used people for personal amusement as was bored with her own lonely existence and formed false friendships to then ridicule and cast scorn behind the backs of people to then amuse and entertain her warped sense of divine image. This woman would let you into her world and then slash and cut you down to size. She had perfected a form of abuse that was so subtle, you didn't even know you had been humiliated until it was too late. She had the art of what bitch women do to other women – the sort of woman who always has that bitch look on their face, the look like they have just sniffed a shit sandwich and their face has stuck in that position. They rarely smile or laugh, and never have a kind word or compliment for anyone other than themselves. They can't stand it if they aren't the centre of attention, and they are always the first ones to start an argument or drama and use the shallowest reason to justify it. It is never their fault and false tears are easily turned on to deflect accusations which are then just as easily turned off. They will never apologise or offer any condolences but will like to patronise instead. They will seem sincere and interested and then skew events to discredit and harm your reputation. Scheming. Spurious. Sly and dangerous. No wonder a lot of men don't trust us women. No wonder a lot of women don't trust other women. You always hear about this "sisterhood" where women are meant to look out for each other. Have each other's backs. I would like to know if this even ever existed.

It feels like a lot of women hate other women. They hate them if they are prettier or hate them if their body is nicer than theirs. They hate them if they can attract more men than them. They seem to just hate for the sake of hating and you get a glimpse of this the more you get to know them.

For some reason they are able to manipulate other people, especially men, and if they can't and they know they can't influence or hurt you in any way, they will hate you anyways, but at least they will eventually leave you alone. A regular woman would be called out as a bully, but the elite bully will hide behind suppressed rage covered up with a synthetic mask of sincerity and get away with it all. Rich bitches are all false smiles and air kisses. They love to stretch the truth and will happily suck you into a meaningless conversation just to gain information that they can later use and stretch out of proportion. They will agree and bluff and emote to cover up their true intentions. Alpha bitches who are more than often rich bitches are usually lazy and idle and unwilling to do most things unless it involves luxury shopping for themselves. Eating, spending hours admiring themselves and playing with makeup, planning vacations and lying in bed for a good part of the day, take up the rest of their time. Some rich bitches do get up early to exercise but that is the most physical they will get during the day and the dirty ones will leave a trail of mess wherever they go as it is beneath them to be tidy and pick up after themselves, and why should they? They are paying someone to do it for them.

My boss was a very special lady and I have never had another one like her. She was very tidy and organised and would even clean her own bathroom and toilet before she would let me near it. She took great pride in her home and with her lovely manners and decent morals it reflected throughout her day, from inside the house and right through to the gardens and fields where the animals lived. She even had the time and interest to make sure she finished her daily duties on time to start cooking her husband's dinner fresh from scratch so it would be ready for him when he came home from the office. She is the only woman that I can remember from all my years of service who would bother to make sure her husband ate a nice homecooked meal and all made by her own fair hand. It's the little things in life that mean the most and cooking your spouse a meal is, although basic care, a sure sign that you are caring and loving.

Food is a basic necessity and providing it with love is a basic human function. Most rich bitches would never even contemplate doing anything as mundane and tedious and would rather they be waited on or be taken out to dine or have something sent in. Bitches wouldn't want to be on their feet for too long and most certainly wouldn't want to ruin their expensive salon manicures.

It is also the first and last time I saw a married couple who were still very devoted and bonded with each other. They would never argue or raise their voices at one another or bicker and moan. They were real soul mates, and they must have loved one another very deeply. They spent much of their time together and shared and laughed and hugged. No one, especially married people, seem to do this in front of anyone, not the ones I have worked for anyways. It seems that a lot of rich couples are just doing what rich people have always done, which is form a partnership based on connections and securing more wealth and producing the obligatory heir and a spare. Their relationships look colder and more formal. Clinical, forced and unnatural. Most are unhappy hence the haughty and horrid attitudes and systematic verbal abuse coupled with the loathsome expressions and the disinterested chat. I suppose they are acting in the same manner as their ancestors did; hundreds of years ago persons of wealth only married to secure more wealth and status and love never even came into it. Oh, how the apples never do fall very far from the tree!

One day, not long after the fiasco of the dinner party when the two psychos went crazy, I was outside my cottage tending to my potted plants. I ended up having a three-hour chat with one of the gardeners who had been working on the estate for the past five years and far from being surprised he listened unflinchingly and then told me that the same thing had happened to all the previous house staff. He said that the only reason he hadn't left was because he worked outside so wasn't privy to the ongoings inside the house and the bullcrap from the in-laws, although the ugly cousin and her boyfriend did like to order him about from time to time. He said that he too was subject to spats of bullying from them when they were drunk, and he only got a hello from them if the boss was around. During the summer months, the ugly cousin would sit outside and sunbathe and attempt to flirt and show off her wrinkled old body, much to the horror of the younger men. He told me that the hag would have done the exact same thing to the previous housekeeper and would continue to abuse any other person who came to work at the estate. She and her boyfriend did not want my boss to have any friendship with the help, as it was beneath her. I thought back to all the Christmas parties and special gatherings when the friends of my boss would attend, and the hag would be in a corner with the horrid in-laws, and they would be pissing and moaning and making fun of anyone she didn't like. The gardener said that he was still friendly with a few of the staff who had left and then added that they were nice people and did their job properly, but they were tired of being harassed and harangued and eventually left. He warned me that the process of my own downfall had started, and the damage would begin when the false rumours and lies spread around the estate and through the family via the bitch cousin and her boyfriend. What a pair of lowlifes! As if people who work for a living are only out for themselves. As if everyone has an agenda just because you have an unstable mind.

Today this has become rather common with young pretenders and over-privileged children that some rich bitches have. They are obsessed with other people's wealth and possessions. Preoccupied on that day when they are going to get their hands on it, as it would never occur to them to get off of their own assess and get a job, which should be very easy after all that expensive education that their parents have bought them. How very predatory and calculating and premeditated. Malice aforethought.

I thought back to when I had first started to work on the

estate, and I had asked the hag about the housekeeper who had been there before me. I had found a curious letter that had been left behind in a box in the airing cupboard by whoever had lived in the cottage before me, and although I felt guilty reading it, I did feel sorry for them. It was words from a friend who told the person to leave the estate and to come and stay with them for as long as they wanted to. It was friendly advice to the poor woman who had lived there before me. The letter begged her to get away from the poisonous atmosphere and to understand that they loved her and didn't understand why she stayed. I was always told that this housekeeper had been very duplicitous and mysterious and that she had been a woman of low character and that she would leave the estate every Friday night and not appear until Monday morning. Her clothes were cheap, and she had fake designer handbags and jewellery. This was the disgusting hag's opinion of a woman she hardly knew and had hounded out of a job and home just because she was friendly and liked by her employer. So, this, dear readers, has summed up what this vile woman was like, spewing hate and judgement on people she didn't know and ridiculing someone's taste in clothes and labelling a woman a prostitute just because they liked to spend their weekends with their friends. She hated her because she couldn't get her over for dinner and drinks and fill her with her hate and negativity.

That poor woman who had been treated so terribly had left the letter for the next person to find. She had left it to warn whoever found it of the hidden danger, a hint of what was waiting if action wasn't taken. The day that I left the job, and the estate was filled with mixed emotions. I was glad to be going and to be starting the next phase, but I was also very sad and when my boss and her husband came to see me off, they brought with them a bottle of champagne and an envelope stuffed with cash to say goodbye and thanks. They knew why I had chosen to leave, and I made a point of telling them that I was loathe to go but a line had been crossed and there was no way back. We all hugged and had tears in our eyes. It was so depressing; but when I look back now, I always smile as they were such a lovely and kind couple, and I was so fortunate to have worked for them and I will never forget them. It must have been embarrassing for them, seeing off another good member of staff and knowing that the next one was going to go under the same circumstance.

I love the old saying that says you can pick and choose your friends, but you can't pick and choose your family. I hope they are living out their retirement in peace and solitude and that their family have cut them some slack and are taking care of them for a change. One can only hope.

TERRIBLE TEMPS
CHAPTER 6
HORRENDOUS HOTELS

It was almost summer time, and I knew I could easily get work in the hospitality sector, hotels, restaurants, pubs and the like. They can be great and fun places to work, especially if you have a friendly and cohesive team who all pull their weight and take pride in the job. It is a pity that many of the hotels and restaurants are the total opposite, and you will find that if you are the new member of staff, you will get the most unpleasant jobs to do; if you are a competent worker, you will have more work heaped upon you while your fellow work mate enjoys longer tea and ciggy breaks or less work altogether.

It's funny how every work place always has that one person who takes the piss, or a group of them, and they always manage to keep their job and will be well in with the supervisor or manager. These sorts are guaranteed to be gobshites who talk crap all day and do the least amount of work. Their life revolves around what happened last night on Coronation Street or what they ate for dinner, and they bitch about their friends and partners and the actual place that you are working for. If you engage them in conversation, especially about the work place, you will find that what you have said will be repeated almost immediately and you will suddenly find yourself in a very cold place or with no job at all. It doesn't matter if you are good at the job, they will find a way to hate you. If you don't fit in or find yourself unpopular with your views on politics, then it will get worse. Bullying is still rife, and most places don't like complaints to the management, and you will be labelled a trouble maker or misfit. Most of the hotels I have worked at are like this and the restaurants and pubs were little better. It's always the same for some reason, no matter how many staff they employ or managers or supervisors, for some reason they are filthy places, and the senior staff just can't seem to see it.

Next time you visit a hotel in the UK, have a little inspection when you first show up. If the reception area is dusty and worn, then expect your room to be too. I always take note of any glass or brass in the entrance and if they are covered in smeary handprints, then I know the place will be filthy. Some managers are clueless and like to think the hotel is well trodden or my favourite, shabby chic. Shabby chic means bohemian themed furnishings, style of interior design that focuses on distressed and antique furniture, sometimes new but made to look older. Think old but elegant. Relaxed, informal and a mixture of old and new but eclectic. Think of silver or pewter, Georgian era objects placed upon a newly painted table in cool pastel shades, distressed and worn and a lamp with a vintage lace shade. Casual and comfortable fabrics and mismatched but stylish furnishings. Floral patterns mixed with earth tones. Rococo style wall panelling and bed frames. Jute. Roses. Rustic. Romantic.

It does not mean stained carpets and dirty skirting boards. Cracked cups and mirrors and uncomfortable soiled mattresses. Frayed towels and dirty rings around the bath tub. Cobwebs and dust in the corners. Old and grey ripped bedsheets and broken shower heads. Spotted tableware and chipped plates. Dripping taps and odious smells from the drains. Shabby chic? More like lazy bastards who don't care and don't mind working in a shithole and probably go home at night to the same filth, oblivious. People who are managers in these types of establishments ought to be sacked along with the useless cleaners. Not all staff are like this, however, and deserve to be respected. Sometimes they are not given enough hours of work to get the work done thoroughly or they are too busy with an unfair workload, or they are being sabotaged by another member of staff. If the hotel is a grimy mess, then it is unlikely that they will attract customers. The people who oversee the other departments within the hotel and who don't care about hygiene and basic levels of standard should not be working in these capacities and should have to take a course, or at least, upgrade their skills set, as this is basic stuff. I guess they don't count on the poor customer noticing and having to put up with their slovenly and pitiful idea of service. If you are in one of these positions and are reading this you should hang your head in shame and remember, your scummy standards reflect you, and you are dragging your place of employment into the gutter. No amount of exquisite advertising or PR work will get you out of the hole. You should start from scratch and be spring cleaning on a monthly basis or pay your poor and unappreciated staff a proper wage and enough hours or at least hire competent and qualified people.

I have worked in five-star hotels, pubs that let out a few rooms, and family run bed and breakfasts. Hotel work is the hardest work I have ever done, and both ends of it take the same out of you. The five-star establishments demand top class standards and a keen eye for detail while the cheaper places, although more relaxed, are usually neglected from years of high turnover and no thorough cleaning. The bed and breakfasts are often better nowadays than the full-on hotels as the smaller owners are more aware of what is comfy and inviting and problems can be corrected faster. It doesn't matter what size or how old or how much it costs, it has got to be clean, and it has got to be friendly and efficient and that is what will bring people back every time. They will want to linger and spend their money if they are happy. It is no use relying on silly and crass gadgets like a TV in the bathroom when the toilet seat is coming off and there are pubic hairs in the hand basin. These are tactics to avert your eyes from the sub-standard conditions. I will get to the horrors I have witnessed in most kitchens of the hotels and restaurants later. Whenever I see Gordon Ramsay freaking out in some pigsty of a kitchen I always laugh as he drops a bollock and screams like a mad thing over the rotten produce or the grease encrusted stove and believe me, he is not over exaggerating, as most places are foul and need a visit from him.

I started the summer working in a hotel near the south coast of England where it was once beautiful and peaceful and very well cared for. Now, it has almost died, and the area is over populated and somewhat of a dumping ground for anti-social families and their feral offspring. The old and opulent grandeur has long since faded, which is a shame, as money could have been spent on it and it would, no doubt, be prosperous and desirable again as a tourist attraction, but now it is cheaper and cleaner to go to Spain.

The hotel was set on a cliff top, and the views were spectacular. The gardens were lovely and mature, and the building was an old Georgian country house. Very secluded and private but very dirty and ruined. Ruined, as in it had been run into the ground and was in dire need of total restoration and a good old-fashioned industrial deep clean. The owner was nonsensical and way out of her depth in the day-to-day running of the place. She would sit at the reception desk all day smoking, talking on the phone to her friends while filing her fingernails and eating her meals, which was so rude as guests would be checking in and trying to ask questions about the area and its amenities. It seemed she was loathe to the very people who were paying to stay and keep her and her dingy house in business. Everything was a hassle for her, and her false smile never appeared on her face again after the first few minutes of meeting her.

I was shown the shabby room that served as the housekeeper's closet and linen store and had a feeling of dread when she told me I'd be shown what to do when the supervisor arrived without even looking at me. The shabby room was dark and depressing and the clean bedsheets had just been dumped in piles on the smelly floor beside the ironing board and beside them sat a pile of pillowcases. I looked into the supply cupboard and was horrified. Boxes of individual wrapped bars of soap and small bottles of shampoo for the guest rooms sat beside boxes of cheap green toilet cleaner. That was it. No other cleaning products or any cloth or tool to use apart from an aging and forlorn hoover that was held together with jubilee clips and a bungee cord.

The door was flung open and a boy of about sixteen years old walked in. He started to fill a bucket with the soaps and shampoos, and he grabbed a bottle of the toilet cleaner and an arm full of pillowcases and grunted at me to bring the hoover and follow him to the top of the stairs. No hello, no names or introductions. How rude! His mobile phone rang, and he dug it out of his cheap tracksuit bottoms and started a highly animated conversation with the caller. Every other word was "fuck" or equally offensive and amongst the grunts and shouts I had the awful feeling that I had met my supervisor, this scruffy and uncouth boy, in charge of me.

We climbed the stairs to room thirteen at the top of the house and I thought this must be an omen, as I couldn't believe what I witnessed in there and I wanted to quit the job there and then and leave, all in the space of fifteen minutes. The room absolutely stank of raw sewage. The bedside lamps were broken and hanging crookedly from the walls and there were huge stains on the carpets and the ceiling. The curtains were torn and held up on the rail with a piece of string.

The boy started to strip the bed and suggested that I start to clean the bathroom, which is the usual ploy you will have to deal with when you are new and starting out at a new place of work. He handed me the bottle of toilet cleaner and a pillowcase and when I asked him what they were for, he got cocky and then angry that I didn't want to use them to clean with. What? Where are the cleaning cloths and the usual cleaning products? Had we left them downstairs by accident? I was shocked and dumbstruck. Here they were, charging £100 a night for a below average room and they were using their own pillowcases to clean out the toilets, bathrooms, and guest areas. When I tried to explain to him how outrageous it was, he just shrugged his shoulders and started to make up the bed which was done so shoddily that I remade it properly with hospital corners when he left to go on a cigarette break. The bathroom was old and caked in limescale, grease and dirt, and hair was stuck to the surfaces. I had to fill the hand basin with water and add the toilet cleaner to dilute it enough to be able to clean with it. I moved into the bedroom and used the same solution and pillowcase to clean the tables and windowsill and skirting boards. The drinking glasses, tea tray, cups and saucers were all cleaned the same way. I wiped the bathroom floor last and by this time the pillowcase was almost black.

I pulled the bed away from the wall and the carpet seemed alive with ancient crumbs and more hair and strange bits of fluff and food wrappers. Someone's lost hairbrush lay there in the crap. I could hear the boy coming along the hallway, bumping and scraping the walls with the hoover and cursing as he dragged it into the room, and I quickly shoved the bed back to its original spot where it had lived for years. He looked around the room and the floor and announced that it didn't need hoovering and it looked fine. And then he left the room again, bumping and scraping his way back down the hallway and down the stairs to the next awaiting room. Another identical and tired room greeted us, and I honestly could not find anything positive or reassuring to say about it. I really felt sorry for whoever would be unfortunate enough to be paying to stay here. The loo had one of those plastic banners across the seat that said it had been sanitised for your protection. The decrepit shower and its curtain were so awful that you didn't want to get in it and the thought of the mouldy curtain, wet and clinging to your body, was the stuff of nightmares. The hallway had rotten floorboards and creaked when you walked along it and there were hundreds of greasy handprints all over the peeling wallpaper. The banister and newel posts had a thick layer of goo, about an inch thick and your hand would stick to it and then smell if you touched it for too long. The ground floor sitting room and common areas were fetid and old cigarette smoke lingered and ash trays were left overflowing.

What is it with modern art inside of old Georgian houses? It is so wrong and just makes it all look cheap and cheerless. Velvet flamenco dancers and bullfighters do not go with period fixtures and fittings. Tribal ethnic art is great, but it doesn't complement chandeliers and candelabra. The dining tables were picnic style, brand new pine but splattered with ketchup and brown sauce and there were old crusty chips underneath that hadn't been swept up. I was amazed that the kitchen was nice and clean but then again, they only served breakfast, so it was only being used for a few hours every morning. Next to the kitchen was the reception area and the wicker chairs for the enjoyment of the guests had been taken over by a pair of stinky but friendly dogs who you really wanted to pet but thought better of it after you caught a whiff of them and then noticed the state of their fur. The poor things, much like the hotel needed a good wash and freshen up. I just can't fathom how people think and why, in their minds, they think all is well and great and wonderful when it clearly is not. It is okay for a bit of slackness in a private home but when you are selling rooms to the public it is a totally different thing, everyone's idea of standards and their expectations are totally different things I know, but please! How can you justify selling your putrid filth? How can you charge £100 per night to stay in a less than mediocre room? I say you are taking the piss or, you are so far up your own arse that the arrogance is off the Richter scale.

I only worked there for a week as there was no way I was going to put up with an insolent sixteen-year-old boy and his theory on cleanliness, or lack thereof, and the fact that I had already secured another job at another hotel a few miles away. I didn't think it could get any more slapdash, but I was surprised that the conditions and the attitude of the staff were little better than the last place. A few of the girls were friendly but reserved and the others were bullies and bitches. It was the same thing; they were very snotty when they realised I was no fool and could quite easily and effortlessly do a good job. The head housekeeper would allot you your rooms to clean but unbeknown to the cleaner, would have entered all the checked-out rooms beforehand and taken any gratuity that had been left for them. The laziest, useless, and less than pleasant member of staff would go into vacated rooms and scout for any food that had been left behind and then would stand there and stuff her face with it. I found out that she had worked there for years, and it had been the only job she ever had. The management knew she was trouble with most of the other staff and a poor worker, but they felt sorry for her and kept her on out of pity. One day I found out that she was one of the bitches who would go into rooms and steal tips, so I did have my revenge on her.

One morning, I had cleaned one of the rooms that had a massive king-sized bed and by the state of the mess, it looked like a couple had done some serious partying in it. The mirror had been taken off the wall and a faint powdery, white residue, was evident. Empty bottles of gin and tonic were here and there and there was a discarded pair of ripped stockings on the bathroom floor, and the toilet and the bin were filled with used condoms. The remains of an Indian takeaway were on the bedside table and a plastic bag of fruit was on the floor next to it. As I threw back the bed covers to strip the bed, I saw a packet of chocolate finger biscuits and a banana lying in the big wet spot in the middle of the bed. The banana looked squashy and was discoloured with streaks of brown poo all over it and the chocolate finger biscuits seemed to be half melted and slightly slimy. I snapped on my rubber toilet cleaning gloves and gathered all the biscuits back inside their box and then put the stinky banana back into the plastic bag of assorted fruits. I changed the bedsheets and cleaned the bathroom and then proceeded to the next room on my list.

I knew the hefty cow would be along soon to say something silly and intimidating and I was ready for her.

Twenty minutes later I could hear her, cursing and talking to herself and moaning that the hallway hadn't been hoovered when she knew it didn't get done until all the rooms had been serviced. I put on my best false smile and turned to greet her, but she pushed passed me and entered the room. She spotted the bags of takeaway and fruits, and I gaily told her that they had been left behind by the guests and, as they were all wrapped up in the bag, would she like to take them? A look flashed across her podgy face like she had just won the lottery and her hand shot out and she snatched the bags and then turned and left the room. I carried on with the other rooms that were on my list and then went to the dingy laundry room which also doubled up as the housekeeper's tea and lunch room.

When I entered, I had to stifle the howl that was brewing inside of me, and I quickly found an empty seat near the back, and I started to eat my lunch. The awful cow was sat there, noshing away with gusto and smacking her lips in between gulps of Indian takeaway, followed up with chocolate finger biscuits and lastly, the squashy, stinky banana. I remember finishing work that day and feeling great, satisfied, and justified. The only way to beat a bully is with kindness and cunning, with just a bit of nastiness to match theirs.

The hotel was very average. It had once been lovely and charming and much sought after back in the day. It was now faded and tired and the overworked rooms and common areas were dowdy and threadbare. It was the same old excuse, the cheapskate owners were going to update and modernise the place but, according to trip advisor they are still saying the same thing and nothing has been done. The hotel was relying on the locals and boring middle class London luvies to keep it going and hoping the "shabby chic" ruse would work. In this case it really meant "incredibly filthy and decrepit". Wealthy modern types on holiday from the city want luxury and opulence when they have time off. They also want value for their hard-earned money and dull and dirty surroundings will not keep them loyal, especially when they are paying top dollar. This "shabby chic" bullshit they were peddling really meant that they were selling a facade. The bedrooms were bodged up with 1970's design and colour. Ugly, scuff marked floors and old bits of food scattered about the dining room, and an inch of dust that had built up over years covered the skirting boards and was ignored by staff. Greasy smears all over the windows and brass fittings hadn't been polished in ages. There were broken clocks and years of grime left in the drawers and closets in the rooms and ancient ring marks left by cups and glasses all over the writing desks. The carpets were mismatched, worn and smelly. There was an odd mix of old and original building that was next to a modern annexe which, although newly built, was tacky and already ruined by not being cleaned properly and one side of it was used by the cleaning staff as a smoking area and it was littered with cigarette ends and food wrappers and unswept leaves.

Someone had come up with the great idea of creating naff and unidentifiable shapes with the towels and then placing them on the unfortunate guest's bed. I think they were meant to be animals and they looked hideous alongside the cheap chocolates that were also left on the old and deflated pillows. The bedspreads were sticky and whiffy. Some of the rooms allowed dogs and, after being walked on the nearby beach they would return, and it seemed their owners would then let them sleep on top of the bed. The bedspread would be given the odd spray of Febreze to keep them "fresh", along with the duvets and both would be covered with numerous spots and stains. Some of the rooms had mould around the windows and vile net curtains trying to hide it. A few of the oldest and damp rooms that were in the original part of the hotel had the misfortune of being attached to the rear of the kitchen and the loud and aging and obsolete extractor fan would rattle and shake throughout the night and start again in the early morning. I felt sorry for the people being allocated these rooms and for having to pay over £100 for the crappy privilege.

There was a pub in the hotel that would fill up and be

overtaken by very loud and unfriendly locals who would get drunk and boisterous and make the paying guests feel uncomfortable and unwelcome. They felt that as it was their local pub, and they were spending their money in it during the off-peak winter months they could act as they pleased and swear and behave like ignorant thugs. The dining room was unappealing and cold and had no charisma and the waiting staff were either untrained and underpaid or they were school leavers who had no interest in the job or hotel and were only there as it was the only place offering employment that was close to their homes. They had no manners and no concept of the aura of the hotel. and they had not been taught what service meant. They were more interested in flirting with each other and gossiping rather than clearing the tables and doing their job; the older staff that had been there for years were jaded and resentful and hated the job but were too lazy or thick to even contemplate looking for another one. In the small-town atmosphere, it must have been difficult to be able to pick and choose work. I could never stay in one area for too long and the town was small, and it only came alive in the summer months. The work was seasonal and low paid and if you were a bit rowdy and well known your reputation would follow you everywhere and it could make or break your chances of employment. I did feel sorry for some of the people there but then again, I didn't feel sorry for the bullies and the bitches and thought that they deserved a shitty and mundane job to go with their shitty and mundane life. I hope they are still there, miserable and sad and still hating everything, including their job but afraid and unwilling to do anything about it. You get out of life what you put in to it. Life is what you make it. If you treat people like crap, you certainly must expect it back in your face at some point, and if you are small minded and ignorant you also deserve a boring and meaningless life.

I stayed in the housekeeping department for the season and was desperately unhappy with the way it was run and the senior staff who just didn't care about anything except power tripping and stroking their own egos. A few of them had been to minor and unremarkable universities and had studied inferior and irrelevant courses and yet somehow thought they were intellectually superior, which was so funny as they couldn't even see how awful and filthy the hotel was.

One day, I was cleaning near to the reception desk and heard some guests complaining about how under par they thought their room was and they were demanding an upgrade or a discount on their bill. I remember the woman looking at me in disgust and obviously thinking that as I was cleaning the tacky hotel souvenir cabinet that I must be the one responsible for cleaning her room. I still wanted the job until I could find a better one, but I knew I had to get away from these awful women who were in charge. I had a big stroke of luck that day as I had found out earlier that the kitchen needed a porter and even more surprised when I was allowed to transfer into the kitchen. If I had thought that the hotel was unclean, I was mortified when I stepped into the kitchen. The smell of it hit you like a punch in the face as soon as the door was closed behind you. Years worth of grease and rotten produce and stagnant water all came together at once and attacked your sense of smell which brought tears to your eyes. Bins overflowed and food waste was all over the floor. The sanitiser had no fluid in it, but it was in constant use and the walk-in fridge was horrific with mould and old blood, congealing and festering. The stack of dirty dishes hadn't been scraped off properly and a swarm of flies was hovering over it.

The chefs, if you could call them that, wore soiled whites and were more interested in the size and shape of the various servers tits and their cigarette breaks than they were about getting orders correct or showing any pride in their so-called culinary efforts. Head chef was so large he could barely stand up and was so bad tempered due to his visible ill health. He was only happy when his pint glass was being refilled. There were more cocky school leavers that were masquerading as Sous Chefs and the mess they made of their work areas proved in an instant the amateurs they really were. Again, I noticed there were hardly any clean and dry cloths, or tea towels. The breakfast chef, who was really very nice, wouldn't talk to the head chef and then the cocky Sous Chefs would be so afraid to offend the head chef they would ignore the breakfast chef and do everything they could to hinder his time in the morning. Their shitty attitude was that breakfast was menial and too basic and anyone could do it, so they treated him like he was stupid. This is so typical of the types of assholes who work in these places and they all like to hide behind each other and bully as a group as they haven't got the bottle to bully one on one.

The behaviour was condoned, you guessed it, by the dismal management and the other wastes of space that were hiding from responsibility in the other senior staff positions. It was normal for these idiots to act as one collective of bullies to intimidate staff to "put up or shut up". I suppose they were all so frightened of losing their jobs that they would do or act as they were told. Some people will always be sheep, but it really isn't right for the people who are meant to be in charge to abuse the power and use it to scare people. It feels like progress has not been made and that certain areas of the country do not realise that there are rules and conditions set in law. I just can't believe that the year 2021 seems like 1921 when it comes to fairness and equality and justice for all. It seems like it only applies to a few, the ones at the top that have the power. The ones telling us what to do and when to do it. It may as well be 1921 for the average worker as we are still expected to accept bullying and favouritism and low wages.

When you are working class, you must accept what job you can and take all the crap that goes with it. There is no union or shop steward. If you don't like it, you go or you stay, however miserable and degrading. Some people can desensitize and become a bully like the management and if not, they suffer and withdraw and are still labelled as weird or stuck up or hard to get along with.

After a few months it was time to go. The whole feeling, in both the hotel and kitchen was very creepy and the fucktards in charge only cared about themselves, what they could do to benefit themselves and how to do it with the least amount of effort. There was never a kind word or gesture or perk to reward you with a job well done and, if the owners of the place did any sort of appreciation day, it never trickled down the line of staff and only the greedy bastards who, ironically were ruining their business, got to partake in any celebration.

When I think of that hotel now, and by reading the reviews, I can tell that the same horrid people are still in charge of it, with their inflated images of themselves, and that the other lowly staff are still afraid of change and still accepting the bullying and the back stabbing. Nothing will ever change, and they will always be thinking that the big time is still around the corner. The filthy hovel will still only manage to be a three-star establishment and, even though they will con people into thinking it is four-star, they know they will never be in any league but the small one that they are in now. Remember, a superb hotel or restaurant does not need gimmickry to get people in through the doors to spend money. They don't need to scheme and trick people. If they try to hoodwink you with words like "quirky", be on your guard as it more than likely means strange, peculiar, and odd. Lame buzzwords like "eccentric" will reveal itself and become abnormal and bizarre. The absolute and top one to look out for is, the most deluded and dreadful, "shabby chic", which I can guarantee will be shabby and a million miles away from sophisticated and stylish. If you do get tricked into staying at a hotel that has bigged itself up in the advert and embellished on its actual criteria, please spare a thought for the poor staff working at these places. You have been lied to in order to get you in the door and if they are prepared to do that, then chances are the lower staff are working under pressure and under dishonest and deceitful megalomaniacs. If you have a complaint direct it at the management or owners as they set the standards and the prices. Lowly staff are always on minimum wage and probably having any tips withheld, so make sure a tip goes into their hand if you are going to offer one. They do deserve it and you don't realise how happy it can make a person feel. They will really appreciate it. It should happen more often.

CHAPTER 7

PRINCESS

I have lost count of how many part time and temp jobs I have had. I always go where the work is and have never stayed in one area for very long except London, as you can always find something to do, and you can always start low and make your way up the ladder if you are prepared to put the work in. It is still the best place to be if you want a high wage and live in accommodation for cook or housekeeper. I left years ago and now only seek employment in the countryside. The more rural it is the better. I do love a quiet life now as I am older and for me, London had changed a lot, and my wild nights of mayhem and madness are well and truly over. During one of the recessions, I did return briefly to temp as I am always for making money rather than to be idle and broke. This time I found myself working near Bayswater for an actual princess. Now it's probably not what you are thinking. It wasn't the likes of a Lady Di type or lesser from the Royal family. She was a rich bitch from a now defunct line of Prussian royalty, but she still acted as if it was relevant today and equal to what we have today in the UK. I never did hold her in any regard or in comparison with any of our royals and she certainly wasn't fit to be anywhere near our lovely Royal Family as she really was a nasty piece of work.

Behind her facade and the polite courtly manner was a hidden and terribly suppressed venom and pettiness. She was one of these wealthy people who can have anything whenever they want but was never satisfied and always wanted more. The epitome of money not making you happy. She lived on the top floor of an exclusive and very expensive apartment block that had views that overlooked Kensington gardens and the building had its own concierge and valet parking. Her apartment was vast as it comprised of two huge apartments, knocked through to make one mega one and it took up half of the top floor of the whole building. Most of the second apartment had been made up as a nursery for her kid and nanny. Lucky nanny, she had a huge area all to herself, complete with separate kitchen and sitting rooms and a private gym. The kid had their own living quarters which also had its own kitchen and sitting rooms and one massive space which was being used for its toy and play area. It is astonishing to think that the kid had more living space than your average family and that it wasn't even walking yet. Some of the toys were life sized and the walk-in closet was already overflowing and really, how many baby grows does one child really need? There were rows of baby shoes and racks of baby sized three-piece suits. The kid already had more clothes and shoes than I have ever owned to this day.

If you think this is way over the top and ostentatious you should have seen the new boss's clothes closets. Imagine the average size of an average family home's main central living room and that was the size of her clothes closet. It was so large that there were sections, all colour coordinated by shades, and all divided up by the seasons. There were separate sections for her ball gowns and suits and hats and accessories. She even had a cold storage box for her fur coats and stoles. Every item of clothing was either in a clothes bag or had a plastic covering. Every season came with a separate chest of drawers for tee shirts, sweaters, socks, knickers and nightdresses. Her bed was super king sized, and it was the largest bed I have ever seen. There was a big jacuzzi hot tub in one of the bathrooms which had had to be brought through into the building by a crane. The whole place was fitted with white marble floor tiles and antique Persian mashad rugs had been scattered throughout. The kitchens were bespoke, and the huge fridges were actually walk in cupboards that had a freezer area and a pantry at the rear. The pantry was large enough to hang a whole leg of Parma ham from a hook and still have enough room for every jar and box and packet of food known to man.

There must have been two hundred cook books on a book rack and there was a separate fridge for wines and champagne. The everyday plates and cups were from Asprey. I was dumbstruck when I saw both the nanny's and the kid's kitchens were, although smaller, exactly the same as the boss's and everything from the walk-in fridge to the Lacanche range and the plates bought in Bond Street were all the same. Talk about opulence! I was glad I wasn't responsible for cleaning any of it as I was afraid to touch anything. I had been employed to do the laundry and the ironing, for ten hours a day, six days a week, for four people.

The laundry room was vast, and I have lived in houses where the square footage was smaller than this room. There were five washing machines and four dryers. Two of the washers and dryers were for the three adults clothes, one washer and dryer were for the kid's clothes and the other washer and dryer was for towels and hand towels. The last washer was for bathmats and kitchen cloths and tea towels. There was a separate clothes hamper for clothes that were waiting to be sent out for dry cleaning and a closet for them to settle in for a few days before being moved onto their racks in the massive walk-in closet next to the main bedroom. There were three large airing cupboards and an old-fashioned drying rail that could be pulled up towards the ceiling. There was a special trouser press like the ones you see in some hotel rooms and an assortment of irons, one being a professional steam iron like the dry cleaners have. One end of the room was taken up by a contraption that ironed and folded sheets. There was a warming box that was designed for drying woollens and was set at the perfect temperature so it wouldn't shrink the garment. There was a sewing machine and a sewing box that contained every hue and shade of cotton on reels that you could imagine and a selection of different sized sewing needles and thimbles and needle threaders. A large Dublin sink with extendable hose and sprayer was in a corner and underneath was a cupboard stocked with every brand and type of washing powder, gel, fabric softener, stain remover, pods, spray and regular laundry starch for every type of fabric.

The laundry room had storage closets which was the home of the family luggage sets. No ordinary samsonite or basic sturdy cabin bags for them, it was all Louis Vuitton cases, makeup boxes, clothes bags, hat boxes, larger suitcases and trunks. Even the kid had their own set of Hermes luggage, small but in four different sizes with matching school satchel even though the child wouldn't be attending school for a few more years. There were shoe trees from Dunhill and extra garment bags, Savile Row for him and Gucci for her. They even had a special steamer for steaming a top hat for when they attended Epsom on derby day or when they went to Royal Ascot. They also had all the various clothes racks and wooden hangers, custom made which fitted nicely in the room and it felt like you were in a smart shop with racks of expensive clothes to choose from when items had been washed and were hanging out to dry. It all sounds very grand, and it was, but this room was where I stayed and worked, ten hours a day and six days a week. It had its own toilet and hand basin and a small closet that you could open out and reveal a counter top with mini fridge, a kettle and cups, toaster and microwave oven, all for my own use when having tea and lunch breaks.

My hours of work were from eight in the morning to six in the evening, with two fifteen-minute breaks for tea and a half-hour lunch break at noon. I wasn't allowed to have any drink outside of these times as Princess Boss didn't want any accidental spillages anywhere and I was also told to provide my own hand towel to use in the toilet. She had pointed out when I started that I was forbidden to use any other toilet in the apartment other than the one that was next to the laundry room. This practice is still very common in today's society, and I have worked for many wealthy families who do not want you sitting on their toilets, even though you are cleaning their house and cooking their food. Segregated toilets are still happening in modern-day Britain and most people will let an occasional builder or painter or gardener use a separate staff toilet, sometimes begrudgingly, and then want it cleaned and thoroughly bleached immediately afterwards. I have worked at many places that provided me with separate accommodation on site and I have still been told to go to my own toilet if I needed it. You could be in the middle of preparing an elaborate four-course meal for a posh dinner party, setting the table and dishing out nibbles and champagne glasses and the boss will expect you to stop everything and go to the separate building and have your pee over there. It doesn't matter if it's pissing down with rain or in the dead of winter, their toilet seat is precious just like they are. Princess Boss informed me how the washing machine worked and what product to use for each garment and what went in the dryer and what was to be hung up to dry. Then, how to fold everything perfectly so it would fit into the custom-made drawers and how to fold the knickers and socks how she liked it. It all had to be just so. It was so unnecessary and patronising, and it felt like I was a child being punished.

The next day was spent the same way and she lectured me on how to wash the bedsheets, at what temperature and cycle, and with what type of detergent. Her sheets were custom-made to go with the custom-made super king-sized bed and only one sheet and two of the pillowcases would fit into the machine at one time. Thank God there were multiple machines, although I wasn't meant to use them. It took forever just to wash her bedding and there would be eight pillow cases to wash along with six smaller ones, and all belonging to the same set of sheets. She told me that her bed was to be changed every day, along with all of her and her husband's towels, hand towels, face cloths and bathmats. The sets of sheets all had to be ironed and folded precisely so that they fit inside their own custom-made cupboard and to make sure she produced a measuring tape and a ruler and instructed me on the exact dimensions so it would all fit perfectly.

Once a month, the enormous and very heavy bedspread would be taken off the bed and sent off to the drycleaner. It would come back and live in the special airing cupboard for a few days and then it would be measured and returned to its custom-made cupboard. It would live alongside three other sets of three bedspreads, twelve in all, one for each month of the year and in four sets of designs and thickness, suitable for every season. The bedspreads that were not in season and not being used were all put into plastic bags, custom-made of course, and had to fit perfectly.

The next day was the turn of the husband's shirts. Once again, a ruler was produced to get the exact measurement for folding so they would fit perfectly into his Louis Vuitton suitcase. He was away most of the week travelling and on business. A few of the more casual shirts were just dried on hangers, ironed, and hung in his closet, but all of his trousers had to be pressed with the professional steam iron and then on the trouser press to ensure a knife edge finish. Even his jeans would have to have a crease on them. Moreover, was the daily washing, drying, and pressing of all the king-sized bedding and baby clothes. Once the sheets were dry it took an absolute age to get them into the machine that pressed and folded them because you had to get them properly folded to go in, so they came out perfect. The only way I could fold them well on my own was to lay them out on the floor and carefully fold them. Princess Boss would have gone mad if she had known this was the way I was doing it, and she would have made me wash it all again even though the tile floor was spotlessly clean. I always waited to do this when I knew she would be working out in her home gym on the other side of the apartment, and then in the jacuzzi and shower for another half-hour, and then a good forty minutes to put on all her makeup and fuss with her hair.

All the pillowcases had to be soaked first and then

starched. Sometimes, depending how much foundation she had applied, the pillowcases had to be soaked overnight to get out all the stains even though she would have taken her makeup off before she had gone to bed. It makes me howl how some women trowel on that makeup! It is the worst thing for your skin, especially if you have it on every day and it looks absolutely ridiculous when the foundation is a totally different shade of colour to your actual skin tone and the neck has none on whatsoever. For some reason it is always a few shades too dark, and it looks hideous on very pale skin and the face and neck never match or they forget to blend it and then they end up looking like some strange cartoon character. The mask doesn't hide their turkey neck and the older they are the more awful it is. Such a waste of money too.

Many of these deluded women spend an absolute fortune on cosmetics only to scrape it all off at the end of the day. I don't know why they insist on pots of super expensive creams and serums from the most expensive department stores. I suggest that if you are going to pack it on like it's Halloween, you are better off popping down to Superdrug and buying some good old Rimmel. After all, why not get the London look? Women out in the countryside don't usually wear it during the day and only tend to slap some on if they are off to the annual hunt ball or other seasonal function. Likewise with the jewellery. Nothing screams blatant vulgarity more than diamonds or other precious stones the size of walnuts being worn and flashed around during the day. Same with a wrist watch. No wonder people are having their £200k Rolex robbed off them along with their ropes of gold and designer bling. Why make yourself a target for the robbers? I can understand that city dwelling women will want to be seen out and about in their fashion queen labels but why would you want to strut around the country lanes in Chanel and Versace? Some of the saddest types of scumbag millionaires are the ones who live in the city all week and then, on Friday, come out to the countryside to their second or third home for the weekend. Instead of embracing the whole ethos of rural life they seem to think they are in the city and spend most of the weekend miserable because of the noise the birds make in the morning or, that the flies and insects like to come in through the windows or that their mobile phone signal isn't powerful enough.

I once worked for a rich, city bitch who always used to say that they had to escape the city every weekend because the children needed fresh air. Well, the spoiled brats hated it, and everything connected to country life. They didn't participate in any outdoor activities, and they didn't like animals. They didn't go outside until they were packed into the car and taken back to their boarding schools for the week. They would stay in the house and play on the Xbox or the iPhone, take selfies of themselves and fight and lay around talking to Alexa. I think the only reason the parents had a house in the countryside was so the kids could go back to their private schools and brag to the other spoilt brats what they did and where they were over the weekend, the same as when they were taken on holidays at half term. It was not really for a holiday as you or I might enjoy. It was for bragging rights and so their friends would tell their parents and it was all done to see whose parents could outdo each other and who had the best one and the most money spent on them. It also made for conversation when the bland and boring parents attended each other's country house for lunch. It was all a competition: who went where, what hotel did they stay in and for how long. Who went to the most exotic location and how many stars was the resort awarded. Fascinating really, when they had all been to the same places and stayed at the most expensive hotels they could find.

Isn't it weird to think that you must live your life a certain way and go through the same old motions just so you can impress people who are meant to be your friends? Some of these wealthy people like to think they are on a par with royalty, and they live their lives around the season and that one does certain things at certain times and that it really matters because other wealthy people are watching them and judging them, and it is all very normal. Can they truly and honestly be happy? If they are like they pretend to be, why do they slag off their so-called friends and strive to outdo them and brag and boast when in each other's company? Why are they so perturbed when one of them is richer or their kids are more intelligent and gets into a better school, or one's just sold the house and made a huge profit, or one's made a fortune on the stocks and shares? Some of them appear to be in one big competition with each other and their kids are exactly the same. They are fixated on who owns what and who knows who and they love to drop names to try to impress and drone on about someone else's wealth or achievement and who is friends with their friends and what they know and what they own. So, what if you live next to a B-List celebrity or see someone on the telly down at the local coffee shop? Why think that seeing a washed-up film star down at your local, overpriced gym somehow connects you with their life and that somehow makes you a better person who commands respect? Why do chumps get star-struck and think that being in their presence makes them special? These so-called celebs are so far up their own arses they couldn't give a toss about anything or anyone except themselves.

Some people who like to think that they have a better pot to piss in always take great pride in reminding you every so often about how great one of their ancestors was. For some reason, if there is a royal connection, they feel that it has obviously reflected onto them and that you should really be fawning over them and licking their backsides. One person who I used to have the displeasure of working for thought that his French ancestry qualified him to act like a little Napoleon. He was a little man, so I figured he had to big himself up in this way as he was probably lacking in other departments. Supposedly, his ancestors had their heads chopped off in the French revolution and he thought this made him superior to us average plebs. What a twat! No! They lost their heads because they were arrogant and greedy and, no doubt, treated others with much contempt. Nothing has changed. I had never worked for such a pompous, racist, and generally dislikeable person as this and hope I never have to in the future. His awful and equally haughty wife hated the fact that she wasn't from distant royalty and that the origins of her family wealth were a bit more ordinary.

They were only middle class and she hated it even though her father had been a successful architect. When the money came, so did the climb up the social ladder, but unfortunately, they left the important aspects of it behind like how to be kind and manners became a distant memory. She wasn't very well educated, and it showed. She ended up getting married to a friend of her father, who was older than her, but he was very rich so that didn't really matter. She acted like an immature and spoilt child, always pouting and shouting and when she kicked off on her husband or her kids or me, I felt like asking her why she chose to have such an empty and meaningless life. She didn't love her husband but was in love with the money and the lifestyle. She had everything and nothing. Everything she owned either came off her father or her husband's back and she had achieved nothing in her life, and she was resentful and hostile and pathetic. She wasn't even a good mother, and her kids were rude and loathsome and as thick as she was. They will inherit their parents' wealth and be married off to other wealthy thick idiots and so the cycle will continue. It is with much astonishment to think that today, all over the world, thick, rich women are still arranging to marry rich men and the same fate awaits their kids unless they discover they are clever enough to generate their own wealth, but then they will still no doubt marry within the same class. If a woman from a lower social class does marry into wealth, she will be slapped with a pre-nuptial agreement to sign and seen as some sort of grifter who is out for her own personal gain. A rich woman who marries into more wealth is seen as clever and deserving, a beautiful one whose breeding and connections automatically qualify her for that life. Your average woman, working class perhaps, is expected to accept her lot and keep her head down.

It is seen to be her own fault that she hasn't bettered herself or worked hard enough to go to university and to climb up the ladder that way. If it is so easy why isn't every woman from every social class and every walk of life doing it and becoming successful? Why is it that today, you are still judged by the type of work that you do, and why are some professions still sneered at and ridiculed? There is dignity in all work, and it is not the kind of work that gives you dignity but how well you do it. A lot of these wealthy women can't even fry an egg properly and they will hire someone else to do it and then eat it, and then complain about it and slag off the poor woman who was hired to cook it. Most rich women, if they don't have their own career, don't even know their assholes from their elbows but will be very well versed in hurling insults and put downs at their staff and be really good at hurting them in a subtle way. They can kill you with one glance of their heavily made-up eye and deliver the coup de grace with a withering look or a nasty sneer from their Botox filled lips. This is their education, their degree that they have learned and passed with flying colours in the overpriced and under-achieving private school that they went to. That, along with the instruction on how and where to bag a rich husband, helped by a mother who went through the same process and daddy's cash.

I arrived at work one morning and found Princess Boss in a state of histrionics. She was shouting and screaming at the nanny and the kid was running around naked and the usually pristine apartment was in a bit of a state. As I walked through, I noticed that the kitchen hadn't been cleaned and there was a stack of dishes beside the sink and that one of the sitting rooms needed a big tidy up. I was in the laundry room and about to load up the washing machines when she came in stomping and pissy and moaning. She was in a rage because the daily cleaner had quit over the weekend and the agency hadn't replaced her yet. Princess started on one, going on about unreliable this and useless that. The audacity of how people can decide what they want to do and when they want to do it. How ill-bred people have no manners and only think of themselves. Really?

I laughed to myself as I watched her face turn purple. I expected her to start foaming at the mouth and to wring her hands. It was fun to see her over react which is normal for these types. The world would obviously end all because someone made up their own mind to end a situation that they felt was a life sentence of hard labour with a sadistic warden.

After half an hour of mock tears and simulated hyperventilating, she finally asked me to do the cleaning, on top of the laundry, and that she would pay me double what I was earning until a new daily could start. I said yes as I had got the hang of all the measuring bullshit, and it wasn't taking as long to do it. I guess some women are scared to chip one of their fingernails or work up a sweat that will ruin their makeup. Maybe the escaping steam at the end of the drying cycle will wreck the hairdo and make if all fizzy.

I finished up and went into the drawing room but not without a further lecture on how to dust and hoover properly and the exact amount of wax to use on the tables and with what cloth to do it with. After I had finished that I watched her walk around the room with a pair of white cotton gloves on, running her fingers along all the surfaces and inspecting them afterwards. My God. How petty and small your world must be. How can you live in a city and be so paranoid about dust and dirt? Fancy being more worried about your clean house and not caring about going outside in the filthy air and breathing it in? Most of you who have lived in a big city and actually walked around and rode the underground or sat upstairs on a bus know how disgustingly dirty the air is. You can see the dirt coming out of your hair when you wash it and see how black your tissue is after you blow your nose. Your clothes usually need a wash after wearing them once and you never ever wear anything that is white if you can help it. If you are so deathly worried about surface dust in your home, why the hell would you bring up a baby there? Why would you have children living in such filthy conditions? If you are that afraid of dust in the city, you are being very selfish and cruel to bring up a child or keep an animal there. Of course, she wasn't that paranoid she was just being pathetic, patronising, and mean.

Over the coming weeks I discovered that she would do really weird and creepy things like hide coins and other small objects under cushions and rugs and amongst her knickknacks, in the hope that I would miss them while cleaning. And then in her weirdo head, she would feel justified to criticise my work and chastise me and have a tantrum and say her house wasn't cleaned good enough, and how awful it was that I couldn't be trusted to do a good job. If you are working for someone who makes it their mission in life to set booby traps for you and hide stuff to try and catch you out, then get away from there as they do not trust you and they do not like you. They have such tiny, warped minds and spend more of their energy on imagining some sort of crime that has taken place and then they will wait for the day that they can catch you out and turn it into an enormous problem that they will constantly harp on about and keep on bringing up until the day that you leave. They will complain and say that you have let them down and that you are useless and unprofessional.

I thought she must have had some form of OCD or maybe she was autistic but, in the end, like a lot of people I have worked for, it turned out that they were suppressing their true selves and so was she. If one of them had been honest and upfront and had mentioned a mental illness, I would have understood and felt compassion, but the elite would never admit anything like that or ever apologise. Sometimes you can work it out for yourself as you may come across a prescription or two for the treatment. The fact is, many have made themselves ill with too many tranquilisers and sleeping pills and all washed down with too much alcohol. The elite like to refer to themselves with terms like "eccentric" or "highly strung" when describing their versions of mental health. The working class and poor are described as "mad" or "deranged". The thought of someone trying to sugar coat a serious issue while ridiculing others is disgusting and if you need help please go and get it. There is no shame whoever you are.

I was so glad that the time was closing in on the temporary position and I started to mark the days off on the calendar. I couldn't wait to escape from the nasty Princess Boss, and I looked around for other upcoming jobs. The past two months had seemed like two years, what with the ten-hour days and the six-day weeks. No wonder the laundress who was on holiday was away for so long. I felt sorry for her, thinking that she would have to endure ten months of slogging her guts out all week long until she could escape away again.

I contacted my agent, and she was happy to say that she had a job on her books that she would send me out for, and she promptly set about arranging a new interview for me in West Hampstead. It was another live out temp position for a month, so I agreed and felt very pleased. I liked the idea of a new area to work in and explore and the money sounded generous. I was staying at a friend's flat that was close to the main bus routes and tube lines so I did have a great sense of freedom as I could leave the job behind at the end of the day and was able to have time out from it. I knew I could handle the last week of working quite easily and I looked forward to what was around the corner.

I smiled to myself and shook my head as I was dusting. I knew where the silly cow would hide the coins and the various objects, and I knew when she would come into the laundry room and inspect the clothing and measure the folded items in the airing cupboard. I had the kitchen cleaned and the sitting rooms tidy, and I had all the days sheets and clothes and towels done on time with time to spare to mop the laundry room floor and clean the toilet. On the last day I had everything perfect, and she was miffed that she could have no reason to start complaining and criticising.

I said goodbye to the nanny and wished her well. She was a cold and stuck-up bitch as well and it nearly killed her to say anything pleasant back to me. She was still fuming at having to take on extra duties when the cleaner quit and that the boss still hadn't found another to replace her. She had the hump because she became responsible for cleaning the nursery, along with her own living space and the en suite bathrooms belonging to the boss and her husband. The nanny said goodbye with a sneer and as she was walking away, she muttered something in French. I never tell employers I can understand French as I like to see if they will be bastards and automatically assume you are stupid and uneducated and that you won't have a clue what the hell they are saying. I heard her say "bon débarras, les incompetant". I felt like booting her hard, right up her scrawny arse but instead turned around and walked away. I felt great because I was just about to walk out of the door forever, and she was stuck there with snooty Princess and her screaming brat. It wasn't worth bothering to say anything back. She was laughing hysterically like a loony, and I waited in the hallway to say goodbye to Princess Boss like I did every weekend, but this time she did not show up.

As it was my last day, I thought it was odd so a few minutes later I ventured towards the kitchen towards the sounds of more laughter and people's voices. I found her and the nanny, giggling to each other and as they turned and looked up and saw me their faces turned sour, and the mood turned to stone. I expected her to hand me my pay cheque and say goodbye, but she didn't and just looked at me blankly and asked me what I wanted. What? How bloody rude! She knew what. I asked her for my cheque, and she shook her head and made up some excuse about not having any cash in the apartment and that she had just at that moment run out of cheques. I looked her square in the eye, and she knew that I knew that she was full of shit and lying. These mega rich people always have a wad of cash on them and a few cheque books to choose from, and they always like to try to get out of giving you what you are owed if they can get away with it, especially if they are the nasty type. They assume that you are always destitute and desperate, and they will use this tactic to humiliate and degrade you. To put you in your place, on a whim to amuse themselves. "Ring me on Monday," she said, with no emotion or empathy or sincerity. She turned away and walked back into the sitting room. No goodbye. No thank you for your hard work. Nothing. The nanny looked at me and gave me an over the top and crazy grin and I was livid, but I didn't lose it and give her any satisfaction. She was hoping I would so she could ultimately go to Princess to report the gossip, but I left the apartment and as soon as I stepped out in to the evening, I felt so happy and relieved that I would never be working in there again. I rode home on the tube and when I got back to the flat, I celebrated with a Chinese takeaway and a bottle of cava. I put my feet up and relaxed. Tomorrow was Sunday and it would feel even better than usual as I would no longer be doing the same boring routine the following week.

On Monday morning I phoned Princess Boss and there was no answer. I called again and again, and still no answer. I spent most of the week trying to call and no one ever did pick up the phone. A few times it did indicate that the line was busy, so I knew that the slag was there. I would have known if she was going away as I would have had to measure her clothes to fit in her Louis Vuitton suitcases and get all her other bags cleaned out and ready.

She finally answered the phone on the Friday and made the excuse that she hadn't been well and therefore couldn't answer the phone. She suggested that she would pop a cheque in the post for me, but I said no. I told her that I would come to the apartment and that she could give it to me personally. I explained that it would be quicker to pick it up rather than wait for the post and then have to wait longer while it cleared in the bank account. She agreed to meet the next day and told me to arrive around noon. The next day, I was there on time, and I was surprised to be met by her husband who gave me the cheque. I had never met him before as he was always working, and I only recognised him from remembering his face in some of the framed photos that I would dust every day. He was a lot younger than she was, which surprised me as it's usually the other way around and it showed when he didn't say a word to me, but just opened the door and held the cheque out to me. So rude!

What is it with people who you have worked for and are owed money, getting shitty with you when they have to give it to you? Do they think that they should be getting the work done for free? Do they think that they are legends in their own minds? After getting the cheque to my bank I found out that it would take a week to clear. This was years ago and things like banking took a lot longer than it does now, so I drew a line under it all and decided it was all done and dusted and glad that it was all over. How wrong was I!

A week later, while at the bank, I checked my account and noticed the money had still not cleared, and to my utter disgust, was told that the cheque had bounced and there was nothing I could do about it. Oh, but there was! As you can imagine, I was about to blow a gasket and I was so angry and in shock that I headed to the nearest pub to have a drink and calm down and think of what to do next. Three pints later, I had made my mind up. I had one more pint for Dutch courage.

I went to the apartment, unannounced and approached the concierge. He looked me up and down and with a withering glance told me, in no uncertain terms that there was no way he was going to let me in the building and go upstairs. I gave him the same look back and told him, very calmly and methodically, that a theft had taken place and please would he be so kind as to telephone the police.

Years ago, the police in London would attend quite quickly to things, including theft or robbery and very quickly if it was an exclusive and expensive address and they came straight around. It was great when they did. Two policemen arrived with lights rolling and sirens blaring, and the concierge looked like he had pissed in his pants. I told the police that I had been conned out of a thousand pounds, which had been my monthly wage. I was so angry and a little drunk that I had forgotten that she owed me more as she was meant to be paying me more for the extra hours I did.

I never did get the extra money that was promised to me. I remember knocking on her door and then, the look on her face when she saw that it was me and that there were two cops standing behind me. She immediately knew that she had no option but to hand over the money she owed me, and she came over all smiles and pleasantries and tried to imply that everything had been a huge mistake and a simple misunderstanding. I was more than wary when she started to write out a cheque while at the same time saying that she didn't have cash at hand. I didn't tell the cops that she had already bounced a cheque on me but thought that at least I had two witnesses in case it happened again. I noticed that she was shaking as she was writing it out and I also noticed it was a cheque book from a different bank, so I did give her the benefit of the doubt again. The cops were really nice, and I thanked them for their assistance. I waved to them when they drove away and as I walked towards the street, I could see a black cab waiting at the curb. By this time, I just wanted to get back to the flat and I was still a bit upset and drunk and I could feel a headache coming on. I walked over to the cab and the driver asked me if I was Simone. Simone?! The awful French nanny bitch who had mocked me and tried to intimidate me.

I told the driver yes, I was Simone, and I opened the door and got in and just as we were pulling away it started to rain heavily, and I could see a lone female figure running through the entrance of the building, shouting and waving her arms and trying to get the driver's attention. I stared at her through the window of the cab as she ran out and into the rain, became soaking wet and was now screeching and stamping her feet. Her evening dress was dripping wet and her carefully coiffed hair was hanging down and clinging to her face. I waved at her and caught her attention and as she recognised me, she stepped into a large puddle and I gave her my best smile, along with a two-finger salute.

CHAPTER 8

THE SHAREHOLDERS

I got off the tube at West Hampstead and walked along the street to the new area that was home to my new temp job. I found the house and walked up the stairs of the grand Victorian terraced house. The door was opened by the PA and I was ushered inside and I immediately fell in love with the cool racing green decor and old Georgian oil paintings of heroic and famous racehorses, each individually lit up with its own brass picture light. I was told by the PA to wait in her office until I was to be shown upstairs and I sat down on a beautiful red chesterfield that had matching chairs. A large walnut desk took up most of the space in the room and there was more equestrian art on the walls, glorious scenes of the hunt in its various progression.

I was summoned upstairs and came face to face with my new boss and her husband, which was a shock as they were nothing like I had imagined, and she looked a lot older than what my agent had described. She wasn't that old, but her clothes and makeup and hairdo had aged her although her mannerism revealed a younger woman who had made unfortunate choices with her wardrobe and style. She looked like she had been dressed by Hardy Amies during the 1970s, all boxy, bland, and unflattering, and she had one of those 1960s bouffant styles that can really age some women. Must have had a bad day out shopping at Harvey Nicks I thought. If she had just had on a pair of nice trousers and a billowy blouse, she would have looked twenty years younger, but the hair looked like a wig. Maybe it was. The drawing room was tastefully decorated, and it really was very impressive.

I only had a ten-minute chat with them and then I was dismissed and told to wait in the PA's office again. When I returned downstairs, I noticed a see-through package of some sort of black and white fabric had been placed on the spot that I had been sitting on the chesterfield and on top of it was a note with my name on it and the word "uniform". I picked it up and opened the parcel and took out its contents which was, a black shin length dress with a white collar and white hems on the sleeves and a white headband which looked slightly 1920s flapper style, but it wasn't when paired with the awful dress. I laughed out loud and muttered, "You have got to be kidding," and at that moment the PA came into the room and said, smiling, "I'm afraid not." We both stared at it and then we both laughed and agreed that it was an outdated practice and belonged back in the 1930s. I pointed out to her that I had on my uniform as suggested by my agent, which was brand new black jeans with a brand new white buttoned shirt and brand new black court shoes with a tiny kitten heel that would be suitable for both day and evening. She shook her head and said it wasn't traditional enough and could I please just put up with it as it was only a temporary position? I ended up saying yes and then proceeded to the bathroom to get changed and it looked more like a costume than it did a uniform. I was amused to think that my new employer had insisted on the awful livery, and I imagined some poor housemaid wearing it in the house which I was standing in now.

This image was reinforced when the PA handed me a white apron to tie around my waist and then told me that the uniform was completed. It came with about a dozen extras, and she told me that I should remember to change it the minute it became soiled or stained. Christ! It was the year 1999 not 1899! What the hell place had I found myself in now! I think a uniform is great if you work for a large company like a hotel chain or a restaurant and the like.

You are representing a company and a brand and if you are working hands on with and for the public it makes you more visible. I don't think that it is necessary if you are working in a private home in the modern day and you are there for one or two people or perhaps a family and they know who you are and why you are there. If you have on clean and functional and appropriate clothing, then I really see no problem. Of course, if you are helping out with a dinner party or an occasion like Christmas then yes you should dress a bit better but for everyday household chores and cooking it does all seem a bit silly nowadays. I have only had to do it a few times while working as a private housekeeper and the people who insisted on it were usually uptight and unpleasant. For me it feels very much like being segregated and suppressed.

I don't see how having to wear an outfit of black and white somehow affects the way you work. I wonder why some private staff still put up with it unless they are on some sort of fabulous wage. Fair enough. Everybody has their limits, but I don't go for the big money anymore as crap like this, wearing a costume is beneath me. I do a good job and I don't go for situations that make me uncomfortable.

The PA made me a cup of coffee while she finished off photocopying what looked like to be a novel sized stack of papers. She then sat at her desk and started to highlight sections of it with different coloured felt tip pens and then checked through them and put it all through a hole puncher and then clipped it into a plastic binder that had a clear cover. She handed it to me, and I was surprised to see that it had my name on it with the underlined words "TO BE READ THOROUGHLY" printed in capital letters. I started to leaf through the binder and noted that it was a dossier on my duties, what to do and when, how often and how important it was and so on and so on. After reading it for twenty minutes I thought that I may as well be at my last job, what with the analness of it all but, also the feeling I was starting to get while sitting there wearing the poxy costume that this new boss was going to be a carbon copy of the last one. For a minute I thought that there must be some great conspiracy against me. Why me? Again? I always do attract the weirdos for some reason.

I started off working in the small sitting room which was the room that the boss would come to after she had had her breakfast which was cooked by her private chef. I was to hoover, dust and plump up each cushion and then place them exactly where they had been, stoke the fire if it was in use and make sure there was plenty of perfectly cut pieces of wood to fill the wood basket with. Then I would move down the hallway and check all the potted plants and flowers for brown or dying foliage and remove it. The main huge drawing room was only used in the evenings, and it had to be dusted and polished daily. The bathrooms had to be wiped down, tissues pulled up from the box into points, loo rolls folded on the ends and hand towels perfectly aligned. Quite a normal routine you may be thinking and yes it was, but it wasn't really. The notes said, highlighted in pink, that I was to wait in the hallway while anyone was in a room and as soon as they left it for whatever reason I was to quickly enter and do the same process each and every time. All day. Six days a week. Each room had to be perfect at all times. Well, I hated the job and I had only done a day's work. I sat on the tube that evening and thanked God that it was temporary, and I knew I could let it all slide and ride it out just like I had done last time. I survived the first week and when I rode home again on the tube that Saturday night, I thought that it was strange that I hadn't done any work on the upper floors of the house and later that night I looked through the binder of household notes and saw that there was no mention of bedrooms or upstairs bathrooms or any upstairs rooms.

I poured myself a glass of wine and started to think back on my last job and pondered why I seemed to be having such bad luck with seeking a normal job. The past year had been shit. I was trying hard to find the perfect situation in between temping and still retain a bit of independence and freedom but I also wanted more security and regularity. I remembered previous job interviews I had been on and some of them made me shudder to think of.

The country house was on the border area of Wales where the family hunted, and I was expected to clean five pairs of boots all with three coats of wax over three days. The mansion near Bath where the outgoing housekeeper was almost in tears and the arrogant groundsman sat in on the interview and started to grill me on my personal life and got really nasty about it. Then there was the estate in Maidenhead that sounded great in the advertisement but actually didn't pay a wage but only a yearly bonus. I could have ended up in any of these places if I hadn't kept my wits about me.

Although I was feeling a bit sorry for myself, I had a rethink and thanked my lucky stars that I was in work and that I knew I would easily get more and that I had seen the hidden dangers and dodged a few bullets. Monday morning, I was back at work in my costume when I met the upstairs housekeeper. She was a lot older, and I could see it was difficult for her to do anything, let alone do it properly. She didn't really stop to chat as she was behind in her chores and was worried that she may not get everything done on time, so I went back to my place standing in the hallway, waiting for the boss to have a sit down or leave a cup somewhere or take a dump. It amazes me when I do work with older women that they always seem to be way past their retirement age but still act like a house slave and think they have to stay with that employer until she dies. They always own their own houses or have secure accommodation and extended families but for some reason they stay loyal to these awful boss bitches for years. If that was my mother, fetching and carrying for some pompous and undeserving spoilt diva, I wouldn't let her do it.

I found out later from the PA that this poor woman was in her late sixties and when there was no downstairs help, she would have to do the whole house. There was no one brought in to help her, as you would think maybe a cleaning company could be used for short periods. No! The diva boss bitch didn't trust or want anyone else in the house and this poor older lady was expected to do it all. I have no idea to this day why she kept doing it and why she was expected to. No empathy or compassion for her whatsoever. This rich bitch boss had inherited a company from her parents when she was still a child. It is a very well-known brand around the world and was once the best and most delicious item you could choose when selecting a sweet treat. The brand remained the best of its kind until a global food conglomerate bought it out from the greedy shareholders and wrecked the original recipe and it has never been the same since. The shareholders made millions each and the UK's favourite for more than a hundred years was gone forever. The stuff nowadays is second rate and sales have plummeted. They don't even make it here anymore as the greedy new owners don't want to pay a living wage and cut into their millions in profit. Stuff the factory workers and the people who helped them become what they were, they can piss off and get other jobs and they will still expect us all to buy their inferior product at a much higher price. I don't buy it anymore and nor do most of my friends. I'm sure that the folks on the other side of the world have no idea it was sold off and now what they are eating has no quality of the original brand. What an awful thing to happen to a legacy that was passed down through the generations. Sold out for the money and still miserable and unhappy. I thought a family legacy, company, or stately home was meant to be enjoyed through the generations and then passed along to the future ones? You have to be some real vacuous and vain piece of work to have the gall to stop it all and claim it all for yourself. Christ, how much is enough for one person to possibly have? Unbelievable.

The PA turned out to be quite nice and we got on well; as I got to know her better, I could tell she was under immense pressure and was on the verge of packing it all in. She told me that she had only recently purchased a house with her partner and that the mortgage was a hefty one and, to top it off, she was expected to take on extra duties outside of her normal hours and for no extra pay. Why do these awful women all seem to do this? Somehow, they all seem to know when you are struggling, either financially, physically or mentally, and like to stick the knife in and start to demand extra work from you. They can all afford to hire extra staff but they never do and seem to be waiting for you to tell them no or refuse them so they can start their power trips and tantrums. Why do they like to take their crap out on other people when they know full well, they can hire extra help and why do they think they should have free labour?

The PA was now expected to come into work on the weekends to go over the next week's schedule and was basically told, in a snotty manner, that she could easily manage it if she started to become more efficient and tidier with her time. I think these bitch boss women just like to see how far they can ride you and if you don't stand up for yourself, they will push you further and further and it's all about control and power and subservience and I really do believe that women who do this are a bit psychotic and perverse. If you stand your ground and refuse to be brow beaten and belittled and treated like an inferior, then it will go one of two ways: They will respect you just a tiny bit more but never let you know it, or they will make the job so difficult that you will walk out and give your notice. I hope you do the latter if this is happening to you. I wish more women would value themselves more and take pride and stop these vile women in authority from treating other women like shit. Men are not allowed to treat you this way at work, so why put up with it from a stuck up, odious, lunatic of a woman?

The PA was also expected to start taking the pet dogs home with her on weekends as the lazy boss who owned them didn't want to look after them or feed them herself and wanted to relax on Sundays. People who won't even feed their own animals shouldn't even be permitted to have any. It is like how children were once treated if they were born into wealth. They were seen and not heard, and the nanny raised them and mothered them. They were brought downstairs for an hour or so each day and presented to the uninterested parents and then they shuffled off to the nursery and were forgotten about until the next day when they were presented again. When they were old enough, they were bundled off to full boarding school and only allowed home during the summer or Christmas and at holidays.

Next, they would have been (if male) sent to university and then, sent to Europe for the grand tour; after that they would be working in the family or a friend's family business. If they were female they would be sent to a suitable college or finishing school which was just a front for finding them rich husbands. They would have lessons on how to please men and what to wear on what occasion and how to act at certain functions. After that they would be presented, which basically means they were shown to society and put on the market for other rich families to consider when selecting an equally rich bride for their sons. They would "do" the season, which is a timetable of events attended by high society, make contacts and network and be very lucky to actually be in love when the time came for marriage. Nowadays it isn't so formal although I can imagine there are some people doing it. Some of these rich women who have had a formal but modern-day version of this upbringing will find husbands and then pump out an heir and a spare or two (preferably by caesarean so as not to ruin the figure) and then hire a housekeeper for the home who will then be expected to become a nanny and surrogate mother on top of her normal duties. Some women will do it properly and hire a proper nanny and have a housekeeper, but some will be cheap and expect one to do all the work. The kids will be packed off to boarding schools and forgotten until the holidays and then sent on a gap year before university, which is always to Africa, where they attempt to make out they are there to make a difference and help the poor kids learn to read and write, but it is really a massive virtue signal and a self-pat on the back and it looks great on their CV when they apply to the universities. Daddy has probably donated a huge amount of cash to secure their thick brat a place and then they will take a meaningless degree like psychology because it isn't that difficult on the scale of things and sounds like it could be taught in a basic comprehensive school. It makes me wonder why we have so much of a problem with people suffering with different types of mental health and why most will never get any meaningful help when surely, there are millions out there who are qualified to be psychologists? Funny, isn't it? After the big piss up at Uni, they will start jobs in daddy's company or mummy will get them a place with someone she knows, and then they will marry into the same social set, same as always.

It's funny, but after working for years in households with teenagers, the parents are always convinced that they are really gifted or really advanced for their age or are destined for greater things. These kids may be able to speak multiple languages or be brilliant on the sports field, but for some reason they can't seem to be able to keep their room tidy or prepare themselves a simple meal or follow basic instructions. They are super at all the latest tech and gadgets, iPods and phones, but they simply cannot operate a washing machine or iron, or even drive a car at seventeen anymore. I guess it is all too dangerous for them nowadays.

My meaningless and dreary days went by so slowly and the work was so mind numbing. Picking foliage off plants that didn't meet the standards and folding endless rolls of loo paper did my head in. Towards the end of my contract, I started to get rebellious and tried to mix it up a bit, get the bitch boss's blood up by folding things in a different way or changing the order of pillows on chairs or placing an object a few inches to the left or right of its normal place. Maybe she would scream at me and sack me or lose her cool and have a tantrum and I would be justified to just walk off into the sunset. How can people live such sedate and regimental lives? I shudder to think what they are like now: older, crankier, and ever more demanding and contemptuous.

The day finally arrived, the day of freedom, and I practically skipped my way down the street knowing I could breeze through the final hours in this house of ludicrous pretension. I couldn't keep from smiling and having the odd whistle while I did my chores and, on this day, I sat down on a chair in the hallway as I waited for the call to remove any trace of normal life from the rooms. The PA came out of her office and told me to go upstairs as the boss wanted a word with me, so I climbed the stairs to her afternoon sitting room and wondered what she wanted to see me for. Perhaps to say goodbye and thank you? Maybe good luck for the future…. No. She started off with a huge lecture about why I had lowered the tone of respectability in her home by having the audacity to sit down while I was on duty. She berated me like a naughty schoolgirl, and I thought that she must have started on the gin already. I couldn't believe it. Who the hell did she think she was? I carried on sitting down until I left a few hours later. There was nothing else to do and Friday afternoon was always a piss up for the awful cow and it was the most normal thing she did during the whole time working for her.

Five o'clock came and I headed for the PA's office to say goodbye to her and to collect my pay cheque and ditch the dreadful costume that was the pathetic uniform. I knocked and entered and sat on the comfy chesterfield while she was talking on the telephone. I felt a little uncomfortable as she had the loud speaker on and was typing a letter at the same time and then I realised it was the boss on the line. She was drunk by now and slurring her words and also sounded very hyped up and agitated. She started telling the PA that she had made up her mind to hire the "menial" the best one after a string of disappointing candidates, and that she wanted the person at the house tomorrow morning at nine o'clock. I felt sorry for the poor unfortunate person who had been chosen and thought what a creep she was by calling them menial, like she was the Queen of Sheeba or Marie Antionette or Imelda Marcos. How ugly and disdainful to say that about someone you were going to hire. How would they be treated after becoming a permanent member of staff? I couldn't wait to escape the atmosphere of antiquated and repressed feeling and vibe. I felt like walking out of the front door, walking to the tube and going home; but I held out until I had the cheque in my hand. I remembered the fiasco with the pay from the last job, so waited and was polite until the telephone conversation had ended.

It felt like I had been punched in the stomach when the PA looked at me with an impish grin on her face and told me that the boss wanted to see me. She must want me back up there for a last scolding and well-aimed torrent of abuse to try to upset me before I left. I got up to go and was looking forward to mocking her and to stand in front of her, arms folded, with an insolent smirk and my best fuck you attitude. The PA saw that I was primed and ready to go and then she softly told me no and that I was wanted for the permanent position. She could tell that what I really wanted to say was not for the faint hearted, especially after hearing the boss call me menial, and we both burst out laughing and shared mutual contempt for her. I told her to please start to look for a new job as there are always lots of PA jobs and she smiled and pulled out a stack of CVs she had photocopied at work and said she had already sent out a few. I was glad she had the bottle to start again, to start to take charge of her life and change it by ending this job that had become a misery to her. She stopped the fear of change and the unknown and repression and turned it around to new opportunity and horizons and to being happy. She stopped the negative feelings and the complacency and was looking forward to experiencing more than she dared was possible, to climb out of the box and explore what extra life is out there and to have the will and the nerve to find it. She longed to become alive and to become herself.

The telephone started to ring, and I looked at her with dread and we laughed again, and she handed me my pay cheque and gave me a quick hug and reached for the phone as I opened the door to leave. We waved goodbye and I was out of the house and on the tube faster than Linford Christie, feeling happy and lucky to be free.

Monday morning came and I was in my kitchen and still in my pyjamas and drinking a coffee when I had a call from my agent asking me if I wanted to stay on at the position full time and it felt fabulous to be able to say no. The agent wasn't bothered and said she understood completely as the client was well known as being difficult and had gone through most of the temp staff and always alleged there was no one good enough to work for her full time. I wasn't surprised when two other agents of mine approached me with the same client, who was also well known to them, and they were having the same trouble with her. Such a high turnover of staff only ever means two things: that they are so awful and unpleasant to work for that people would rather leave as quickly as possible, and that they will never be satisfied with anything anybody ever does. Avoid them like the plague and find an employer who will value you and the job you do for them. You are worth it.

CHAPTER 9
DESPOT

One of my more recent temporary jobs was in the west country and it was on an estate whose history went back to the civil wars. Several houses had been built over the previous ones that had burned down and the last one went in the last quarter of the nineteenth century. The building that was being used as the family home was the former stable block which had been built during the Georgian periods and, to this day, is one of the most beautiful and unpretentious houses I have ever been inside, and I have been inside quite a few. The gardens were lovely and tranquil and largely unspoilt by over clipping and mowing and there was a lot of it left for wildflower meadows to flourish as it would have been years ago. I do hate it when country houses are ruined by overzealous gardening. Why have straight even lines mowed into lawns and precisely pruned hedges when you are outside any town and in the middle of nowhere? Why even have lawns and formally laid out gardens unless they were there originally, which means they were very grand houses back in their day as newly built. Unless Capability Brown designed your country house gardens why would you want it all regimental and tamed? I think a garden is much more natural when nature can be left to take over occasionally.

The family that I was to temp for were the owners of a large and well-known insurance company that also had a monopoly on the franchise of a well-known fast-food outlet. I only met my boss once as she was always engrossed in her work, but she seemed pleasant and appreciative and was only there on the weekends. She would commute to the city in her private helicopter and had a landing pad for it on one side of the property and it was camouflaged on the golf course. She had nothing to do with the everyday running of the house or the estate and it was being supervised by her new personal assistant who had been brought over from America. She had only started to work there a few weeks before I arrived, and it seemed like she had turned the whole place upside down and facing the wrong way. She had managed to create an atmosphere of silence and fear from what used to be a happy and productive environment, and I was left wondering if I would even be able to work the whole length of my temporary contract.

What is the problem with some people who are given a little power within their job and then use that power in a negative and Machiavellian manner? Why take the route of being nasty and wily to achieve results from other people who would, no doubt be quite open to negotiation and constructive problem solving if only approached in a calm and friendly way? You expect men to be a bit ruthless in these roles but when it is a woman it all seems very rehearsed and I always think of Alexis in the old television show Dynasty, talking down to the plebs in the boardroom, but not as glamorous or convincing. Maybe Hyacinth Bucket, angry and belligerent and ordinary, but trying to hide behind a perceived echelon of society that nobody cares about anymore nor is impressed by. What do they think they look like, strutting about and acting like a feminised version of Gordon Gekko, but without the style or charisma. I hope women can see through these types of women who act like they think a man would towards other men. Surely, they must realise that they are being laughed at behind their backs and that they are a source of great amusement and ridicule amongst the recipients of their sad displays of righteous self-importance.

The new PA had unleashed a torrent of systematic abuse towards every member of staff in every department of the household. I met all the staff who, although very nice and good at their jobs, were all new to it as the older staff who had been there for years had all been dismissed or had left on their own volition after being told they would be taking a pay cut or leaving if they objected to it. The new staff had all been hired from the local agency and the PA had been given a reduced fee due to the volume of workers she had taken on. All the agency staff were being paid less than the original staff and the rumour was that she was being paid a massive bonus on top of her normal wages to reflect how much money she could trim down from the estate's annual outgoings along with any money she could claw back from any sector of the expenditures. She had threatened the farmer who had lived and worked at the estate for thirty years and turfed him and his family out of their tied cottage. The farmer had worked on the estate for the previous owners and was a much liked and respected member of the community and the county. He left before he was pushed and then she had hired in a few stockmen on a daily basis to tend to the cattle and the fields. The management of most of the land and its upkeep was left to the gardeners and they would either have to learn how to tend to it during their own time or they too could also leave the estate and seek other employment if they didn't like it. The domestic staff consisted mostly of laundresses and daily cleaners, cooks and nannies, and this had also been reduced to two laundresses and an occasional cleaner to come in twice a week to do the holiday lets and cover for staff sickness and holidays, and the new housekeeper would be taking on the additional roles of cook and nanny. Well, that's what she thought.

I did like spending time with the two laundresses. They worked in a separate building that was across the courtyard of the main house, which was very old and would have been the storage area for the feed and hay and carriages for the stable block. They were very jolly and friendly, and we had fun slagging off the awful PA who would try to browbeat us and assault us with her verbal diarrhea. They told me that she was having trouble finding a housekeeper and I quickly understood why. If you aren't intimidated enough or are unwilling to sacrifice your dignity and integrity, then you aren't going to even be considered for the position. So, from then on, I did the same thing I always do and decided that the job was below my standards. I lost interest very quickly and didn't bother to do any extras or even care about them. Play stupid and disengage from any emotional attachment to the area you are in or the people you are working with. I knew then that this wasn't a temp job at all but just a drawn-out job interview and that I was being used to do a bit of cleaning and then could be dismissed at any minute but was I so glad that I had sussed her out and was one step ahead of her.

While I was there, I was staying in one of the outbuildings which had been part of an old cow barn and one part of the house still smelled faintly of milk and cattle and hay. It was next to the PA's house, and I found out later from one of the gardeners that there was a concealed door inside that opened into a larger house and that the PA wanted it all to herself, which was the real reason why it was taking such a long time to acquire a housekeeper. Apparently, she didn't want to hire a daily housekeeper, as part of her plan was a live-in would then be asked to take on more hours, her hours, so she could take more time off when her boyfriend from America came over to visit. She had done this to the last housekeeper who had been there and had unsuccessfully tried to bully her into becoming an answering service in the evenings for any problems that may arise on the estate so that she could go off and have fun. She also wanted the housekeeper to assist the part-time housekeeper to clean out the other cottages and buildings on the estate that were used as holiday lets to the public, so essentially it worked out to be a seven-day a week job. I was tipped off that she was lying to the job applicants and that their happiness and wellbeing went out the window if she thought that an extra buck could be made to go into her bonus at the end of the year.

The old and nasty trick of reneging on an employment

contract would be used and a zero-hour contract would be given, either with no added accommodation or a very basic type, which meant that you would be expected to share accommodation with another member of staff.

Accommodation is supplied in most domestic situations in the UK, especially if you are working at a large residence and it is part of your wage and is for the enhancement of ease in your duties. There are jobs that still only offer a room in the main house, but the majority do have separate detached or purpose-built flats for the domestic staff to live in while in the job. An au pair or nanny can expect just a room and a senior or highly experienced member of staff can expect proper detached accommodation and both should be fully furnished.

If you are a driver and the job requires you to use a car for part of your duties like grocery shopping and other errands, a car is usually provided for use and a generous employer will let you use it on your time off. If you have your own car, you will be provided with a petrol allowance if you find that there is no car available.

One day, one of the laundresses birthdays was celebrated in the laundry house and at lunch time we had planned to get together and have a little informal party. The day before, the PA had announced that she would provide the sandwiches and place an order with the posh bakery that was in the nearest village and go and collect them in time for our lunch time break. The birthday girl was asked what type of cake or pastries she desired and the rest of us agreed to provide some crisps and other snacks to make up the party food. Seeing as it was her fiftieth birthday, we had asked the PA if we could, just for that day, forfeit our two other tea breaks and use the time to add on to the lunch break so that the party could last an hour. We couldn't believe it when she said yes and at that moment, we all thought that she may not be the stuck-up ice maiden that we all thought she was and maybe had been a little too hasty to judge. Oh, but how wrong we were!

We had our little celebration, and it was nice. The birthday girl was very touched, and we all enjoyed the relaxing of the tight rules and regulations, and we ate the food and looked forward to hopefully healing the rift with the PA that we all felt was the only part of the job that was disliked. We finished up and got on with the rest of the day's work and then we all went home. The next day I made my way to the laundry room as this was where I had started to have all of my breaks as it was nearest to the main house, and I couldn't believe what I had found there. Three envelopes had been left and propped up beside the kettle and toaster with our names typed on each one. The laundresses had waited until I got there to open them; as I reached for mine, they both looked over my shoulders to see what it could be. To our surprise, it was a receipt for the sandwich that I had had the previous day, and when the birthday girl opened hers, she found that she had two receipts: one for her sandwich and the other for the cake. Now I am sorry, but if someone (especially a senior member of staff who has control of the petty cash) asks you if you would like something as trivial as a lunchtime sandwich that you haven't asked for, I would assume that it is a nice gesture and a little perk that one may partake on a rare and special occasion. We couldn't believe it, and all agreed how cheap and nasty this woman was and then we laughed at how pointless it was for her to have even offered anything when she knew full well that it was just another shitty trick to show that she was in authority.

In the end we all chipped in and paid her the measly ten pounds with as much small change as we had on us. As we sipped our tea on our break, we looked out of the window at our boss's new custom Range Rover being delivered and wondered out loud at the small injustice we had experienced and guessed if she even had been aware what the PA had done, and if so, did she agree that we were not worth ten pounds to her? The gloves were off again when it came to the PA, and we all suspected that the boss wouldn't have been so stingy and thoughtless. We knew then that our suspicions had been confirmed and that we were wasting our time feeling like valued members of a team. I decided I wanted to leave as soon as possible and was sick of being treated with distrust as if I was a school leaver on her first day at her first job.

After work I went for a walk around the fields and just happened to bump into one of the gardeners who was on his way home from work on his pushbike. The events of yesterday and the realisation that considering staying any longer than I had to seemed hopeless and I struck up a conversation with him, partly as he was quite friendly, and also to see if I could gain additional information about what had happened to the farmer who had left abruptly after thirty years and of the general upheaval that had been orchestrated. He warned me about the huge lies that would unfold once the temp job was over, and I would be offered full time if I wanted it. He told me that at one time there was separate accommodation for all the staff and that himself and the head gardener once shared one of the cottages on the estate.

The cook and regular housekeeper each had their own cottage near to them and the laundry staff had shared a large flat that was above the laundry room. Since the PA had come along, everyone had been evicted and left to find their own private rental or leave altogether. The new housekeeper was to share the flat above the laundry room with the two laundresses as all the old staff cottages were now being let as holiday cottages and the house that I was staying in would be reclaimed and used as the extended part of the PA's house by removing the concealed doorway. This was the reason why they couldn't find a mature and experienced housekeeper that wanted to stay because who in their right mind would want to share a flat with two others and be expected to share bedrooms and bathrooms? Maybe when I was in my late teens and early twenties I wouldn't have minded so much, but now I did and, as you know, the added luxury of your own private space is a much-needed thing at the end of the working day. I know a lot of people wouldn't mind this, but I hadn't shared a bedroom with others since I was sixteen and living in London in a shared flat and I wasn't going to start again now. Or ever. I really couldn't understand how all these separate dwellings that were on the estate and rarely used were once home to happy staff and now just empty until they were rented so that the PA would have more towards her bonus. They had been used for years by the estate workers and now that had been taken away there was little incentive to attract decent staff who would want to stay and love the job. The boss obviously didn't need the money from any one-off weekly holiday let and the wage offered would not compensate for someone having to rent privately in the area which would be very expensive as renting in the countryside is – that is if you can find something to rent.

After having witnessed how cold and calculating this woman PA was, I knew I would not have the piss taken out of me any longer. I had no reason not to believe the gardener and the other members of staff when they told me of what was going on and I realised that if things were as rosy as was being portrayed, then they would have found the perfect housekeeper by now and not be interviewing and needing temporary help. To this day I still don't know if the boss had any idea what was really going on with how the staff were being shit on by her own PA. This is very common, though, and I will touch upon this type of vile behaviour in an upcoming chapter. I always thought our employment laws and regulations had stopped a lot of this form of bullying and deception towards staff in the workplace, but I have found that private households seem to be exempt, and you are on your own if you have any type of grievance. It is up to you to provide your own legal representation if you want to go the legal route and take the matter to court. You will basically never have a leg to stand on unless you are willing to fork over a lot of money and you will find that your boss will have a Barrister on their side, and you will be shut down quickly. Forget the idea of legal aid as you will be laughed at if you try and apply for that too.

I ended up leaving that evening after confronting the PA and telling her, in no uncertain terms, where she could stuff her job and I wasn't going to stay and let her humiliate me anymore with her sneaky lies. I wasn't going to feed her ego by letting her think I was going to sweat and grovel for the chance of a job, a job that were plentiful and could take my pick. It amazes me how some women get star-struck so easily. They become dazzled by wealth and opulence and power, and they seem to grasp it with everything they have, but they are desperate to get up that ladder of success and they will but only part of the way. These thick and shallow sheep don't realise that although they have a foot in the door, they will never be able to fully enter the higher echelons of the world they aspire to. Unless you are born into and of that social class to begin with, you haven't got a chance in hell of getting on the pedestal. It is such great fun to watch them try and it is even more fun when you know they will never get what they covet.

BAD LUCK COMES IN THREES
CHAPTER 10
THE BOHEMIANS

A few years had passed since my last temp job, and I tend to avoid them now. I have had a lot more than is mentioned here but most of them were very pleasant and the people and families I worked for were very nice and a pleasure to work for. I wouldn't want you to think that I am just a moany old cow venting my woes to the world as I really have had a good variety of situations and experiences on the job front. I wouldn't continue as a housekeeper and I really do enjoy doing it, but I have had a lot of bad luck too, meaning I have had the displeasure of finding myself in jobs that were all down to luck. Many times, I have had a choice of two or three at one time and have picked the most rotten of the bunch.

I have had more good ones than bad ones, but unfortunately when it comes to reading books like this, you want the blood and guts rather than the happily ever after dialogue. Nice is all very well and good, but it just isn't meaty and satisfying enough. Most people want to read the down and dirty rather than the cherry and the icing. I would like to write more about the nicer experiences but there isn't that much to say, as in the job was easy and the bosses were a dream to work for with no drama and that I remember them all with much fondness. I am still very good friends with some of the other staff that I worked with and sometimes we have a good old reminisce about the place and person we worked for, and although it may not have been a great experience, we agree that it was good to have met each other and could share the memory of particular events that helped to shape our ethics and attitudes that we carry forward today and use, not only in the work place, but also in our everyday lives and when dealing with certain scenarios and situations. An example of this (as I have told you of in parts of this story) is whenever I start to feel any inkling of poor treatment or verbal scorn, I switch down a gear and go into neutral. I won't go above any extra effort I need to perform a basic service, but I will not go under my basic standard either.

Likewise, if I am spoken to and treated well, I will go over and above my duties and take the time to bother with the little extras and not worry and watch the time as I do it. It is a sign of happiness on the job when you never look at the clock and fret about going over your time. I think it is unnecessary to time watch when you are doing something you enjoy and, in turn, make someone else's life a bit better by caring about them. It doesn't seem like work and when you achieve some sort of gratitude in the simple form of a smile or some pleasant conversation or a gesture as small as a cup of coffee made for you, it all makes it worthwhile and the feeling of being appreciated and valued is one of the best feelings you can have. It is all such a shame as, in the real world, nothing lasts forever, and you must take all the good times along with all the bad.

This new job sounded fabulous, and I felt that maybe my luck was changing, and I would be happy but, as you know, if it sounds too good to be true, then it most certainly will be. I have had many jobs that were great in being the straight forward and simplistic type, great wages and hours, weekends off and gorgeous accommodation, but then you will usually get difficult people to work for or a type that will never let you get on with it and will be a constant thorn in your side, micromanaging you and generally bitching about everything. I like to work on my own with no supervision or help from extra staff as you know your own standards and you can rely on yourself. So, when someone tries to tell you how your system should work and then suggests you do it a different way or in a different order, I think it is rude and disruptive and see it as someone's way of controlling you, even if you are doing the tasks that the controller would never actually do themselves. As a rule, I generally do not "do" children, as a nanny has a totally different role to a housekeeper and nowadays it is a generic term for a person who is expected to look after kids along with all the duties of a housekeeper, unless the nanny is a proper Norland nanny or has taken a course or degree on the subject. Occasionally, I will agree to work in a house that has teenagers, but teens nowadays seem a bit younger than they are and the more pampered and cosseted they have been while growing up the more work they are. I will often agree to work in a home that only has one child, because you will find that an only child can be a bit more savvy and older than their years. You discover that they have had more time and attention spent on them and they are keen and bright and engaging. If they have been over indulged and spoilt, they can be annoying and imperious and a little shit, and in this case, this new job, it became apparent from the beginning that there was something very wrong.

My newly found dream job was anything but, and I like to trust my gut instinct and I like to give people the benefit of the doubt when starting new jobs. If you become too picky and fussy you will find it harder to get work and luck does come into play. I like to think that not every new employer will automatically be an asshole and that you should be able to get along with the majority. I am an open and generous type of person and always look for the good in everyone, and always go into new situations feeling optimistic and hopeful. I really had high hopes for this new job as the female boss was quite artistic and seemed very carefree and creative. I was looking forward to working for someone who was inspiring and easy to relate to and I couldn't have found a more disruptive and chaotic scenario than I'd let myself in for. What would be relatively normal was the complete opposite. Everything started out fine as usual and within a week I knew that all was not well inside the little farmhouse out in the glorious countryside of southern England.

The new boss was very modern and open minded and liked to be seen as a messiah Mother Nature type, into yoga and health, organic everything and no boundaries when it came to art and expressing one's opinion. Free speech and revelations ruled the day. Charity and fund raising were also a big part of her life and each month would bring in a new worthy cause or enthusiasm for another project all geared towards helping others and giving support to all manner of people and animal welfare. She was a strict vegan and liked to buy ethically sourced items like fairtrade goods and clothing made from hemp and woven fabrics with the least amount of man-made dye and human involvement. She had an artist's studio on the grounds in an old cottage that had once been a stable and she had a potter's wheel and a kiln next to it in the pottery shed. I always wanted to have a go on it, but I never got to as it had never been used and seemed to have been abandoned after her idea of organic pottery didn't come to fruition and she chose to give up on it rather than create other items with it. There were other outbuildings on the property that had been turned into mini production plants that had also been promptly abandoned as the realisation of failure loomed its head, a shed set up to press and bottle raw organic fruit juices, free range organic eggs, a loom for weaving linens that had been dyed using organic veg, an organic herb garden, all abandoned. It could have all been working and productive if a little effort had been put into it. It was meant to be the provider of the source of income for the charity fundraising, but it looked like it was all a bit too much for the hectic lifestyle of this new dingbat who I was working for.

While I was there, nobody ever set foot in any of the outbuildings and none of the ventures would ever make any profit. Instead, fundraisers became a never-ending round of coffee morning and the odd gathering of the local village ladies who lunched would meet in the dining room for afternoon lectures on jam making or starting a local seed bank, or other eco-friendly projects that they could think of.

The new boss had an outlandish and bizarre taste in art so it always made me laugh when some of the older residents of the village would pop by during a coffee morning and be sat there, red faced in a room with featured artists like Aubrey Beardsley and other sets of prints of the Kamasutra and African fertility symbols. Above the old fireplace was a huge modern painting of three figures engaging in a very energetic and vivid display of oral sex, and this one really was the show stopper. The old ladies would be spluttering their coffee onto the saucers and pulling their husbands away from the offending spectacle. There would have been very little respite found in the small toilet that was on the ground floor and used for such gatherings as its walls were home to a very nice but equally graphic collection of prints by Tom of Finland, which were my favourites. No wonder people were usually long gone after one cup. I think they preferred to drop some money into the collection boxes and get the hell out of there rather than stay and study the walls. You never would have thought that a traditional old farmhouse out in the countryside in a tiny chocolate box village would boast such a large collection of pornographic art that could rival any gallery in Amsterdam. She must have had a massive collection of erotic art as most of it was in her house in London and she had brought down to the country house what wouldn't fit on the walls. She had only been living in the village on and off for two years so every now and then someone would come into the house and see it for the first time.

It was hilarious to see people's expressions change as soon as they clocked what was on display, but one Christmas, two old ladies came for a sherry and mince pie fundraiser for the local donkey sanctuary and were soon in tears and slightly traumatised after a visit to the toilet and I felt awful for them, and after that I didn't look for anyone's reactions. After the novelty had worn off, I found the art to be a bit naff and couldn't see the point in any of it. The shock value of it had worn off and as it didn't affect me the first time, I came to see it as a bit boring and the lowest form of art in that it was basic in any response of creativity and debate. Basic as it is a common function, performed by every living thing and on par with daily rituals, like going to the toilet and other habitual norms that collectively make up our daily routines. Now that we can just turn on the television or the computer at will, nothing has been left to the imagination and it has all become sanitised, repetitive, and boring. The thrill has gone. Pornography in any of its guises is as mainstream and bland and uninspiring as watching some decrepit and predictable old soap opera on television and has lost its taboo status long ago.

Whenever I dusted and polished the large collection of glass and stone vintage dildos and sex toys that were displayed in a cabinet in the master bedroom, I often wondered who owned the collection? Was it his or hers or was it shared? Were they still in use or did they stay permanently in the cabinet? One of the guest bedrooms was home to a collection of leather gimp masks and bondage gear and several large mirrors, and there was an assortment of whips and handcuffs attached to the walls with chains. It would have made perfect sense if it had been in a loft in the city, but it seemed so contrived and silly out in the wheat fields of a sleepy village. Why do people bother to collect things? Why do people start new projects and buy all the necessary equipment and tools and then abandon all interest in it as quickly as they got into it? What is the point of starting something and then starting ten more projects and never seeing what became of the first? Are some people really that bored with life? Can you imagine never having to work or worry about any type of bill or expense and being able to do whatever you wanted to, all day and every day? All of this wasted effort and energy that was spent on vanity could have easily been turned around and used to someone's advantage. My God, can you imagine just rolling out of bed in the morning, when you wanted to and having a choice of what activity you wanted to do that day and every other day without any concern. The facade of work, covering up the fact that you really have no intention of exerting any mental or physical willpower at any time and are quite happy to let others think that you are some sort of workaholic and trying to make a difference for those less fortunate, when actually, you are a lazy idiot who is desperate for approval and will spout your virtue to whoever is gullible enough to buy into it. What is the point of chasing a few pennies for half-hearted attempts at dreary tat that you have made, so people can be in awe of you and your pretended persona of empathy? Some of these types of people are so good at lying and concealing their true colours and it makes me so angry when you witness the other idiots, their friends and family, fawning over them and showering them with false praise. I feel like shouting and causing a scene and letting anyone who is close enough to hear that the truth really is that only a few minutes ago they were acting like spoilt brats and swearing at the staff and criticising the very people they were pretending to want to help. I thought that if one group of people needed help then so be it. You cannot treat one group of people in a certain way and then dismiss the next group who also need help, just because you think they are less deserving or because their plight isn't trending or being discussed as often in the right circles? How can that be right? Surely, everyone who needs help deserves it and the people trying to help them should not be segregating them into who gets what and who doesn't get anything? Who are these people in charge of what should get approval and who is going to be seen doing it? It always seems to be someone with more money than sense and someone who is very average and has failed at life in general. So, what better way to rebrand yourself as a modern-day prophet, a guru, a charlatan, and make believe to yourself and others that people are your passion. But only the right sort of people. The others who you don't like and are beneath you can fuck right off! All of those carefully chosen and popular traits of diversity and inclusivity have just gone right out of the window.

If you or anyone cares about any human rights, then it must include the whole of humanity otherwise, once again, we will have to start to segregate people as has always been the case. It doesn't seem to be going away and we have still haven't learnt any lessons. Here we are today, still categorising skin colours and judging people by religions. Grading people by their status at birth and then further tests of social and material status as they get older. And if that isn't bad enough, you've got self-righteous assholes with enormous pretensions and privilege, giving out praise and charity to meaningless causes at the same time as treating and speaking to their poor hired help with utter contempt – the exact opposite of the persona of person they are so desperately trying to be. How fake and synthetic. Why are we wasting time trying to pigeonhole people? No one can help when or where they were born and into what type of household and environment, an advantage or disadvantage. The same person will go through life living and thinking and generally trying to be a good person based on whether they had the advantage or disadvantage.

The school of hard knocks or the never-ending silver spoon treatment. I think you must experience the bad to truly understand and empathise with the disadvantaged in society. If you have never had to feel what it is like to have to choose between paying your rent or paying your bills and eating or never having extra cash after paying your wages out on just living, then I don't think you should be giving advice or brow beating anyone about anything. Politicians are a prime example of this, and it seems ridiculous to place one of the elites privileged into a position of say, social welfare or social housing or anything else that claims to protect vulnerable people. They have no clue how to relate to the people and therefore are merely patronising them but on a very large scale. The elite and privileged are very good at appearing to be caring and generous to their own class but when they are dealing with someone of a lower class, they become hypocritical bigots.

This was the new boss. She would preach and purge and compare herself with Mother Nature. She would only use natural and ethically sourced goods and she would ride her bicycle to the village high street to cut down on her carbon footprint. She only ate organic food and once a week her masseur from London would arrive at the house along with her nutritionist and they would work out an eating plan for the week for her to follow. On the other hand, she was constantly in the city visiting her Harley Street doctor for seemingly common ailments and therefore was always on one or two different prescription drugs, along with her fondness for sleeping pills this amounted to quite a lot of chemicals every day. She thought nothing of whizzing up and down the motorway in her diesel Volvo estate, into the city and back to the countryside. When it came to holidays, she always made sure she left enough time to spend in between each one a few weeks away at her house in Provence. Once a year she would visit her mansion in the Cayman Islands and every Christmas was spent in the Maldives or the Caribbean.

Her husband never seemed to speak and certainly never initiated conversation or action of any kind and quite happily remained in the background, very unassuming and invisible. I think he only spoke to me on a half dozen occasions and only to say good morning or give the odd thanks. He worked at Canary Wharf and would only come down to the countryside on Friday evenings and then leave again on Sunday night. He did not like socialising or engaging in conversation or any form of a gathering of people that would require him to talk or make eye contact or reveal his personality. Although I do like this quality in people, the type who are a bit mysterious and do not tell you their entire life story in the first ten minutes of meeting them, it can be very frustrating and annoying when educated adults are such hard work and bordering on rudeness. I think he only showed up on weekends as he could not cope with his wife who was the complete opposite to him, and their child seemed to be a combination of both of their psyche.

Now as you know, I am not a mother and although I did have a brilliant childhood, I cannot ever compare any other child's experiences, but sometimes what you think is advantage or privilege is anything but. Just because a child has wealthy and highly educated parents does not mean that it is automatically going to make that kid successful in anything. Sometimes it is the complete opposite. It is like working-class people trying to claw their way up the ladder with a higher paying job and not realising that they will never become middle class overnight. You can win millions in a lottery, and you are still going to be working class and you will never be accepted into another group. You can be born into wealth and the upper classes and have every advantage given to you, but if you are not very bright, there is nothing anyone can do. No extra tutor or special school or mentoring can change that. Daddy will still get you a top job somewhere and you will be protected in it when you come of age. It happens all the time and just look at the state of some of our MPs and other CEOs and managers of industry, and you will see what I mean. If your kid is of normal ability and is an average student, then so be it. If they are happy and kind and an all-round good person, then why would you try to change them? I know that the competition is fierce out there and they have to be the best and stand out from the crowd to get on in life, especially in this day and age; but why would you make their life a misery and change them into nervous and nasty wrecks, just so they can achieve what the parent thinks is best for them? It seems like an awful lot of parents these days are all behaving like stage mothers, constantly pushing and screaming from the sidelines and taking utter control of every aspect of the kids being. It is really sad to see kids' spirits being broken by overzealous parenting and watching them transform into shells of their former selves, being shouted at and brow beaten and treated like machines. Yes, they need discipline and guidance, but they also need to be children too. In the space of eighteen months, I watched this child turn into an aggressive and arrogant little shit who had been taught by his mother that his sole purpose in life was to achieve, win, compete, and that only losers lose. This was the earth mother who had done this, the woman who liked others to see her as a beacon of natural wholesomeness. The epitome of health, wealth, and success.

When I started the job, the child was eight years old and seemed like most other kids the same age. There was already a massive amount of pressure being heaped upon him and I slowly started to see how it was affecting him as he struggled with school and being accepted by his peer group and awkwardly trying to fit in. He had started at a new school after transferring from an expensive but very informal and alternative form of education, and the sudden change seemed to be very stressful and alien for him. Overnight he had swapped a classroom size of twelve to twenty-five and was having to conform to a uniform and tie instead of the comfy casual attire he could choose for himself each morning. He was not used to an alarm clock and hated to wake up early, which is strange in young kids this age. It is usually the older teenagers who don't like to get up until noon.

Dressing himself was a puzzle and he could never match his socks or button his shirt symmetrically. Jumpers would be put on inside out. The same confusion continued at breakfast and there was indecision on choices and tantrums and tears when milk was spilled, and the discovery of crumbs on his clothes would send him into a rage. This resulted in his mother whisking him away upstairs where she would lock them both into either the kid's bedroom or his en suite bathroom. The routine was always same every morning and he would be brought back downstairs twenty minutes later, his face swollen from crying and silent and docile, he would be bundled into the car and driven to school. It was my job to pick him up from school later in the afternoon and usually he would be angry and in a foul mood, which would turn to floods of tears as we got nearer to home. I asked my boss about his behaviour as I had never witnessed such despair from an eight-year-old and was always told that it was due to his sensitive nature and, as an artist and creative being, he was trying to deal with the soulless and chaotic conformity of the private education system.

This went on for months and one morning after a tantrum that lasted for almost an hour, I was finally going to make it my business and find out what really was going on behind closed doors. In some ways I hadn't, and to this day there is nothing I could have done legally and pursuing it may have cost me my career. That morning, I crept up the stairs towards the locked bathroom and listened at the door and the thought of it still makes the hair on the back of my neck stand up and fills my mind with dread for how that kid grew up. It makes me wonder how he is now as he will be in his late teens and how it must have affected him as a person. Daily he was subjected to humiliating treatment, and some would argue that it was abuse, a mixture of sexual, psychological, and mental abuse – and all of his strange and unexplainable behaviour suddenly made sense.

I remembered the small harness that was kept under his bed that his mother said was part of a fancy dress costume, and the cloth nappies that were kept in the bottom drawer of his bathroom cabinet. I remembered the strange questions asked after any length of time she was away from him or when she got home late at night, and I had babysat for the evening. She would always ask if he had soiled himself and had I checked his bottom? I remembered the kid pleading with me not to go into his bedroom to tuck him in and not to make him take his trousers off or accompany him to the toilet, and the relief on his face when I assured him I wouldn't. I remembered while listening at the bathroom door, his mother stripping him down and forcibly placing him on the toilet. The cries and sobs while she scrubbed him in the shower and then struggled with her while she applied cream and after inspecting his backside and fitting a nappy onto his lower parts. The scary thing was that he didn't have a problem soiling or wetting himself or wetting his bed. After she had finished with him in the bathroom the poor kid would be crying and hysterical at this stage, and then she would tell him to hug her and thank her, while he was pleading for forgiveness, telling her that he loved her and then the crying would stop.

A few weeks after I had decided to make the boy's misery my business, I was getting ready to move on to my next job. I had contacted my agent who had placed me there and told her the whole horror story, adding that I had no problem giving statements to the police or social services. I was basically told to shut up and to keep what I had seen to myself. In no uncertain terms was I to get involved and to keep my nose out of others domestic affairs and that it was no concern of mine. I was also warned that I would never survive in a courtroom unless I somehow had a better barrister than my employer and I was to give up and get out of there if I didn't like it. *Do not bring shame on the agency or the client. You are not a mother so you cannot judge.* I couldn't believe the shitty attitude from the agent, and I am glad to say that I am no longer with them, and it still angers me to think that that kid was thrown under the bus and made the scapegoat because of money. The agent didn't want to lose potential commission by being associated with any whiff of scandal and I felt awful that I couldn't do anything for him. As I had no proof of abuse it was apparently all hearsay. I hadn't witnessed or seen any signs of physical abuse, so it was futile to find a solicitor and pursue any justice. I would be way out of my league and then crushed by trying to take on the establishment. I made a vow to never work with young children ever again.

I look back on my own childhood and remind myself how lucky and blessed I was to have such a grounded upbringing. Both my parents worked blue collar jobs and gave my sister and I everything that they never had. Sometimes we did go without and sometimes they did fight, but we were never treated like an object and expected to become some fictional character that would be a facade for their expectations.

I cannot imagine how it must feel to be pressured at such a young age to perform and become someone that has been manufactured. How can you be forced to master Rachmaninoff on the piano when you can't even tie your own shoelaces or tell the time on a clock? How can you study for exams when you don't even know your left from your right or your own address and phone number? I know that times are tough, and more children have to be able to shine at strategic points in their education, but at least let them have some form of normal childhood. There are poor kids living in extreme poverty in some parts of the world that are having to work instead of play and learning and that has carried on in another form in the Western world as academic pressure has replaced economic pressure. Only a few lucky ones will reach the top. Let the kids be kids. Let them be happy and progress on their own terms and learn to love life before they realise what it is.

CHAPTER 11

THE HORRIBLE HOUSE GUEST FROM HELL

The happiness and excitement that comes with finding and obtaining a new job lasted all of two weeks and once again I started to look for a new one. I didn't even unpack any of my possessions or bother to explore the area and I gave up most of my agents and started to apply to employers directly via the internet. The new job could have been fantastic and who knows, I may have still been happily employed there. The wage was more than generous, and the new government workplace pension had just kicked in and that had started to accumulate quite nicely. The new boss was alright at first and the other staff seemed friendly, and then the horrible house guest from hell came to stay.

The house was huge, and it looked like something from a set in a Merchant Ivory film and it was surrounded in extensive woodland which was lovely to walk in. It was an old Georgian property and was stunning from a distance or from outside, but the interior had been refurbished and modernised and filled with modern art, and it really was awful. Some of the rooms were beautiful and left from the 1930s, all art deco style and some were older, stuffy and Victorian, and it was all crammed with ugly modern art that didn't make sense. Vile glass structures that had no purpose and probably made by some unknown artist who wasn't really an artist but someone who was bored and wealthy and was doing it to feel relevant and who was lucky that some fool was buying it and liking it. There was wooden African art next to papier-mâché creations, which were next to hideous stacks of old suitcases and tacky mobiles made of wire hangers were hanging here and there. I know each to their own but why would you have the odd priceless antique inter mingled with trendy tat?

There were several outbuildings and one huge barn that was rented out for parties and events and the odd coffee morning. The coffee mornings were for charity fund raising and I found out later after being hired that I would be expected to work at these events for nothing and that us staff were included in the rental fee.

The same applied to the private hire party barn. What is it with charity fund raising being done by people who only do it for their image and reputation? These types are usually very abrupt and mean to their own staff but like to project an image of respectability and piousness. Behind the closed doors they are bitter and cold and also very self-centred. I don't know why they carry on with the charade that they clearly hate and dread and just don't make a large donation (tax deductible of course!) and make sure that their name is mentioned somewhere along with the donated amount rather than put on a grim display of pretence.

When I was hired, I was looking forward to cooking for the private parties in the party barn, but after the first few weeks went by, I knew I wouldn't be staying, and I had to pretend that I wasn't up to the standard they wanted, and I started to underperform in the kitchen. This was all down to one woman, this house guest who was coming to stay, and I was lucky to have a bit of warning from some of the other staff. I knew it must be bad, hearing it from the gardeners, as they work outside and rarely come into the house, but they knew all the inside gossip and gleefully let me in on all of the family secrets including this woman who was about to arrive. It is so funny when you hear gossip from men as you always associate it with bitchy women who are bored, but these middle-aged guys got down and dirty, and complained and moaned like seasoned pros. They made me laugh when they explained how they changed their routine and adopted different patterns of work when this woman was around, and they made sure they did work that needed doing at the furthest corners of the estate and around the perimeter rather than be near the house and outbuildings. They told me to be on my guard as she would know that a new housekeeper had arrived, and she would be watching me very closely.

As my new boss travelled a lot and had multiple properties worldwide, they were often away for long periods of time and this house guest woman would be brought in to "keep an eye on things", but she had taken it the wrong way and would patrol the grounds and buildings and intimidate the staff on a daily basis, thinking she was keeping some sort of order, but really making herself look like a complete lunatic and control freak. I was warned she had clashed with the previous housekeeper and as they were still in touch with her, they actually phoned her while I was with them, and she basically told me to run for my life. I didn't know what to think at first as I had just started working there and hadn't even got my bearings yet. I thought back to previous interviews where the outgoing housekeepers had warned me by the dead expressions on their faces and in their eyes and their emotionless responses and one-word answers to my questions relating to the job. I knew that this new job was doomed, but I also knew I needed it until I could find another one, so I decided to get on with it and take whatever was coming my way from this awful woman who I hadn't even met yet.

As the estate and house were so large there was always a lot to do, and I promised myself to not let anything bother me. So, I busied myself with my chores and lingered in the woods while walking the dogs and hung out with the chickens while collecting the eggs and cleaning out the coops. It was summertime and the weather was gorgeous. There were no children to mind and not a lot of day-to-day cooking day to do, so I could really take my time while polishing the oak staircases and wandering through the flowerbeds selecting blooms and foliage to create massive seasonal displays. When other staff members tried to befriend me, I kept my distance and avoided socialising with them. Some may think that sounds rude and anti-social, but over the years I had learned that when working with and living near people you wouldn't normally have anything in common with, the best policy is to keep to yourself and not enter into their drama or into any involvement outside of the job. If you are living on an estate or in a small village, people can't handle not knowing everything about you and there will always come a time when any knowledge is used against you if there is a falling out or a little too much alcohol is involved or a little too much favour is bestowed upon you which makes them jealous. As you get older it is not so important to be as open and carefree as you were in your youth. A lot of people nowadays like to think they have an advantage over you, and they are not afraid to use it to undermine you in any form for their own gain. As you get older you are usually a better judge of character as well and you realise that only a small handful of family and friends are the only ones who really have your back and are reliable and loyal. Those of you who own a pet are lucky to have a sentiment being who loves you unconditionally and will stick with you through thick and thin.

I went into hibernation mode in my head and started to build up a wall of protection, ready for the onslaught of mental and psychological abuse I would be fighting off and I learned how to switch it all off as soon as I finished my work for the day and got back to my private accommodation. I vowed to not let anyone buy my soul just because they were paying my wages, and I only did as much work as I had to.

The first time I had to cook for a private party was a lot of fun and I liked the fact that the paying guest chose the menu and then personally sat with me and went through what was required of my time and then provided me with a typed-out timetable of the function, step by step. They would bring in all the food, supplies and decoration and I would cook what they wanted in the kitchen that was joined onto the party barn and then serve it if there was a small party or set it out on trestle tables buffet style. The paying guests had decorated the barn and had spent the day setting up tables and chairs with matching floral arrangements and table cloths and candles and had brought in a collection of small trees and large potted plants that were adorned with twinkling fairy lights and it made the room seem like it was an enchanted forest, which had enveloped the barn. When the doors were thrown open it all came to life and the sounds and smells of the countryside summer evening filled the barn and lifted everyone's spirits.

People were beginning to arrive and soon the barn was filled with the sounds of glasses clinking and soft peals of laughter. The murmur of conversation would rise and fall, and I would notice it in between the last-minute preparations and presentation of the dishes I had made. Just as I was getting ready to transfer it all to the awaiting buffet table, I heard someone beside me say, "That's not the proper way to do that." I stopped and looked at the woman who had appeared from nowhere and I instantly knew that I had met *the woman*. From that moment until I had finished cleaning down the kitchen counter tops and unloading the dishwasher, she was complaining and criticising everything I had cooked and presented, despite the guests eating everything and continuously thanking and praising all my culinary efforts. Everybody was happy and grateful except for her. She hated me on sight and hated the fact that I handled the evening's events with aplomb and ease, and she hated the fact that I was able to do this job without any help from anyone, especially her. She made the extra effort to talk down to me in front of the guests and degrade me in every way possible. She told me, with great pride, how she had made the previous housekeeper cry and how she treated her like dirt, and how the poor girl took it and eventually left the house in the middle of the night not telling anyone. She ranted on about how only she could run a house such as this one and how the staff were frightened of her and how it was the only way to control people, so they didn't take advantage.

Well, I have found that over the years most people don't. Most just want to get on and do their job with minimum fuss and then get home to their own lives. You do get the odd one or two who are shit stirring and lazy, but you can find these types of people in any type of job. I can't believe that there are still people out there who think that treating people like crap and generally being nasty and intimidating towards them will make them respond with gratitude and thanks for making them feel awful and that they deserve it and that they should be grateful and let themselves be degraded and not feel worthy of anything. Keep people frightened so they don't step out of line and start to think for themselves. Tell people how to think and feel and shame them into producing more or giving more so that they maintain some sort of privilege. Let them think they are lucky to have a job and that they can be easily replaced, and that the replacement will be able to do it better. If you are employed by a company or person who has adopted this attitude then please, realise it is against the law and you must find another job or harden yourself up and let all the words and hurtful treatment slide off your back and carry on regardless. I think a lot of the workers nowadays must adhere to the latter out of necessity and that, although illegal, times have not changed one bit on the scale of things when it comes to modern employment rules and regulations. Some job seekers are so cut-throat that undercutting the competition is now normal and employers are canny to exploit this, especially if you are hiring private staff for the home.

Desperate times call for desperate measures. I've never stayed with an abusive or nasty employer just for the sake of a wage or a nice place to live. Life is too short to live like that and yes, before you question me, I have been in desperate situations before when I have had to decide on which bill to pay before any food was bought or how much food I would be able to buy after said bills. I know how it feels to make do with old shoes and clothes and having to live with a toothache for a few months because the car needed repairing. I know how it feels to cobble five part-time jobs together to make one liveable wage and how hard that is physically and how terrible it feels to sleep on a cushion on the floor of my sister's home for a year because that is all she could provide for me while I was homeless, and how very grateful I was for it.

If you find yourself in dire straits and feel there is no hope and no light visible in any tunnel, please do not think that your life is over. It is only a temporary glitch and instead of focusing on lack of resources, try to become more resourceful. It may seem like you are stuck forever but you truly are not if you decide not to be. I know it is hard but keep going and make the extra effort, do the menial job, do the extra hours. It will eventually pay off in the end. Realise that what you think makes you respectable and successful is probably material and therefore doesn't. A mansion and an expensive car and a luxury lifestyle most probably is fun for a while, but it will not make you happy. Most of the wealthy women I have worked for and who had everything and anything whenever they wanted it, were some of the most miserable and unpleasant people I have ever met and wouldn't want as friends; the more they had the more they wanted, and they were never happy or fulfilled.

You must remember that you are already rich if you have family and friends who love you for you and not for what you have or own or what you can do for them. You are rich if you have an income and a roof over your head and food on the table. You are rich if you have your health and strength in knowing and loving yourself. We live in the Western world and almost everything we do or experience or own or even how we live is a world away from most of the people on the planet. So, next time you are depressed because you haven't got the latest iPhone or laptop or that you live in a less desirable area or you cannot afford to eat lobster very often, please stop moaning because these are first world problems and most of our fellow human beings cannot imagine the luxury we have, even though you may think that you have nothing. Do not think that life is easy and that you will be handed things on a plate, unless you do have an inheritance coming (lucky you!), then expect it to be a struggle and when you look back at a later time and see what you have created for yourself, you will smile and see that it was achievable and you made it happen for you. Staying happy is key and changing bad and harmful habits and routines will really make a huge difference in how you feel about yourself and your life. Life is all about change and you need to see that there is always a solution or different path to choose to achieve personal happiness. You have to love and respect you and then how you perceive problems and obstacles will become so much easier to navigate. How you relate to and deal with negative and mean-spirited people and situations will become so much easier and simpler to have to experience.

Whenever the awful house guest woman came into my sight or when her name was mentioned I could immediately switch off and cut her nasty energy out before I had even begun to focus on my job duties. In a way I guess it was retreating into survival mode. I just kept thinking to myself that one day soon I would be a million miles away from her and that her hate was ingrained in herself and that whoever took the job after me would be treated exactly the same way, which in turn made me feel liberated and that I was going to be fine whatever happened. I would move into the next room if I heard her coming and I would avoid eye contact and being near her physically. I made it clear that I didn't appreciate her manners, but she kept on being loud and intrusive and belligerent. Sometimes she would follow me through the house and constantly complain about the method or progress of my work, and other days she would not even appear. Then, after I had left for the day, she would make a huge mess and leave it all for me to clean up, which was usually in the kitchen after every utensil had been used and left to stagnate and go crusty on the countertop overnight. Food would be all over the floor and stove top and the bins would be overflowing and stinking in the heat of the aga and summer sunshine.

A few times she didn't walk the dogs before bed so they had relieved themselves all over the hallway during the night and then she would casually step over it in the morning while ordering me to clean it up. Other times she would leave the cupboard open where the dog food was kept, and the dogs would gorge on the contents of the ripped open bags and then throw up all over the hallway and then casually step over while ordering me to clean it up.

I often wondered if my boss knew what type of person she was leaving in charge during her absence, and if she had any idea how this woman was treating her staff. Was the new boss a heartless and patronising bore who had let her new wealth and status go to her head, or did she think most of us were beneath her and therefore stupid and inferior compared with her privilege and superior class she had bestowed upon herself when she acquired her new job in the city? I thought about the rushed interview I had had with her. She had the annoying habit of staring at my chest instead of looking into my eyes and she had never asked me anything about myself and how it was all about her and what she wanted. It was all very cold and clinical. There was no warmth and no feeling of any sort, and I realised then that this awful house guest woman who had been brought in while she swanned off around the world was an extension of herself and I was about to see it firsthand that very weekend at her milestone birthday party.

The birthday party had been in the planning for months and friends and family were jetting over for it from various far-off places and different parts of the country. Extra beds had been bought and were being delivered to fill the numerous bedrooms and every other spare room in the house was being transformed into sleeping quarters. Several large and elaborate tents had been erected throughout the lawns and magnificent marquees had been hired to hold all the dining guests, including toilet and washroom facilities. Only the immediate family were staying in the house and its use was limited to the catering staff, teams of florists and the entertainment, which included a band and a few professional actors to mingle with the guests and make merry when they became bored with each other, and the awkward silences went on too long. There were a half dozen nannies to set up a creche in one of the wings of the house and a car load of party planners had arrived to supervise the function in its entirety and to allot the staff their individual list of duties and tasks to be performed during the party. I remember being given my list by the awful house guest woman and not being allowed into the meeting with the other staff members and I was shuffled off to the kitchen to make tea and coffee for everyone. I didn't think it was odd at the time as I had been given my list, but what happened that evening made clear the extent of the sabotage and manipulation this woman was prepared to put me through and all I can think of the reason why was because she could, and nothing could stop her. I wasn't afraid of her, and she couldn't control me so she now took it a step further and did all that she could to ruin my reputation and turn my boss against me.

Guests started arriving shortly after lunch, which I had prepared for the family and a select group of their friends who had already stayed the night. I had made a surprise birthday cake the day before and had hidden it in the pantry inside a tin that no one was meant to find. But as I went to retrieve it, I noticed the tin lid was open and the cake was gone. I thought that perhaps one of the guests in the middle of the night had come down to the kitchen looking for a snack and had found it, but later that day, while taking a bag of garbage out to the wheelie bin, I noticed it had been thrown in the bin. Not in a bag, but just thrown in on the top so whoever next took out the garbage (me) was sure to notice it right away. It pissed me off as I had spent ages making it and decorating it in my own time and to see all the hard work just thrown away really annoyed me. However, I soon forgot all about it as I was so busy dealing with the party and the list of tasks I had to do, which were all timed to coincide with the events and stages of the party and as it was only 3pm by now I had a lot to do before I could finish around midnight.

I cleared the lunch dishes away and started to prepare the tea time items that the guests and children would be eating in the far end wing of the house that had been turned into a creche for the duration of the weekend. They were basically having fancy sandwiches and cakes and biscuits, but the nannies had to have a proper hot meal. So, I started making them their separate meals, and as I was cooking it, the awful woman appeared and surprised me by saying that she would be happy to help with the children's tea as she knew I had a lot to do. I thanked her as I then had to make up separate covered trays that the actors and members of the band would be eating when they were on their breaks later in the evening.

After I had finished in the kitchen I returned to my own accommodation and took a shower and changed clothes, and then was straight back to the house, checking bedrooms and making sure the guests had enough clean towels and supplies, and I made up some of the extra beds that had been brought in. I kept the list I had been given in my back pocket and took it out and re-checked it every hour, as I was so busy, and I didn't want to forget anything. As I was checking it, I could hear shouting in the kitchen, and I went to see what was going on. As I got closer to the kitchen, I could hear my name being mentioned and then I realised it was the woman shouting at my boss.

I entered the room and was met by both of them screaming at me: "Where the hell is the food for the children?" and "What the hell have you been doing?" I should have known not to trust her, but I had, and now I was paying the price. The woman had told barefaced lies and said she would gladly do it and was now stood there with a demonic half smile on her face with her arms folded over her chest, revelling in the chaos she had caused and letting my boss believe it was all my fault for not adhering to the list. At that moment I just felt like leaving and screaming back at them to do it themselves, but I kept calm and started making the sandwiches. It was at that moment, two weeks after I had started, that I knew I was out of there and they could poke the job up their arses. No wonder the last housekeeper had told me to run! No wonder the other staff I had spoken to seemed to dislike the boss and were only there for the money. No wonder they had absolutely nothing nice to say about any of them whatsoever.

Several hours later I had calmed down somewhat, and I went outside for a break in the hot summer evening. The party was in full swing, and the majority of the guests were in the big marquee that had been turned into an indoor dining area. I could hear them taking turns to make toasts and laughing before there was a lull and then the odd murmur while the food was served, and they began to eat. I drank a bottle of cold beer in the garden and then found an empty bathroom to freshen up in before checking the list and starting the last round of room and toilet clean up. By now it was around 9pm; it was still very hot and sunny. I moved through the house quickly as by now it was empty of guests except for the creche wing and as the nannies had been served their dinner, I didn't disturb them and carried on tidying and cleaning. I thought I had made up some time now, and having had to redo the children's food, I then reached for my list, but soon realised I didn't have it and had to backtrack through every room I had been in to find it. But I never did.

I can remember last seeing it while I was in the bathroom and it being on the counter beside the sink, but I never found it, even after looking in the bins and in the closet used for storing all the cleaning supplies and cloths that I had been in and out of most of the day. I knew someone must have taken it and I also knew who it must have been. At this point I really didn't care anymore, and I started to laugh. It was 11pm and I didn't care about any list or schedule or responsibility anymore. I laughed at the thought of being so wound up about it and running around like an idiot, worrying about other people's comfort when I had just been treated like shit, and I laughed even harder when I knew there were more things on the list that I was meant to be doing before I finished for the evening, and I didn't care.

I went back to my flat and fell into a deep sleep. I had been working for over fourteen hours on my day off and had only had one half-hour break and an extra ten minute one that I had had to sneak. I would not be getting paid any extra for it and I had been screamed at and ridiculed. *Yeah, stuff your job where the sun doesn't shine*. Even though the next day was also meant to be my day off, I had to begin the big tidy up and help other staff prep the breakfasts for the guests who had stayed overnight. The extra staff were all agency staff who had been hired and I was the only regular member of staff who was expected to work that day. For nothing. After being told to cook about ten pounds of bacon slices, I had to assist the waitresses with serving breakfast and then was told to go and clean out the disgusting portable toilet block that had been hired and brought on site by a private company who would have supplied their own specialised cleaner and cleaning products. But the cleaner decided she would mingle into the breakfast queue and line up for a free meal followed up by over-the-top ass kissing to my boss and keeping her talking until I had finished doing her job. I could tell that my boss was really pissed off at me by the way she was giving me withering dirty looks and didn't say good morning or speak to me at all that day. I did eventually find that party list about a week later. It had been scrunched up into a tight ball and had been hidden underneath a wad of tissues that had been pulled out of the box and stuffed back in; it was beside the sink in the bathroom that I had used to freshen up in during the evening of the party. The box of tissues had been used up and as I replaced the box with a new one, I could hear the paper ball rattling around inside the empty container.

There was only one person who would have done that. Any sane person who had found it would have either left it there or put it in the bin. Since that weekend of the party, everything went downhill, and I knew that this awful house guest from hell had gone all out to cause me as much damage as she could. I noticed that the boss and her husband rarely spoke to me and now, other members of staff avoided me too. I knew it was their problem and I was outside of the little clique they were all in, and I was all the happier for it. There was a lovely older gentleman who worked in the office who never said much, and I only had one conversation with him while I was there, and it was during the final week and the last time I had to clean the area where his desk was. He knew what had happened and he knew what this awful woman could get away with, just because she was the boss's friend. He sympathised with me, but also warned me that it would only get worse and that I didn't have to put up with such shoddy treatment. He agreed with me when I told him it was best that I just moved on to another job and he suggested I should try to reason with the boss and tell her exactly what had happened and the extent to what her friend was up to. In the end I decided not to say anything and to just get the hell out of there as soon as I could. Experience reminded me that there was no point, especially if it involved one of their personal friends or a family member, and if they were so easily persuaded to blame and turn against me, then why bother to reason with them? Best to save anymore heartache and sleepless nights and move on. Put it down to more experience and put it all in the past and look forward to new horizons. Laugh. Change. Rejuvenate. I didn't want to have to stoop to their level and start to play the blame game. That was too easy, and soon I found myself on another new path and ready for another new start. I longed for that feeling you get after you get home from being on vacation, that feeling that nothing in the past mattered and from now on everything looked, smelled, and felt different. I wanted change and a new perspective and that meant becoming a new me. The new me would never let herself be chastised and abused and treated like a second-class citizen ever again. The new me started to love herself as an honourable and good person, a person who deserved just and fair treatment, like any other human being has every right to.

CHAPTER 12

LORD AND LADY MUCK

I was now in my twenty-fifth year of service and apart from earning the top money that most people enjoy at this point in their careers, I had reached the top in as much as experience goes. The money has never driven me. I know it is nice to have and to feel secure and to feel to be able to flash it on your friends, but for me all that matters is a nice balance and quality of life. I prefer to work less hours and have a nice place to live as part of my wages rather than the big bucks and chasing all the extra hours and overtime. As you get older you realise that you can't have any of that time back that you eagerly traded off for cash and your own personal space and down time is worth so much more. Physical labour for years on end also plays a part as arthritis was diagnosed in my early 30's and now I am in my mid 50's it is starting to hurt and affect my life, especially in the colder months and I prefer not to take the prescribed medication. I always tend to ride pain out and have a few shots of whisky or a hot toddy before bed, which usually works for me.

In this line of work, you tend to find employers get rather annoyed if you are off sick and many times I have had to grin and bear it and struggle through the day when all I wanted to do was to lay down and die. Once I had broken my baby toe while playing with the cat. I was chasing her around the lounge with a cowboy hat on my head which she adored, and I ran into an old metal shipping trunk that was doubling up as a coffee table and I caught my toe on the edge, and it broke.

I was in absolute agony and although I did manage to get the day off, I was expected back the next day and I had to wedge on a tight-fitting pair of trainers to work in, and I hobbled for about a week before I could start to bear weight on it properly again. Even when you look and sound and move around like death, people will still think you are pretending and make like you are trying to pull a fast one ripping them off. It seems that if you are in private service, you are somehow exempt from any illness, physical or mental, and I have had to on a few occasions provide a sick note from my doctor even though the boss could see I was really suffering.

When the boss is ill, it is a totally different set of rules. The latest new job and boss turned out to be a mixture of everything that was mostly bad that I have ever encountered in all my years as a housekeeper. It was a shame, as my new surroundings seemed beautiful, and I found myself in a lovely village which was set in an area of natural beauty. The job was part time, which usually means that you work a few hours during the weekday or spread over to include a part of the weekend, which is usually light housekeeping and some cooking. Sometimes most of the hours are on the weekends as some people like to be waited on and these types are always the least pleasant.

This arrangement worked for a year and although the new boss and family were very messy and demanding, I didn't mind as they would all disappear on a Sunday evening to one of their other houses and not be seen again until the following weekend. It all started to go pear-shaped when Lady Muck started to feign illness, which was anything but a bad attempt at hiding the fact that she was very lazy and addicted to online shopping. She would spend most of the day in bed, creating a mess and ordering things she didn't need, and she became hysterical when the instant gratification wore off which was then fixed with more shopping. I knew it was a real form of addiction but had little sympathy for her. When I first saw her dishevelled and roaming around the kitchen with no makeup on and looking very pale with a wild look in her eye, I thought there was something wrong and she played on it until I figured out what was really happening. She would lie in bed until noon and become nasty and shout if anything woke her up. She would take a tray of breakfast up to her bedroom and not appear again until 2pm and either start shopping online or, if going out somewhere, leave in a foul mood, complaining of being late and leaving a trail of mess and destruction behind her.

Once she accused me of making her late for an appointment because one of her socks had been left inside out before being put away in the sock drawer. Another time was because I had not ironed a shirt properly and it had been difficult for her to fold and pack into a bag. Once she had finally left the house it would look like a bomb had gone off and through it. Every room would be trashed and every item of clothing, both clean and dirty, would be mixed and thrown onto the floor. The bed would have food and crumbs in it and the bathrooms had more food and clothes and wet towels thrown all over the floor. Garbage that had overflowed from the bin would also be on the floor and mixed in with the food and clothes and towels and all left there for me to pick up. The sinks and mirrors would be covered in gob and toothpaste and the toilets would be full and unflushed. The sitting rooms had more food thrown around and stains had been left all over the stairs and sofas and carpets. A bottle of red wine would be knocked over and just left there for me to deal with.

The kitchen was in a perpetual state of chaos and more food and every item of cutlery, plate and pan, seemed to be constantly dirty and left to congeal and pile up in the sink or left on the counter top despite there being three dishwashers to choose from. I know it is my job and I know some people are not very good at keeping things neat and tidy, but there really is a limit and when things constantly go over the limit, it is time to question reality and come to some sort of answer. The husband and adult children contributed to the disorder too, so I had to conclude that they couldn't possibly be doing this to degrade me and that they truly had to be the most repulsive and utter scumbags that I had ever had the displeasure of working for. There really is no need for people who are supposedly educated and privileged, to behave this way.

You really couldn't make it up, and I have been inside the homes of some of my friends who haven't got two pennies to rub together, and they are spotless and clean enough to eat your dinner off the floor. How could it be that poorer people are clean and have pride in what they own and how they live, and their home reflects their lovely down to earth and genuine selves? Surely the wealthy people should know better how to treat people and empathise and reflect their good manners beyond their social status to others, on all levels and display aspects of dignity and pride for their possessions and household and living standards? How can you trash your own house on a continual basis and then just move on to stay at another one with another set of staff and trash that, and so on…. How can you live like animals and then act like Lord and Lady so and so, and then pretend that you live and lead a perfect life?

One day some workmen came to the house to paint some of the exterior and they had passed by the kitchen windows and seemed quite concerned as I took them out a cup of tea and a biscuit on their mid-morning break. They had noticed the absolute wreckage that was the kitchen and had thought a burglar had been in and had ransacked the place. I found out from people in the village that other housekeepers before me had never lasted long working there, and there were rumours of years of high staff turnover and illegal work practices and unreasonable treatment and expectations. None of their neighbours liked them and even their dog had run away from them. I found all of this out over the time I worked there from the locals at the village pub, and I believed all of it as locals at village pubs are always up to date on the village gossip and are not afraid to air their complaints or give newcomers the heads up, especially a newbie coming to work for a difficult or unliked member of their surroundings. I remember being told by my boss not to venture into the village pub as they didn't want anyone to know who I was and who I was working for. I am not the type of person to name names or make anything obvious or draw a lot of attention to myself, but I thought *screw you!* I can drink where I like, and as a responsible adult, I can hold my own in a room full of strangers. So, I knew then that something was odd and that skeletons would be getting dragged out of closets.

I became a regular and became friends with people who had worked for them in the past and learned what dreadful human beings they really were. Most of the previous housekeepers had been foreign and many had come to this country with little or broken English, and they were terribly exploited, shouted at and belittled, and paid in cash below the national minimum wage. They had been working seven-day weeks and didn't realise that they were entitled to days of rest and paid holidays, and they were subjected to vile treatment inside their own on site private and separate lodgings by way of being spied on with phonic surveillance in the form of covert listening devices and motion activated front door cameras, without their knowledge or consent. These women were constantly being reminded that they could become homeless and blacklisted if they didn't perform the job and they were frightened and unaware that what was happening was highly illegal.

The most frightening thing about it was knowing that the boss knew it was illegal but had kept on with the method of treatment to more and more women. That is until I started to work for her, and I made sure I was paid correctly and above board and had proper holidays and time off. Looking back on it all now, it seems like they didn't like the fact that I knew my own worth and my human and workplace rights, and they still carried on with their abusive behaviour, but in a different way, and that way was a continual display of malice, contempt and disdain. They thought they could hurt me, but they never did and they continued to be selfish and bitter towards me. They would openly discuss business of their friends and family with scorn and in front of me, and by the way they criticised and demoralised them, I knew that they must detest me, and I realised how the whole family were toxic. It seemed like overt narcissism was a family trait and delusions of grandeur and snobbery were legitimate qualities that made them unique. I don't think they realised how hateful and unnecessary all the charade was and how dysfunctional and damaging they were to themselves and their children, and how that was going to affect them in how they see and treat others in the future. How sad to live like that and think that it is acceptable, treating people like dirt and being able to sleep at night. It just goes to show that money cannot and will not make you happy and it can't seem to buy you a heart either. You can't hide behind a polite and courtly manner, gushing and acting posh when lurking beneath the surface is awful and petty suppressed venom just aching to come out as the real you. The term elitism may be used to describe a situation where power is concentrated in the hands of a limited number of people. An elitist is a bully who has power over you. A psycho is a bully who has power over you. They tried to break my spirit and demoralise me, but I would never let them anywhere near my tipping point and I would laugh at them when I was alone in my thoughts.

Once again, I started to go on the odd job interview and took extra time to look out for a new position that really appealed to me and would be suitable for what I wanted and needed instead of the old habit of winging it and hoping for the best. I always used my day off so they wouldn't know where I had gone, and I never used the telephone or my mobile inside of the house or on the property. I lost count of how many interviews I attended and always felt guilty when I was offered a job but had to turn them down and make up excuses why I didn't want it. Usually, it was the way in which the person acted or spoke or looked at me, which would remind me of a previous boss, a situation, or a feeling that was awful, and it had stuck in my mind, and I vowed to never let it happen again. It is easier to get a job when you are already employed, and I used it to my advantage. I knew I could afford the time it took to find what I wanted, and all the nasty treatment, words and general atmosphere of contempt rolled off my back and I continued working. Except now I had a huge smile on my face as I knew it was just a matter of time and a bit of luck and I would be on my way to another new chapter of my life. Whenever voices were raised and the yelling started, I laughed. Silly complaints and sarcastic remarks made me laugh out loud inside my head. It was hard to keep from smirking and maintain eye contact when the shrieks and over the top theatrics were being badly performed in front of me.

Things started to get even crazier, and Lady Muck started to spend more time at the weekend house, preferring to sleep all day and then roam around the house at night. She would cook and leave a mess, deciding to sort out various drawers and cupboards and just emptying the contents out into a pile in the middle of the room and then drape a sheet over it so I couldn't tidy it up, and then it would sit there for weeks. Eventually, it would all get shoved into one of the spare bedrooms that had been turned into a storage room and it looked like something a hoarder would be proud of. She spent more time lying and eating in bed. When the time came to clean out the bedroom and change the sheets, it would look like a junkie had been occupying it. There was food in the bed and plates and trays on the floor, along with more dirty clothes and used tissues and various prescription pills that were scattered all over the room.

The en suite bathroom was worse as you can imagine and the same detritus carried on in from the bedroom along with wet towels and face flannels, thrown and mixed in with garbage and used Q-tips and cotton balls, which had been used to scrape makeup off with. The walk-in closets were a shambles and expensive new garments had been taken off and thrown to the floor, and shoes and boots had been kicked off into the corner and left in a heap. A pile of cashmere jumpers lay in front of the full-length mirror, pulled off inside out and dumped next to a pile of soiled knickers, socks, and stockings. All of this meant extra hours of work and I was still expected to do all my usual hours, as well as fit all the extra work it would take to clean up after her and have the house ready and the food cooked on time for the weekend when all of the other family members would show up with all of their dirty laundry. They would sometimes show up with dirty pots and saucepans that they couldn't manage to rinse out after taking leftovers away with them from the previous weekend.

I was expected to do all the extra time and hours in the original hours I was being paid for and there never was any mention of a pay rise in almost three years although the terms and conditions changed all the time to suit them. They started to change my day off and my start times on a weekly basis and thought nothing of phoning me late at night or on my day off to request a taxi service (me) to pick one of their useless adult children up from the train station, with so much of a thank you, or proper wad of cash in lieu of inconvenience to me. One week everything would be fine, and the next Lady Muck would have a massive flip out and tantrum and screaming fit if her clothes had not been folded properly or her sock drawer wasn't symmetrical, or her towels hadn't been fluffed up enough. There would be a terrible scene, and everything would be changed back to how I had been doing it for years and Lord Muck would buy her more trinkets from Chanel and there would be peace and harmony again for a few weeks. The bag of Chanel goodies would sit unopened on the closet floor and be joined by others over the coming months, all unopened and unloved and not appreciated at all.

Lady Muck was so feckless and boring and insignificant that she couldn't even muster any empathy to do anything charitable with all her spare time and unlimited wealth. She hated to give anything away to charity shops as she didn't like the fact that she wasn't in control of who she thought was deserving enough to receive it. She loved to scorn the poor, especially if uneducated and refused to acknowledge their plight, although she did take pride in teaching the children about poverty by loading them into the Audi and driving them past the tower blocks in the less affluent parts of the city. She loved the fact that today, the class system was alive and well and that anyone below her was a loser. She taught her kids the same ethics and, having the rules of class drummed into them, she then sat back on her wide arse and installed an Alexa in every room so that she didn't have to be disturbed by them when they had a question they needed answering or help with their studies. If it wasn't related to chocolate or haute couture or shopping or luxury holiday resorts, she really didn't want to know about it. She would walk away or turn her head and ignore you, which was infuriating if you were in the middle of a conversation with her.

There was little or no respite when they all went away on holiday either. The build up to the departure day was absolute torture and drama was the order of the day. As usual, Lady Muck would lie in bed until the last minute and then rush around screaming at everyone to help her pack and get ready and she would get so nasty she would be swearing and foaming at the mouth. Havoc would be wreaked throughout every room of the house and most of her clothes would be on the floor in heaps and strewn around the house as she decided to pack an item and then discard it for something else, so it also was thrown on the floor. When the family had departed the house would fall silent and then the scale of destruction would suddenly hit you. Even during holidays, when I was given a few days off it never really was a proper holiday for me as so much time would be needed to put the house back together along with the laundry and ironing and beds and cooking that needed doing before they got back again. I dreaded the arrival as it meant a mountain of dirty laundry and more ironing and cooking, and it seemed never ending. If Lady Muck was in the middle of one of her flips, I was forbidden to use the dryer, which was crazy given the amount of wet clothing that needed drying, which was utter lunacy during the winter time. I would have to wait to use it when she left the house along with the other appliances and often I would just re-iron clothes that had only been worn for a few hours until being put in the dirty clothes pile. A spray of Febreze and a nice fold up and back in the cupboard and no one is the wiser for it!

I started to mind the time and looked for the quickest and easiest ways to fit so much work into a few hours and I restructured how I did everything from the method I used to clean the house and rooms and the way in which I cooked certain recipes. I usually had to cook the same dishes every weekend so I stopped doing it the traditional way and looked online for the speedier and easier way to cook and prep and substitute ingredients so I could save more time by not having to drive into town to get them if they weren't already in the fridge. I hated to do it and it seems so petty and mean, but there was no way that I was going to be put upon and used by this Lady Muck who had already decided it was my lot to be at her beck and call and to hurry up while I was at it. The last year I was there I had noticed how nasty and selfish she was becoming, and she neglected to remember my birthday and my day off, and to reimburse me for money I had spent while popping to the shops because she hadn't ordered online. There was never a compliment or a kind word from her, only criticism and complaints about the quality of my work and sometimes Lord Muck would chip in with his opinion, but it was never to my face, and he would moan to her and then I would get it back twice as bad. The pair of them would argue and then involve me and take it out on me and then turn it around so that I was the cause of it all, either something I did or didn't do that wasn't good enough. Imagine being blamed for someone's failed marriage and bad life choice? I knew the problem lay with Lady Muck who was twenty-five years younger than her husband and that the marriage was most probably convenient for her. After all, what could a pretty and young twenty-year-old woman, possibly find attractive in the fat, balding, ego centric, forty-five-year-old stock broker? No wonder she was so miserable. All the money and the multiple houses full of stuff and the luxury vacations will never make you happy. Only you can make you happy. Be happy for who you are and what you have, and what you have experienced.

We are all human beings, and we all deserve and require dignity and respect and basic rules when it comes to our human rights. There is no higher being unless you are religious and even then, the Gods would offer the same treatment for all, rich, poor, sinners and saints. It is medieval to think that money and wealth instantly places you on a pedestal and the people beneath you are somehow unfit for any purpose. How can people still be thinking this way and still be getting away with treating others with this serf and master mentality? It is so sad and so very small minded. I have concluded that people who think like this are to be pitied and that there is something broken and dead inside their hearts. They have no soul, and they truly are the real dregs of society. The lowest of the low. Scumbags. Scumbag millionaires.

The final straw happened one morning in the springtime and within two minutes of blurting out my intention to quit my job, I immediately felt the weight come off my shoulders and the little cloud that had been hovering over my head for the past year suddenly stopped raining. It had all happened because I had forgotten to plump up the cushions in the conservatory after spending the whole of the previous day cooking for ten for the dinner party that was to take place that evening, and even though I had time to do it later, Lady Muck had gone mad and had flipped. I could feel the cool feeling of relief and ease and I automatically started to imagine a new start in life, and I couldn't wait to finish for the day and start to search for it. I didn't care that I had no luxury of taking my time to select a new position and now I just wanted out and to get away and the sooner the better. I knew I would be taking another huge leap of faith into the unknown and that I would be at the mercy of fate and luck, and timing, and I couldn't wait to see what the wheel of fortune would be steering me towards this time. I wasn't afraid of failure anymore or of heartbreak or unfulfilled expectations.

I approached the situation head on and within a few days I was already in familiar territory and had been offered two interviews for live-in cook/housekeeper and the same old feelings started to creep into the back of my mind. I had thoughts of self-doubt and panic but briefly, as usual, they gave way to an enormous sense of relief and wellbeing. I knew I would be okay and employed again and with a roof over my head, which really is the biggest worry to anyone. It is one of the worst things in anyone's life to become homeless and I have known the feeling many times in my life and how it can destroy all other rational thoughts. It is one of the biggest drawbacks when you have chosen a career in private service, but over the years I have learned to turn fear around and now see it as an opportunity to live in a different part of the country, and in a way, it has made me a stronger person. A new start and a change are as good as a rest, and you really can recharge and reinvent yourself with a new atmosphere and new outlook on life and things in general. I always remind myself that nothing lasts forever, and life is all about change, and every time you can change you should do so and feel good about it. If it doesn't work out the first time, try again and again and eventually it will. Be positive. Be optimistic. Be a good person. Let the past go and step forward into a new life. We are only here in this world for a very small amount of time, and we must make the most of it. Make the best of it. Heal and love and believe in yourself. There is only one you. Dare to believe that anything and everything is possible. Never limit yourself or your expectations. Turn your dreams into reality and ride the crest of the wave towards your destiny. Refuse to surrender your ambitions and remember that tomorrow is going to be another beautiful day to try all over again.

CHAPTER 13

EPIPHANY

There really is a world out there where you wake up every morning eager to spring out of bed and greet the day with all the cheer and vigour and euphoria that the birds sing about as you pull open the curtains and throw open the window to the beautiful sunshine. Believe that your hopes and dreams really can come true and then they will. I was prepared to resign myself to a never-ending cycle of putting up with second best and always going through the motions and thinking you are happy and that everything is okay, when it is anything but, and you always think it in the back of your mind but suppress it and pretend the opposite. I was ready to go into my new job and my newfound happiness lasting a month or so before reality set in and I began thinking the same old patterns of thought that followed me throughout most of my working life, ending any chance of peace and fulfilment. I waited for it to happen and thought something must be terribly wrong, but it never did, and I felt a new sensation of hope and contentment. I started to look forward to each new day and I began to love waking up early in the morning again.

I had finally found a boss who treated me with kindness and compassion and who valued me as a person, who was also a fellow human being, and not just there for a specific purpose or to be used and dismissed and then forgotten about until needed again for any random reason. It felt like I had stepped through a portal into a new life and that the further I walked along the path the sunnier and more abundant my surroundings became. My spirit guide had finally found me and had taken my hand and was leading me towards a great feeling of warmth and joy and I felt like I was truly at home after being lost out in the wilderness for years. I could feel myself smiling. I had become me again.

Everyone's happiness and destiny are out there waiting to be discovered and the tools to find it are already instilled within you. So, find the courage and inner strength to make your life a life of success and wonderful experience and realise that you are blessed. It is never too late to try, and it can and will happen if you really want it to. And keep smiling.

Milton Keynes UK
Ingram Content Group UK Ltd.
UKHW021055020924
447770UK00016B/1025

9 781835 634408

- I am strengthening my spirit every day.

- I am freeing myself from the chains of addiction.

- I am growing emotionally every day.

- I am living my life with authenticity and joy.

- I am finding my purpose and direction.

- I am at peace with myself and my decision to change.

- I am discovering my true potential.

- I am choosing growth over complacency.

- I am learning to successfully manage triggers.

- I am overcoming the barriers that once held me back.

- I am grateful for my strength and determination.

- I am building a life filled with love and hope.

- I am learning from my challenges and triumphs.

- I am choosing life and leaving addiction behind.

- I am trusting in my ability to change and heal.

- I am letting my heart guide my path to recovery.

- I am finding joy in the simple things in life.

- I am embracing the process of change with gratitude.

- I am proving that I am stronger than addiction.

- I am working towards achieving my goals.

- I am filled with hope for the future.

- I am learning to manage stress in a healthy way.

- I am living a life free of guilt and regrets.

- I am letting go of excuses and taking action.

- I am focused on my well-being and happiness.

- I am letting go of everything that holds me back.

- I am surrounded by positive energy.

- I am learning to enjoy the simplicity of life.

- I am grateful for every opportunity to improve.

- I am committed to my healing process.

- I am transforming my life with every choice.

- I am discovering new ways to feel alive.

- I am celebrating every victory, big or small.

- I am rebuilding important relationships.

- I am leaving behind the mistakes of the past.

- I am seeing my life from a new perspective.

- I am on the path to a free and happy life.

- I am learning to be patient with myself.

- I am creating a life full of meaning.

- I am letting self-love guide me.

- Every small step brings me closer to success.

- I am changing my story with each sober day.

- I am open to change and growth.

- I am learning to love myself.

- I am letting go of negative thoughts.

- I am creating a new version of myself.

- I am strong and capable of facing any challenge.

- I am leaving behind negative influences.

- I am proud of myself for choosing recovery.

- I am focused on building a better life.

- I am overcoming my fears and doubts.

- I am learning to trust my ability to change.

- I am grateful for every day of sobriety.

- I am developing positive and healthy habits.

- I am building a strong support network.

- I am making decisions that reflect my worth.

- I am enjoying the mental clarity that sobriety brings.

- I am choosing self-love over addiction.

- I am seeing progress in my life every day.

- Each day without cocaine is a victory.

- I am proud of the steps I am taking.

- I can overcome any urge or craving.

- My life is better without cocaine.

- I am committed to my recovery.

- I have the strength to say "no."

- I am freeing myself from negative patterns.

- I am taking control of my life.

- My mind is growing stronger every day.

- I am surrounding myself with supportive people.

- I am leaving behind everything that harms me.

- I am an example of courage and determination.

- My life has purpose and meaning.

- I am letting go of guilt and shame.

- I am capable of building healthy habits.

- I am healing my body and mind.

- I am learning to enjoy life fully.

- I am full of energy and determination.

- I am choosing what is best for me.

- I am discovering new ways to be happy.

Mental reprogramming phrases.

- I am stronger than any temptation.

- Each day, I move closer to freedom.

- My life is valuable and deserves care.

- I have the power to change my story.

- I can overcome any obstacle I face.

- I am in control of my decisions.

- Every positive choice makes me stronger.

- My body and mind deserve to be healthy.

- I am creating a life full of peace and joy.

- I am capable of overcoming addiction.

- My recovery is my priority.

- I am surrounded by love and support.

- I let go of the past and focus on the present.

- I am worthy of a happy and healthy life.

- Cocaine does not define who I am.

- I am resilient and brave.

- I am building a bright future.

- My emotional and physical well-being matters.

- I am learning to manage my emotions wisely.

36

Powerful phrases for mental reprogramming.

This process focuses on changing thought patterns and beliefs that perpetuate addiction, replacing them with more positive and constructive ideas and approaches.

It is based on neuroplasticity—the brain's ability to form new connections and habits through repetition and conscious focus.

This is a key tool in recovery, as many people struggle with automatic, negative thoughts that drive them toward substance use.

Mental reprogramming combines techniques such as positive affirmations, meditation, and visualization.

It also incorporates cognitive-behavioral therapy (CBT) to redirect mental and emotional patterns toward a state of empowerment.

It requires consistent practice, but over time, it can transform how challenges are perceived, helping to build confidence and resilience.

A practical example of mental reprogramming is identifying a recurring thought like "I will never be able to quit cocaine" and actively replacing it with "Every day, I am getting closer to a life free of addiction."

By repeating this new thought, the mind begins to accept the change, weakening the impact of previous negative beliefs.

Every great change begins with a first step, and you have already taken it.

Quitting cocaine is not just about giving up a substance, but embracing a new life full of possibilities.

Allow yourself to imagine a future filled with joy, health, and inner peace.

You deserve that life, and with every positive choice you make, you are one step closer to achieving it.

Change is possible, and the future is waiting for you.

Don't give up.

Cocaine does not define you.

You are so much more than this struggle, and within you lies a strength you may not have fully discovered yet.

Every effort you make, no matter how small it may seem, shows that you have the capacity to build a life filled with purpose, peace, and genuine happiness.

Seek support, because no one has to face this alone.

Talking to people who understand your experience-whether in support groups, with therapists, or through friends and family can ease the emotional burden and provide practical tools to overcome tough moments.

These connections will remind you that there are people who believe in you, even on days when you may doubt yourself.

Imagine the life you want for yourself: waking up every day with mental clarity, building strong relationships, pursuing your dreams, and feeling proud of who you are.

That life is within reach, and every choice you make toward recovery is an investment in that bright future.

You can rediscover your passions, find purpose, and enjoy the freedom of being fully yourself without relying on cocaine to face life.

If you ever feel like you can't go on, remember how much you've already overcome to get to this point.

Recovery is a journey of strength and courage, and every day you choose to fight is a testament to your determination.

Believe in yourself, even when it feels hard to do so.

35

Words of encouragement for the reader.

Quitting cocaine is a monumental challenge, but it is not impossible.

If you're reading this, you've already taken the first and most courageous step: recognizing that you want change.

That desire to transform your life is a powerful spark that can ignite the fire of recovery.

Although the journey may seem daunting, remember that you are not alone.

Countless people have faced the same challenge and have overcome it, finding a fuller, freer life.

You can do it too.

It's important to remember that recovery isn't about perfection; it's about progress.

There will be hard days, and it's okay to stumble—the important thing is to get back up and keep moving forward.

Every small step you take toward a life free from cocaine is a triumph.

Every sober day, every time you choose your well-being over substance use, is a victory that brings you closer to the freedom you deserve.

Your worth is not defined by the mistakes of your past but by your willingness to work for a better future.

INSPIRATION TO
EMBRACE A LIFE FREE
FROM COCAINE

The twelfth step involves sharing the experience with others, helping newcomers to the program, and applying the principles of the 12 steps in daily life.

For instance, someone who has been in recovery for a year might become a sponsor, guiding a newcomer through the program and demonstrating through their example that recovery is possible.

The seventh step involves asking for help from that higher power to overcome identified weaknesses.

For instance, someone struggling with resentment toward a loved one might seek support to develop empathy and forgiveness, replacing negative emotions with constructive attitudes.

The eighth step is about making a list of people harmed during substance use and being willing to repair those relationships.

For example, someone might write down the names of friends they neglected while prioritizing drug use, acknowledging the need to restore those connections.

The ninth step calls for action, making amends whenever possible.

For instance, a person might sincerely apologize to a family member they deceived to obtain money and commit to never repeating such behavior.

The tenth step encourages ongoing maintenance, meaning regularly evaluating one's actions and correcting mistakes as they arise.

For example, someone who realizes they acted rudely toward a coworker could promptly apologize and strive to improve their behavior moving forward.

The eleventh step involves seeking a deeper connection with that higher power through practices like meditation or prayer.

For instance, a person might dedicate time each morning to reflect on their goals for the day and ask for strength to remain sober.

For example, someone initially skeptical about the idea of a higher power might choose to trust the collective experience of a support group, observing how others have successfully overcome their addiction.

The third step involves deciding to trust that higher power and stop trying to manage everything independently.

An example would be a person who stops blaming themselves for relapses and instead commits to following the suggestions of their sponsor or mentor in the program, such as attending meetings regularly and working through the steps.

The fourth step is a personal inventory, where one conducts a deep analysis of their actions, emotions, and behavioral patterns.

For instance, someone might reflect on how their cocaine use was tied to avoiding emotions like sadness or fear of rejection, identifying patterns that perpetuated their addiction.

The fifth step involves sharing the findings of the inventory with another person.

This could mean confessing to a sponsor that, during their drug use, they lied to their family and stole resources to fund their addiction.

This act of confession not only alleviates emotional burdens but also fosters accountability and honesty.

The sixth step requires a willingness to work on one's character flaws.

For example, a person might acknowledge that their impulsive behavior contributed to their problems and be open to developing patience and self-control as part of their recovery.

34

The 12-step program.

It is a structured and effective approach that has helped millions of people overcome addictions, including cocaine addiction.

This program, adapted from Alcoholics Anonymous, is based on principles of self-exploration, mutual support, and spiritual or personal growth, depending on individual beliefs.

The steps are interconnected and encourage continuous progress toward recovery.

Each step includes a practical component that can be illustrated to understand how it applies in real life.

The first step involves admitting that control over cocaine use has been lost and that life has become unmanageable.

For example, an individual may acknowledge that, despite repeated attempts to control their usage, their addiction has damaged family relationships and led to job loss.

This recognition is a crucial starting point as it opens the door to change.

The second step focuses on believing that a higher power can help in the recovery process.

This higher power does not necessarily need to be religious; it can be the support group, the principles of the program, or even the individual's own desire to improve.

Adopting a growth mindset involves replacing these limiting beliefs with affirmations such as "I am learning to handle this situation" or "Every day, I am getting closer to my goals."

A growth mindset also fosters gratitude and recognition of progress.

Celebrating small victories, such as a week without using, learning to manage a trigger, or building a healthy relationship, reinforces the idea that every effort counts.

This creates a positive cycle where success fuels more success.

Adopting a growth mindset requires practice and patience but offers significant benefits for those seeking to overcome cocaine addiction.

It enables individuals to face challenges with an attitude of learning and resilience, focusing on progress rather than mistakes.

With this mindset, people can not only overcome addiction but also build a richer, more meaningful life aligned with their values and aspirations.

With this mindset, individuals can not only overcome addiction but also build a richer, more meaningful life aligned with their values and aspirations.

It is a powerful tool for transforming obstacles into opportunities for growth and demonstrating that, with effort and perseverance, change is always possible.

33

Adopting a growth mindset.

This concept is based on the idea that our abilities and qualities can develop through effort, appropriate strategies, and support.

It allows individuals to face the challenges of recovery with resilience and optimism.

For someone seeking to overcome cocaine dependency, a growth mindset can be a transformative tool that strengthens motivation and commitment to change.

The first step to adopting a growth mindset is recognizing that addiction does not define the individual and that recovery is a process that fosters learning and progress.

Instead of viewing relapses or difficulties as failures, a growth mindset interprets them as opportunities to learn and improve.

For example, if someone experiences a relapse, they can reflect on the circumstances that triggered it.

They can then develop new strategies to handle similar situations in the future, rather than punishing themselves or giving up.

A key component of this mindset is changing the internal dialogue.

Many individuals in recovery struggle with negative thoughts like "I'll never overcome this" or "I'm not strong enough."

Each time a high-risk situation is successfully managed, confidence in the ability to remain sober increases, reinforcing the commitment to recovery.

Identifying and avoiding risk factors is an active and dynamic strategy that requires self-awareness, planning, and a willingness to make changes in one's environment and relationships.

With a mindful approach, appropriate support, and practical tools, it is possible to significantly reduce the likelihood of relapse and move toward a fulfilling life free from cocaine dependence.

For example, a person struggling with loneliness might join a book club or volunteer, which not only provides social interaction but also offers a positive sense of purpose.

Advanced planning is also key to avoiding risk factors.

This involves developing a plan of action to handle high-risk situations before they arise.

For instance, if someone knows a social gathering will include people using cocaine, they could choose to attend with a supportive friend, set a time limit for their stay, or have an exit strategy ready if they feel uncomfortable.

Having a clear strategy reduces the likelihood of falling into an environment that encourages use.

A practical example is John, who identified loneliness and boredom as his main risk factors for relapsing into cocaine use.

To address them, he developed a daily routine that included morning exercise, afternoon art classes, and evening support group meetings.

He also removed people from his life who encouraged drug use and cultivated new friendships in healthier environments.

Thanks to these measures, he was able to stay focused and avoid situations that put him at risk.

It is important to recognize that avoiding risk factors doesn't mean living in isolation or constantly fearing relapse.

Instead, it involves building a balanced and meaningful life that minimizes exposure to triggers and strengthens the ability to resist them.

If certain places or people are associated with drug use, it may be necessary to set clear boundaries or even avoid those environments altogether.

For example, someone who always used cocaine at a specific bar might choose to avoid that place and seek alternative activities, such as attending support group meetings or engaging in sports.

Social pressure is a common risk factor, especially if a person's social circle includes friends who still use cocaine.

In such cases, it's important to learn how to say "no" assertively and surround oneself with people who respect and support the decision to stay sober.

Having prepared responses to refuse drug offers can be helpful.

For example, someone might say, "Thanks, but I don't use anymore. I'm focused on my health."

Replacing harmful relationships with new connections in support groups or healthy activities can make a significant difference.

Negative emotions, such as anxiety, depression, or loneliness, are frequent triggers that can increase the risk of relapse.

Learning to manage these emotions without turning to cocaine is essential.

This might include seeking therapy to address underlying issues, practicing mindfulness to stay present and balanced, or developing hobbies that provide emotional fulfillment.

32

Identifying and avoiding risk factors.

Understanding what triggers the desire to use cocaine makes it possible to develop an effective plan to confront and overcome these challenges.

Risk factors vary from person to person but may include stress, negative emotions, social pressure, certain environments, or activities associated with drug use.

Recognizing and learning to manage these factors is crucial for maintaining long-term sobriety.

A first step is conducting an honest analysis of past consumption patterns.

This involves reflecting on when, where, and why cocaine was used, identifying specific situations or emotions that acted as triggers.

For example, someone might realize they turned to cocaine after family arguments, during periods of work stress, or while attending parties with certain friends.

This type of self-reflection provides valuable insights for anticipating future risks.

Avoiding risk factors doesn't always mean avoiding them entirely but finding ways to confront them in healthy ways.

For instance, if work stress is a significant trigger, techniques like meditation, regular exercise, or deep-breathing practices can help manage it effectively.

MAINTAINING LONG-TERM SOBRIETY

A key component of his recovery was therapy and his commitment to structured programs such as the 12-step approach, which provided him with the tools needed to maintain long-term sobriety.

These programs not only helped him manage cravings and avoid relapses but also allowed him to rebuild personal and professional relationships that had been damaged by his addiction.

Additionally, Tyler embraced a healthier lifestyle, prioritizing his physical and emotional well-being to stay focused on his sobriety.

The results of his transformation have been extraordinary.

He not only overcame his addiction but also led Aerosmith to new heights of success and longevity.

The band, which at one point seemed on the verge of dissolution, experienced a resurgence with successful albums like Permanent Vacation and Pump, solidifying its status as one of the most iconic rock bands of all time.

Tyler, with his unmatched charisma and talent, became a symbol of resilience and reinvention in the music industry.

31

Steven Tyler.

The legendary lead vocalist of Aerosmith faced an intense battle with cocaine addiction and other substances throughout much of his career.

In the 1970s and 1980s, Tyler was immersed in a rock-and-roll lifestyle where drugs and alcohol were part of the daily environment.

Cocaine became a constant presence, fueling both his creativity and self-destruction.

His addiction severely impacted his physical and mental health and jeopardized Aerosmith's stability, causing tensions among the band members and threatening to end their musical legacy.

In his own words, Tyler admitted that his addiction was "as big as his career."

The turning point in Steven Tyler's life came after multiple failed attempts to overcome his addiction.

An intervention by his family and bandmates ultimately led him to seek professional help.

Realizing that his dependence was affecting not only himself but also those around him, Tyler entered a rehabilitation program—a crucial step marking the beginning of his recovery.

During his treatment, he worked to address the underlying causes of his substance use, such as the pressures of fame, the stress of touring, and the emotional void he tried to fill with drugs.

Through acting, he found a creative outlet that allowed him to channel his emotions and stay away from the temptations of substance use.

The intensity and commitment he brought to his work helped him regain his confidence and build a solid career.

The results of his transformation are extraordinary.

After overcoming his addiction, Samuel L. Jackson became one of the most respected and successful actors in the film industry.

His ability to portray a wide range of characters, combined with his charisma and on-screen presence, solidified him as one of the most influential figures in modern cinema.

He has appeared in some of the highest-grossing films in history, including the Marvel franchise and Pulp Fiction, and is renowned for his work ethic and professionalism.

30

Samuel L. Jackson.

One of Hollywood's most iconic and prolific figures, Samuel L. Jackson faced a tough battle with cocaine addiction before achieving success in his career.

During the early years of his life as an actor, Jackson struggled with deep personal issues that led him to rely on drugs as an escape from emotional challenges and the difficulties of establishing himself in a highly competitive industry.

His substance use escalated to the point of jeopardizing his health and relationships, culminating in a critical moment when his family found him unconscious at home due to substance abuse.

The turning point in Samuel L. Jackson's life came through the intervention of his family, who took him to rehabilitation following this alarming incident.

This act of unconditional support marked a pivotal moment for the actor, who finally acknowledged the severity of his situation and decided to commit to his recovery.

During his time in rehabilitation, Jackson began to confront the emotional and psychological roots of his addiction while acquiring the tools needed to maintain sobriety.

A key pillar of his recovery process was redirecting his focus to his passion for acting.

His dedication to his craft became a way to keep his mind occupied and his energy focused on something constructive.

Additionally, her commitment to philanthropy and humanitarian activism became a central part of her life, providing her with a sense of purpose and connection to global causes.

Through her work with the United Nations and her focus on human rights and refugee aid, Jolie not only distanced herself from drug use but also transformed her life into a vehicle for creating positive impact.

The results of her transformation have been remarkable.

Angelina Jolie not only left her drug use behind but also became one of the most respected and renowned actresses in Hollywood.

Her work in acclaimed films and her ventures into directing have solidified her as an influential figure in the film industry.

At the same time, her dedication to humanitarian causes and her role as a UNHCR Goodwill Ambassador have inspired millions, positioning her as a symbol of resilience and purpose.

29

Angelina Jolie.

A renowned actress, director, and humanitarian activist, Angelina Jolie faced a past marked by drug abuse, including cocaine, during her youth.

Raised in the entertainment world and influenced by the complex dynamics of her family and personal environment, Jolie began experimenting with substances at an early age.

Her search for identity, combined with an intense personality and a tendency to explore limits, led her to use various drugs, including cocaine.

This period was characterized by a sense of emptiness and disconnection, where drugs became a means to escape her emotions and the pressures of her surroundings.

The turning point in her life came when Angelina began to deeply reflect on her purpose and future.

Her growing interest in building a meaningful career and finding a greater cause that connected her to the world made her realize that her drug-driven lifestyle was neither sustainable nor compatible with her ambitions.

This moment of introspection marked a turning point, as she decided to distance herself from drugs and redirect her energy toward goals more aligned with her values and aspirations.

Angelina found in her career as an actress and director a way to channel her creativity and emotions constructively.

A crucial aspect of his transformation was his connection to his spiritual faith, which became a source of strength and purpose.

Clapton has spoken openly about how he found comfort and guidance in spirituality, allowing him to address his addiction from a deeper perspective.

This faith helped him find inner peace and reconnect with a sense of purpose beyond music and material success.

The results of his commitment to recovery were extraordinary.

Not only did he achieve sobriety, but he also used his personal experience to help others.

In 1998, he founded the Crossroads Centre in Antigua, a rehabilitation facility designed to provide treatment for individuals struggling with drug and alcohol addiction.

This project reflects his desire to give back and support others on their path to recovery.

28

Eric Clapton.

One of the most legendary guitarists in music history, Eric Clapton faced a long and difficult battle with addiction to cocaine and other substances during the 1970s and 1980s.

His substance use began as a way to cope with stress, the pressures of fame, and emotional struggles, including deep insecurities and personal losses.

As his career flourished, so did his dependence on drugs, particularly cocaine, which became an integral part of his personal and professional life.

Substance abuse not only affected his physical and mental health but also jeopardized his career and closest relationships, isolating him from those who cared about him.

Clapton's turning point came after numerous failed attempts to quit drugs and alcohol.

He recognized that he needed a structured approach and external support to overcome his addiction.

He found a path to recovery through a 12-step program, which provided him with a framework to maintain sobriety and connected him with a community of people facing similar struggles.

This program was instrumental in helping Clapton understand that he was not alone in his battle and that he could learn from the experiences of others to strengthen his own recovery process.

Through therapy and structured support, he learned to manage his emotions and stress without turning to substances, laying the foundation for his recovery.

A key component of his transformation was redirecting his focus toward charitable causes and activities that gave him a renewed sense of purpose.

Elton became deeply involved in philanthropy, founding the Elton John AIDS Foundation, which grew into one of the most prominent charities in the fight against HIV/AIDS.

This work not only allowed him to give back to the community but also helped him stay focused and committed to his sobriety.

He found in activism a way to channel his energy and passion positively, which strengthened his resolve to remain drug-free.

The results of his commitment to recovery have been remarkable.

Elton John not only overcame his addiction but also revitalized his music career, releasing successful albums and embarking on world tours that further solidified his status as a music legend.

Additionally, he became an outspoken advocate for mental health and well-being, using his experience to inspire others to seek help and break the stigma associated with addiction.

27

Elton John.

One of the most influential and renowned musicians in the world, Elton John faced a tough battle with cocaine addiction during the 1980s.

At the height of his career, when his fame and success had reached global levels, the pressures of the music industry, the stress of constant touring, and internal struggles with his identity and self-esteem led him to turn to drugs as a form of escape.

Cocaine became a central part of his life, providing momentary euphoria but with devastating consequences.

His addiction not only impacted his physical and mental health but also endangered his personal relationships and began to erode his creative abilities.

The turning point in Elton John's life came when he finally recognized the severity of his problem.

After years of substance use, episodes of erratic behavior, and a growing sense of emptiness, he decided to seek professional help and committed to entering rehabilitation.

This step was not easy, but it marked the beginning of his transformation.

During his time in rehab, Elton worked not only on overcoming the physical dependency but also on understanding the emotional and psychological causes that had led him to rely on cocaine.

The actress also focused on transforming her life by adopting a holistic approach to well-being.

She began prioritizing her physical and emotional health, dedicating herself to activities that promoted balance, such as exercise, meditation, and spending quality time with her family.

Her commitment to recovery not only allowed her to overcome addiction but also helped her rediscover her purpose and redefine her personal and professional priorities.

The result of her efforts has been extraordinary.

Jamie Lee Curtis has maintained her sobriety for decades and has used her personal experience as a platform to inspire and educate others about the dangers of addiction and the possibility of recovery.

She has spoken openly about her story in interviews and public events, breaking the stigma surrounding addiction and offering hope to those facing similar challenges.

Additionally, her continued success in the entertainment industry, combined with her authenticity and dedication to activism, has established her as an example of resilience and transformation.

26

Jamie Lee Curtis.

A renowned actress and activist, Jamie Lee Curtis has been open about her struggle with drug addiction, including cocaine, a challenge she faced during a difficult period in her life.

Coming from a prominent Hollywood family, Curtis was exposed to the pressures and temptations of the industry at an early age.

Her substance use began as a way to cope with stress, personal insecurities, and external expectations related to her career and public image.

In her case, addiction was also fueled by easy access and a culture that normalized recreational drug use within the entertainment industry circles.

The turning point in her life came when she realized the negative impact cocaine and other substances were having on her health, relationships, and overall well-being.

She decided to seek professional help, marking the beginning of her journey to recovery.

Jamie Lee Curtis entered rehabilitation programs and began attending support group meetings, where she found a safe space to share her experiences and learn from others facing similar challenges.

These groups provided her with essential tools for maintaining sobriety, such as the importance of establishing healthy routines, identifying triggers, and developing skills to manage stress without turning to drugs.

Running became a way to relieve stress, manage cravings, and restore his physical health.

Eminem mentioned that he initially ran compulsively, covering up to 17 miles (27 kilometers) daily, which not only helped him overcome the residual effects of drugs but also provided a positive focus and a structured routine.

Exercise allowed him to channel the energy he once dedicated to substance use into a healthy and constructive activity.

Additionally, he focused on rebuilding his personal and professional life, distancing himself from negative influences and restructuring his environment to support his sobriety.

He worked on his music as a form of expression and therapy, allowing him to channel his experiences and emotions through his lyrics.

Eminem released his album Relapse in 2009, addressing themes related to his battle with addiction, followed by Recovery in 2010, a project that marked his triumphant return and solidified his message of overcoming adversity.

The result of his effort and commitment to recovery has been remarkable.

Since 2008, Eminem has maintained sobriety, regaining not only his physical and mental health but also his creativity and artistic success.

He has released award-winning albums and has proven to be a model of resilience, using his story to inspire others facing similar challenges.

25

Eminem.

One of the most influential rappers of his generation, Eminem faced a tough battle with drug addiction, including cocaine, at the height of his career.

His substance use began as an attempt to cope with stress, the pressures of fame, and intense emotions stemming from traumatic events, such as the death of his best friend, Proof, and struggles in his personal relationships.

As his career soared, his substance abuse escalated, involving not only cocaine but also pills like Vicodin and Ambien.

The addiction severely impacted his physical and mental health, creativity, personal relationships, and artistic productivity, leading him into a dark period where he even considered retiring.

The turning point in Eminem's life came after a near-fatal overdose in 2007, which put his life at risk and forced him to confront the severity of his addiction.

The overdose was a wake-up call, making it clear that if he didn't make a drastic change, he wouldn't survive.

It was then that he decided to seek professional help and committed to a rehabilitation program to detox and work on his recovery.

This critical moment marked the beginning of a challenging but transformative process.

As part of his recovery, Eminem embraced physical exercise, particularly running, as a central tool to maintain sobriety.

Her story highlights that recovery is not a linear process, as she has faced relapses along the way, but it also demonstrates that every step toward healing is valuable and achievable with the right tools.

This marked the beginning of a deeper commitment to her recovery.

Demi found effective tools in structured programs like the 12-step approach, which provided her with a supportive, community-focused framework for working on her sobriety.

Therapy played a central role in her process, helping her address the underlying causes of her substance use, such as emotional trauma and struggles with self-esteem.

Additionally, she prioritized her mental health, including treatments for her bipolar disorder diagnosis, which allowed her to better manage the triggers that had led her to use drugs.

Demi also incorporated self-care practices, such as regular exercise and meditation, to maintain balance.

Another important component of her recovery was her willingness to be transparent about her struggles.

Sharing her story publicly not only helped her find support and understanding but also turned her into an advocate for mental health and addiction recovery.

This act of vulnerability connected her with millions of people facing similar challenges, inspiring them to seek help and break the stigma associated with addiction.

The result of her efforts has been a remarkable personal and professional resurgence.

Demi has returned to her career with strength, releasing music that reflects her experiences and her journey toward healing.

Additionally, she uses her platform to advocate for the importance of mental health care and recovery, helping to destigmatize these topics.

24

Demi Lovato.

An internationally recognized singer and actress, Demi Lovato has been open about her struggle with cocaine and other addictions, a battle that began in her teenage years.

Exposed to the pressures of the entertainment industry from a very young age, Demi faced high levels of stress, self-demand, and constant criticism—factors that contributed to the development of her mental health issues and substance abuse.

She started using cocaine and other drugs as a way to cope with her emotions and the pressure, a cycle that quickly became self-destructive.

Additionally, her struggles with eating disorders, bipolar disorder, and episodes of self-harm intensified the complexity of her situation, making her a public figure privately dealing with multiple personal challenges.

The turning point in Demi Lovato's life came after several critical moments, including a particularly dark period when her substance abuse threatened not only her career but also her life.

After facing legal and personal issues that highlighted the severity of her situation, Demi entered rehab several times to address her addiction and underlying mental health problems.

A key moment was an intervention by her close team, who showed her how her behavior was affecting both her life and the people around her.

A pivotal moment came through his relationship with Susan Levin, who would later become his wife.

She set clear boundaries and offered unconditional support but made it clear that she would not stay with him if he continued using drugs.

This ultimatum, combined with his desire to rebuild his life, became a significant catalyst for his recovery.

Downey Jr. adopted a comprehensive approach to overcoming his addiction.

He committed to following a strict recovery program that included rehabilitation, group therapy, and professional support.

Additionally, he incorporated practices like meditation and yoga to manage stress and anxiety, factors that had contributed to his substance use in the past.

These tools not only helped him maintain sobriety but also provided him with a new perspective on his physical and emotional well-being.

The discipline in his daily routine, along with Susan's support, were key elements in his transformation.

The result of his commitment to recovery was extraordinary.

Not only did he achieve sobriety, but he also revived his Hollywood career in an impressive way.

With his iconic role as Iron Man in the Marvel Cinematic Universe, Robert Downey Jr. became not only one of the highest-paid actors in the world but also a symbol of redemption and resilience.

23

Robert Downey Jr.

A renowned Hollywood actor, Robert Downey Jr. is a quintessential example of overcoming addiction to cocaine and other substances that nearly destroyed his career and life.

For years, he struggled with drug use that began at a very young age due to his family environment, where access to drugs was common.

His father, filmmaker Robert Downey Sr., introduced him to marijuana at an early age, marking the beginning of a self-destructive path.

Cocaine, along with other substances like heroin and alcohol, became a constant in his life, severely impacting both his personal and professional life.

Despite his undeniable talent as an actor, his drug problems led to multiple arrests and time in jail, turning him into a controversial figure and putting his Hollywood career at serious risk.

Robert Downey Jr.'s turnaround did not happen overnight.

He went through multiple failed rehabilitation attempts and periods of relapse before reaching a breaking point.

The arrests, legal consequences, and damage to his reputation forced him to confront the reality that he needed to make a radical change to save his life and career.

STORIES OF TRANSFORMATION

Rediscovering your passions and pursuing meaningful goals is a powerful way to fill that void, reconnect with yourself, and create a life rich in purpose, creativity, and personal fulfillment.

This process not only transforms your recovery experience but also prepares you for a future full of possibilities.

For instance, if you value helping others, you might consider getting involved in community work or volunteer projects.

Engaging in activities that promote physical and emotional well-being can also help you rediscover your passions.

Exercises such as running, swimming, playing sports, or walking outdoors not only improve physical health but also stimulate the release of endorphins, boosting emotional well-being.

These activities connect you with nature, your body, and your mind, creating space for introspection and creativity.

Social support plays an important role in this process, as talking with friends, family, or therapists about your interests and aspirations can provide new perspectives and encouragement to explore your passions.

Additionally, joining communities or groups with similar interests can inspire and keep you motivated.

For example, someone who discovers an interest in photography might join a local photography club, where they can learn from others and share their work.

Finally, celebrating every step you take toward rediscovering your passions and goals is essential.

Acknowledging your achievements, no matter how small, reinforces your self-confidence and strengthens your motivation to keep moving forward.

Recovery isn't just about quitting cocaine; it's about building a life that inspires you and makes you feel whole.

Recovery offers a unique opportunity to try things you've never considered before.

You could enroll in a dance class, learn to scuba dive, practice yoga, study a new language, or participate in volunteer work.

For instance, someone who never considered gardening might discover it as a therapeutic way to relax while caring for something living, reinforcing their sense of purpose.

Setting clear and achievable goals is another vital component of this process.

Goals provide structure, direction, and a sense of accomplishment, which is crucial for maintaining motivation during recovery.

These goals can start small, such as reading a book, attending a class, or completing a weekly walk, and then progress to larger objectives, like resuming studies, securing a fulfilling job, or developing a professional career.

For example, someone who always dreamed of learning to play the guitar could start with basic lessons and practice regularly, seeing their skills improve over time.

Reconnecting with your values is fundamental to rediscovering your passions and goals, involving reflection on what truly matters to you and what you want in life.

This might include relationships, contributions to the community, personal growth, or simply finding inner peace.

Identifying these values provides a solid foundation for setting goals aligned with your priorities, helping you move toward a more meaningful life.

22

Rediscovering your passions and goals.

This is a crucial step in the process of quitting cocaine, as prolonged use of the drug tends to divert attention away from what truly matters, such as personal interests, dreams, and life goals.

Addiction not only consumes time and energy but also diminishes motivation, creates disinterest in activities that once brought joy, and leaves a sense of emptiness.

Reconnecting with passions and redefining personal goals not only provides renewed purpose but also serves as an anchor to remain steadfast in recovery.

The first step to rediscovering your passions and goals is reflecting on what you used to enjoy before cocaine became part of your life.

Think about activities, hobbies, or projects that once excited you.

For example, perhaps you loved painting, playing an instrument, writing, cooking, or playing sports.

Returning to these activities can serve as a bridge to reconnecting with yourself and your most authentic interests.

Even if you don't feel the same level of enthusiasm at first, giving these activities a chance can help you rediscover the joy and satisfaction they once brought you.

Exploring new activities is also essential for opening doors to interests and talents you may not have known about.

Engaging in activities you are passionate about reinforces the belief that you are capable of creating and contributing meaningfully.

Another effective strategy is reflecting on past achievements and recalling moments when you overcame challenges or demonstrated resilience.

Recognizing your ability to face difficulties in the past can provide confidence to tackle current challenges.

For example, if you once successfully achieved an important goal, such as completing a complex project or getting through a tough period, remembering that experience can remind you of your strength to overcome the recovery process.

Finally, regaining self-confidence requires patience and consistency.

This process doesn't happen overnight, but every step forward strengthens your self-esteem and belief in your ability to change.

Self-confidence not only helps you face the challenges of recovery but also lays the foundation for a fuller, more balanced, and meaningful life.

By focusing on your strengths, celebrating your achievements, and maintaining a learning mindset, you can rebuild a solid sense of confidence that enables you to face the future with hope and determination.

Setting small, achievable goals is essential for rebuilding self-confidence.

Each time you complete a task or reach a goal, you reinforce the belief that you are capable of keeping commitments and overcoming challenges.

For example, if resuming daily activities feels overwhelming, you can start with something simple, like maintaining a consistent sleep routine, attending a support meeting, or completing a task at work.

Every success, no matter how small it may seem, becomes a building block for self-confidence.

Self-compassion is a key tool to counteract self-criticism and guilt, which often accompany addiction recovery.

Practicing self-compassion means treating yourself with the same kindness and understanding you would offer to a friend in a similar situation.

This includes recognizing your achievements, validating your emotions, and avoiding self-punishment for mistakes.

For instance, instead of criticizing yourself for a difficult day, you could say, "Today was hard, but I'm doing my best to improve, and that deserves acknowledgment."

Strengthening your skills and abilities can also help rebuild confidence.

This might involve learning something new, returning to a hobby, or developing skills that interest you.

For example, if you enjoyed painting before your substance use, returning to that activity not only gives you a sense of accomplishment but also reconnects you with positive aspects of your identity.

21

Regaining self-confidence.

This is an essential aspect of the process of quitting cocaine, as addiction often erodes self-esteem and creates doubts about the ability to change.

During substance use, it is common for individuals to experience feelings of guilt, shame, and failure due to the negative consequences of their actions, such as broken promises, relapses, or damaged relationships.

This cycle can make it difficult to believe in one's ability to overcome challenges, further reinforcing harmful behavioral patterns.

However, rebuilding self-confidence is possible through a conscious and progressive approach that combines self-compassion, achievable goals, and practical strategies.

The first step to regaining self-confidence is accepting that recovery is a process, not a single event.

Recognizing that it is normal to make mistakes along the way helps release the pressure to be perfect and shifts the focus to learning and personal growth.

For example, instead of saying, "I've failed because I relapsed," you can reframe that thought as, "I've learned from this relapse and am taking steps to prevent it from happening again."

This shift in perspective turns setbacks into learning opportunities and strengthens confidence in your ability to adapt and improve.

Finally, it is important to remember that not all relationships can or should be restored.

In some cases, it may be necessary to accept that certain bonds will not recover, especially if the relationship was harmful or toxic.

This is not a failure but an opportunity to focus on building new, healthier connections.

Rebuilding personal and family relationships is a process that requires time, honesty, and dedication, but the effort is worth it.

Strengthened relationships not only provide emotional support during recovery but also offer a network of love and connection that can be a constant source of motivation and purpose.

This type of exchange can help heal wounds and build a foundation of mutual understanding.

It's also important to establish clear boundaries in relationships, which may involve the person in recovery communicating what kind of support they need and what behaviors from others could be harmful to their sobriety.

For instance, someone might ask their family to avoid using alcohol or drugs in their presence or to refrain from constantly bringing up past mistakes in a negative way.

Participating in shared activities is another effective way to strengthen relationships.

Spending time together doing things everyone enjoys, such as cooking, playing sports, or simply talking, can help create new positive memories to replace difficult moments from the past.

For example, someone who became distant from their children during drug use might start taking them to the park regularly or helping them with homework as a way to reconnect.

A practical example is Mariana, who lost her sister's trust due to years of broken promises during her addiction.

After starting her recovery process, Mariana decided to have an honest conversation with her sister, apologizing for her past behavior.

She also started following through on small but important commitments, such as arriving on time for family gatherings.

Over time, her sister began to notice the change in Mariana, and gradually, their relationship grew stronger.

Actions, in addition to words, are fundamental for rebuilding relationships.

Keeping commitments, being honest, and maintaining consistent behavior are ways to demonstrate that the change is real and sustainable.

For instance, if someone promises to spend more time with their family, they should ensure they follow through by attending family gatherings or actively and meaningfully engaging when present.

Patience is essential in this process, as the emotional wounds caused by addiction do not heal overnight.

Some friends or family members may need time to process their emotions and learn to trust again.

In such cases, it's important to respect their pace and show understanding, remembering that rebuilding relationships is a long-term effort.

For example, if a family member remains distant or skeptical, the person in recovery can continue to demonstrate their commitment through consistent actions without expecting immediate results.

Family therapy can be an invaluable tool for repairing damaged relationships.

A trained therapist can facilitate difficult conversations, help family members express their feelings constructively, and teach effective communication skills.

For example, in a family therapy session, a parent might express their pain over their child's lies during drug use, while the child could explain how addiction drove them to act harmfully.

20

Rebuilding personal and family relationships.

Lies, broken promises, erratic behavior, and isolation are common behaviors during substance use that can erode trust and create emotional barriers between the person in recovery and their loved ones.

However, with time, effort, and an honest approach, it is possible to repair these relationships and build healthier and more meaningful connections.

The first step in rebuilding relationships is acknowledging the impact cocaine use has had on others.

This involves taking responsibility for past actions without justifying them or blaming others.

Sincerity in this process is key to starting to rebuild trust.

For instance, someone might approach a close friend or family member and say: "I know that during my drug use I did things that hurt you, like lying or not keeping my promises.

I'm working on changing, and I want you to know how sorry I am for causing you pain."

Sincerely apologizing is an essential part of the reconciliation process, as an effective apology acknowledges the harm caused, expresses genuine regret, and conveys a commitment to change.

For example, instead of simply saying "I'm sorry," a meaningful apology might include: "I regret breaking your trust by not keeping my promises. I'm working to regain your trust and hope to show you that I'm committed to my recovery."

REBUILDING YOUR LIFE

This includes remembering why the decision to quit cocaine was made and focusing on the long-term benefits, such as improved health, meaningful relationships, and personal growth.

For example, someone might write a list of reasons to stay sober and review it regularly to reinforce their motivation.

Resisting social pressure is a process that requires self-awareness, preparation, and support.

It doesn't necessarily mean abandoning all previous relationships or environments, but it does involve prioritizing personal values and well-being over external expectations.

Over time, each situation faced strengthens confidence in the ability to stay sober, demonstrating that true strength lies in choosing a path aligned with health and personal growth.

For example, someone might decide to avoid gatherings where they know drug use will occur and instead seek new activities or social circles that promote a healthy lifestyle.

Setting clear boundaries is another crucial strategy.

This involves assertively communicating the decision to quit cocaine and not yielding to others' expectations.

Practicing prepared responses to decline drug offers can be helpful in confidently handling uncomfortable situations.

For instance, someone might say, "Thanks, but I don't use anymore. I'm focusing on taking care of my health."

Having these phrases ready can make interactions easier and reduce anxiety in moments of pressure.

Developing new friendships and participating in drug-free activities also helps resist social pressure.

Joining sports teams, creative workshops, or volunteer groups not only provides a positive distraction but also creates opportunities to meet people who share similar interests and support a substance-free lifestyle.

For example, someone who joins a climbing club might find a group of friends who value physical activity and health over drug use.

Self-confidence and self-esteem are also fundamental to resisting social pressure.

Working on these areas enables individuals to face others' opinions and judgments with greater assurance.

19

Resisting social pressure.

Social pressure can manifest in various forms, from friends who use and offer drugs to environments that normalize or glorify their use.

Learning to navigate these situations is essential for maintaining sobriety and building self-confidence.

One of the primary causes of social pressure is the desire to belong to a group or fit into a specific environment.

Many people start using cocaine in social contexts where the drug is portrayed as a means of fun, success, or acceptance.

For example, someone might feel pressured to use cocaine at a party to avoid seeming different or boring in front of their peers.

This need for acceptance can be a significant obstacle, but it is important to remember that true belonging should not depend on substance use.

To resist social pressure, the first step is to identify environments and people that encourage drug use.

This includes recognizing friendships or social circles where cocaine is present and evaluating whether those relationships are healthy.

Although it can be challenging, distancing oneself from people who do not respect the decision to quit is an essential act of self-care.

For example, someone who distanced themselves from their family during drug use could start rebuilding trust by calling regularly, attending family gatherings, and showing reliable behavior.

Facing guilt and shame is a process that requires time, patience, and effort, but it is a vital part of personal growth in recovery.

When managed in a healthy way, these emotions can be transformed into catalysts for change, reconciliation, and the strengthening of self-esteem.

For example, someone might tell themselves: "I've made mistakes, but I'm learning and working to do things differently now."

Social support is also key to addressing these emotions.

Talking openly with trusted people, such as friends, family members, or participants in a support group like Narcotics Anonymous, can help ease the burden of guilt and shame.

Hearing the experiences of others who have faced similar situations also helps normalize these emotions and reinforces the idea that no one is alone.

For instance, at a support meeting, someone might share their shame about losing a job due to drug use and receive empathy and words of encouragement from others who understand that pain.

Therapy, particularly cognitive-behavioral therapy (CBT), is another effective tool for managing guilt and shame.

CBT helps identify recurring negative thoughts, challenge them, and replace them with more balanced perspectives.

For example, someone who frequently thinks, "I've let everyone down, and I'll never be able to repair the damage," could work with a therapist to reframe that thought as: "While I've made mistakes, I have the opportunity to learn from them and rebuild relationships with time and effort."

Taking concrete steps to repair the damage caused can also help alleviate guilt and reduce shame.

This might include sincerely apologizing to those affected, taking responsibility for past actions, and demonstrating a commitment to change through consistent actions.

Healthy guilt can serve as a guide to take corrective actions, such as apologizing or changing harmful behaviors.

For instance, someone who feels guilty for neglecting their family during drug use might decide to express their regret and start rebuilding trust through consistent actions.

In contrast, toxic guilt, which is based on an exaggerated sense of responsibility, should be confronted and challenged with the help of a therapist or counselor.

Shame, often more deeply rooted than guilt, requires a similar approach.

Many people in recovery carry a sense of unworthiness or not being "good enough" due to the consequences of addiction.

To address shame, it is helpful to remember that addiction is a complex medical condition, not a moral failing.

Shifting the internal narrative from "I am a bad person" to I am a person working to overcome a challenge" can make a significant difference.

For example, instead of thinking, "I've ruined everything and don't deserve a second chance," someone might remind themselves, "I'm taking steps to improve and repair what I can."

Self-compassion is a powerful tool for managing guilt and shame, as it involves treating oneself with the same understanding and kindness one would offer a close friend in a similar situation.

Practicing self-compassion does not mean justifying mistakes or avoiding responsibility; it means recognizing one's humanity and accepting that everyone makes mistakes.

18

Facing guilt and shame.

This is a central aspect of the process of quitting cocaine, as these emotions are often significant barriers to recovery.

Guilt and shame can arise from actions taken during drug use, such as lying, damaging relationships, missing opportunities, or facing legal consequences.

While these emotions are normal and understandable, they can become obstacles if not managed properly, fueling feelings of worthlessness, hopelessness, and isolation that could lead to relapse.

Guilt, which relates to remorse over specific actions, and shame, which impacts self-perception as a person, are natural human reactions.

However, when these emotions become overwhelming, they can paralyze progress and reinforce a negative self-image.

To face guilt and shame, the first step is to acknowledge and validate them as legitimate emotions.

Suppressing or ignoring them only increases their power, while accepting them allows the process of addressing them to begin.

For instance, someone who feels guilty for lying to a loved one might recognize this feeling as a sign that they value honesty and wish to repair the damage.

It is important to distinguish between healthy guilt, which motivates repair and change, and toxic guilt, which perpetuates self-criticism and stagnation.

Resuming participation in recovery activities, such as attending support group meetings or returning to therapy sessions, is vital for managing a relapse.

These activities reinforce the commitment to sobriety and remind the individual that they are not alone in their journey.

Additionally, hearing the experiences of others who have faced and overcome relapses can be a source of inspiration and motivation.

Finally, it is important to remember that every relapse is a lesson, not a defeat.

With the right mindset, it can become a tool to strengthen recovery.

Rather than focusing on the setback, the most valuable approach is to concentrate on the progress made and the steps that can still be taken toward a healthier, fuller life.

Managing a relapse is not just about getting back on track but also about moving forward with greater knowledge, resilience, and determination.

These actions not only help stabilize the body after a relapse but also improve mood and rebuild confidence in the ability to recover.

For example, someone feeling physically and emotionally drained after a relapse might benefit from taking a walk outdoors or preparing a nutritious meal.

Accepting relapse as a learning opportunity means identifying what can be done differently in the future.

This involves exploring how cravings were managed, which strategies worked and which did not, and what emotions were not adequately addressed.

For instance, someone who realizes that a craving was triggered by loneliness could plan healthier social activities, such as attending support group meetings or spending time with friends who support their recovery.

A practical example is Luis, who, after six months of sobriety, experienced a relapse during a business trip.

Luis identified that work-related stress and isolation in an unfamiliar environment were key triggers.

Immediately afterward, he called his sponsor in Narcotics Anonymous, who helped him process the situation without self-judgment.

Luis then worked with his therapist to adjust his recovery plan, adding specific strategies for managing work-related stress, such as practicing daily meditation and setting clearer boundaries in his work schedule.

He also decided to avoid traveling alone and, in the future, to seek travel companions who would support his sobriety.

This analysis helps identify what went wrong in the relapse prevention plan and how it can be improved.

Seeking immediate support is key to managing a relapse.

Talking to a therapist, a sponsor in a support group like Narcotics Anonymous, a trusted friend, or a close family member can help ease the emotional burden and provide practical guidance.

For instance, someone facing a relapse might call their therapist to schedule an additional session and discuss specific strategies for managing future triggers.

Reviewing and adjusting the recovery plan is another essential step.

A relapse often indicates areas that need strengthening or factors that were not adequately addressed.

This might include adding new strategies for managing stress, setting clearer boundaries in certain relationships, or avoiding high-risk situations.

For example, if a relapse occurred after visiting a place associated with drug use, the solution could be to avoid that environment and seek alternative activities that reinforce sobriety, such as joining a hiking group or learning a new skill.

An important tool for managing a relapse is practicing self-care.

During this time, it is crucial to prioritize physical and emotional health.

This includes maintaining a balanced diet, engaging in regular physical exercise, and establishing a healthy sleep routine.

17

How to handle a relapse.

Although a relapse can be a difficult moment, it does not signify definitive failure but rather an opportunity to learn, adjust strategies, and strengthen the commitment to sobriety.

Addiction is a chronic condition that affects the brain, and relapses are common due to the challenges of overcoming physical and psychological dependence.

What matters is how the situation is handled and the steps taken to get back on the path to recovery.

The first step in managing a relapse is to acknowledge it without falling into excessive self-criticism or paralyzing guilt.

Feelings of guilt or shame can fuel a negative cycle that increases the likelihood of further use.

Instead, accepting what happened as part of the process allows for a more constructive attitude.

For example, someone who has relapsed might say to themselves: "This is a setback, not the end of my recovery. I can analyze what happened and move forward."

It is essential to identify the factors that led to the relapse.

This includes analyzing triggers such as situations, emotions, people, or places that may have sparked the urge to use.

For example, a person might realize they attended a social event where they felt pressured to use drugs or experienced an intense stress situation without having sufficient tools to manage it.

OVERCOMING OBSTACLES

With the help of a therapist, Anna began establishing a nighttime routine that included turning off electronic devices an hour before bed, drinking lavender tea, and practicing 15 minutes of gentle yoga.

During the day, Anna managed her stress by dedicating time to outdoor walks and journaling to process her emotions.

These practices not only improved her sleep quality but also provided her with effective tools to face daily challenges without turning to drugs.

Activities such as running, swimming, or playing sports helps release endorphins, which improve mood.

Additionally, it helps channel accumulated energy in a constructive way.

For example, someone who used cocaine to cope with work pressure might start taking daily walks after work to release the tension built up during the day.

Setting boundaries and learning to say "no" are other key strategies for managing stress.

Many people in recovery find that much of their anxiety stems from taking on too many responsibilities or not expressing their needs effectively.

Practicing assertiveness can help reduce stress-inducing situations.

For instance, someone feeling overwhelmed by social commitments could learn to decline invitations respectfully, prioritizing their well-being.

Techniques such as therapeutic writing can also be beneficial.

Keeping a journal to express thoughts and emotions not only helps release tension but also allows for the identification of stress patterns and potential solutions.

For example, someone writing about a recurring workplace conflict might discover more effective ways to address the situation.

A practical example is Anna, who faced difficulties sleeping and high stress levels after quitting cocaine.

Another effective approach to improving sleep is limiting caffeine and other stimulants, especially in the afternoon.

Additionally, avoiding the use of electronic devices such as phones or televisions before bed can be beneficial.

The blue light they emit interferes with the production of melatonin, a key hormone for sleep.

Incorporating a relaxing bedtime routine, such as reading a book, taking a warm bath, or practicing meditation, can also help prepare the body for rest.

For instance, someone might establish a nightly ritual that includes drinking a cup of calming herbal tea, like chamomile, followed by 10 minutes of deep breathing to reduce tension.

Managing stress without drugs is equally important, as many people turn to substances like cocaine to cope with anxiety or daily pressures.

One of the most effective techniques for reducing stress is the regular practice of relaxation exercises, such as mindful breathing, meditation, or yoga.

These practices help calm the mind, lower cortisol levels (the stress hormone), and promote emotional balance.

For example, someone feeling overwhelmed by a stressful situation might practice the 4-7-8 breathing method: inhale for four seconds, hold the breath for seven seconds, and exhale slowly for eight seconds.

This method is known to induce an immediate sense of calm.

Physical exercise is also a powerful tool for managing stress.

16

Improving sleep and managing stress without drugs.

Cocaine disrupts the central nervous system, interrupting normal sleep patterns.

It also increases stress levels by causing overstimulation, anxiety, and neurotransmitter imbalances.

As the body and mind adapt to the absence of the drug, it is essential to implement effective strategies to restore healthy sleep and learn to manage stress naturally.

Sleep is one of the most affected areas during cocaine use and the recovery process.

Many people experience insomnia, difficulty falling asleep, or frequent awakenings due to the chemical changes in the brain caused by cocaine.

To improve sleep, it is crucial to establish a consistent routine.

Going to bed and waking up at the same time every day helps reset the body's circadian rhythm.

Creating a sleep-friendly environment is also essential; keeping the bedroom dark, quiet, and at a comfortable temperature can facilitate falling asleep.

For instance, someone struggling with insomnia might try using blackout curtains, white noise machines, or fans to create a relaxing atmosphere.

Finally, both nutrition and exercise are powerful tools for reducing the risk of relapse.

A balanced diet helps maintain stable blood sugar levels, which can reduce irritability and mood swings that often trigger cravings.

Exercise, on the other hand, not only relieves stress but also fosters a sense of achievement and purpose—key elements for a successful recovery.

For example, someone in recovery facing cravings can use exercise as an effective distraction.

By going for a run or completing a gym workout, the individual is not only redirecting their attention but also establishing a positive routine that supports their healing process.

Regular exercise also improves cardiovascular health, counteracting the negative effects of cocaine on the heart and blood vessels.

A practical example is Carlos, who, after years of cocaine use, decided to seek professional help to quit.

As part of his recovery plan, he began working with a nutritionist to create a weekly menu that included foods rich in essential nutrients.

Carlos incorporated fruit and spinach smoothies into his breakfast, balanced lunches with lean proteins, and light dinners featuring vegetables and whole-grain carbohydrates.

He also started attending yoga classes three times a week, which not only improved his flexibility and strength but also helped him reduce anxiety and manage cravings.

Additionally, nutrition and exercise can help stabilize sleep patterns, which are often disrupted during cocaine use and withdrawal.

Eating foods rich in tryptophan, such as bananas, turkey, and dairy products, can help the body produce serotonin, a precursor to melatonin that regulates sleep.

Regular exercise, especially when done in the morning, also helps reestablish a healthy circadian rhythm, promoting deeper and more restorative sleep.

Complex carbohydrates, found in foods like oats, brown rice, and sweet potatoes, provide sustained energy.

Meanwhile, healthy fats from avocados, nuts, and oils such as olive oil support brain function.

Fruits and vegetables are essential for supplying antioxidants, vitamins, and minerals the body needs to detoxify and repair the damage caused by cocaine use.

For instance, fruits rich in vitamin C, like oranges and strawberries, can help strengthen the immune system.

Leafy greens, such as spinach and kale, are rich in magnesium, a mineral that can reduce anxiety and improve mood.

Drinking enough water is also crucial to keep the body hydrated and assist in flushing out toxins, as cocaine use can cause dehydration.

Exercise is equally important in recovery, as it not only helps restore physical health but also has a positive impact on mental well-being.

During cocaine use, the brain becomes accustomed to artificially high dopamine levels, reducing its ability to naturally experience pleasure.

Physical exercise stimulates the release of endorphins and dopamine—neurotransmitters associated with well-being and happiness—helping to counteract this deficiency.

Activities such as running, swimming, cycling, or practicing yoga can reduce stress levels, improve sleep, and boost self-esteem.

15

Nutrition and exercise for recovery.

Nutrition and exercise play a fundamental role in recovering from cocaine addiction.

This is because they help repair the physical and mental damage caused by prolonged drug use.

Cocaine severely impacts the body, depleting essential nutrients and disrupting sleep patterns.

It also weakens the immune system and damages the cardiovascular system.

Incorporating a proper diet and a regular exercise routine can accelerate the healing process, improve overall well-being, and reduce the risk of relapse.

One of the most common causes of physical deterioration in people who use cocaine is poor nutrition or lack of appetite.

Cocaine suppresses hunger, which can lead to malnutrition, weight loss, and deficiencies in vitamins and minerals.

This affects energy levels, concentration, and the body's ability to recover.

To address this, a solution is to design a balanced diet plan that includes all necessary nutrient groups.

For example, consuming protein-rich foods such as chicken, fish, eggs, and legumes helps repair tissues and stabilize energy levels.

RECOVERING PHYSICAL
AND MENTAL HEALTH

Through visualization exercises, she imagined speaking to her younger self and offering the emotional support she lacked at the time.

This process helped her recognize that she could seek recognition and validation internally and through healthy relationships instead of turning to cocaine.

From the perspective of biodescodification, solutions involve identifying and resolving unprocessed emotional conflicts, rebuilding self-esteem, and learning to consciously manage emotions.

It also includes connecting with the body to identify how emotions physically affect the individual.

For example, a person might notice tension in their chest whenever they feel anxiety and, through relaxation techniques, release that tension to reduce the urge to use drugs.

While biodescodification may be an interesting approach to exploring deep emotional aspects, it should not be considered a substitute for evidence-based medical and psychological treatments for cocaine addiction.

However, as a complement, it can provide valuable tools for those seeking to understand the emotional and symbolic dimensions of their drug use.

For instance, someone undergoing cognitive-behavioral therapy to manage triggers might find in biodescodification an additional way to explore the deeper meanings behind their behavior.

Biodescodification aims to identify the emotional and symbolic causes of addiction.

A biodescodification therapist may work with an individual to explore significant life events that may have triggered drug use.

For example, if someone began using cocaine after a traumatic breakup, the therapist could help them examine unexpressed emotions from that experience, such as abandonment, guilt, or loneliness, and consciously release them.

The idea is that by processing and releasing these emotions, the subconscious drive to turn to cocaine diminishes.

One cause that biodescodification might attribute to cocaine use is the search for a quick and artificial solution to complex emotional problems.

This can include the desire to escape stress, the need for social acceptance, or the inability to cope with failure or pressure.

Instead of addressing these emotions at their root, the person uses the drug as a temporary fix, perpetuating the cycle of dependency.

To address this, biodescodification proposes techniques such as guided visualization, focused meditation, and symbolic exercises that help the individual reconnect with their emotions and find healthier ways to meet their emotional needs.

A practical example would be Laura, who identified that drug use gave her a false sense of control and recognition-something she had deeply longed for since childhood.

14

Cocaine and biodescodification.

Biodescodification is an alternative therapeutic approach that suggests diseases and addictive behaviors, such as cocaine addiction, originate from unresolved emotional conflicts and subconscious patterns that affect the body and mind.

From this perspective, cocaine use is not only considered a physical or psychological dependency but also a manifestation of internal conflicts that the individual has not processed in a healthy way.

Although biodescodification lacks widely accepted scientific validation and does not replace traditional medical and psychological treatments, some people find its techniques useful as a complement to a comprehensive recovery approach.

In the context of cocaine addiction, biodescodification suggests that drug use may be linked to a need to escape an emotionally painful reality, seek a false sense of power or euphoria, or fill a void related to a lack of recognition or love.

For example, a person who grew up in a family environment where they constantly felt judged or inadequate might turn to cocaine to experience a temporary sense of confidence and well-being, momentarily compensating for those emotional wounds.

From the biodescodification perspective, these behaviors are interpreted as unconscious attempts to heal emotional wounds, albeit in a dysfunctional way.

For example, a therapist might explain how cravings decrease over time and provide specific strategies for managing difficult moments.

Seeking professional help not only addresses the addiction itself but also promotes personal growth, improves relationships, and fosters a more balanced and fulfilling life.

Although the process can be challenging, the tools, support, and strategies provided by professional treatment make recovery possible and sustainable.

By committing to this path, individuals can overcome cocaine dependency and build a future rooted in health, stability, and purpose.

Comprehensive treatment programs, such as outpatient or residential rehabilitation programs, are another effective option for those facing severe cocaine addiction.

These programs combine multiple approaches, including psychotherapy, counseling, addiction education, and wellness activities, in a structured environment.

For example, someone entering a residential program might participate in daily group and individual therapy sessions, life skills workshops, and physical activities designed to enhance overall well-being.

This holistic approach not only addresses the addiction but also helps rebuild a balanced and meaningful life.

Family therapy can also be beneficial, as addiction often impacts the entire family unit.

This type of therapy allows family members to express their emotions, learn how to support recovery, and address dysfunctional dynamics that may contribute to substance use.

For instance, a family that previously avoided discussing the problem might learn to communicate openly and constructively, strengthening the recovering individual's support system.

In addition to therapy and medical treatments, education about addiction is an essential component of professional help.

Understanding how cocaine affects the body and brain helps individuals make informed decisions and be better prepared to face the challenges of recovery.

For example, someone experiencing a strong craving to use could learn in ACT to acknowledge the urge without acting on it, focusing on their personal values, such as health or family, to make decisions more aligned with their goals.

Individual counseling is another form of professional support that can complement psychotherapy.

Addiction counselors provide a safe space to explore the emotional, social, and situational factors contributing to cocaine use.

For instance, a counselor might work with someone to identify family dynamics or toxic relationships that foster drug use and help establish healthy boundaries or develop communication skills.

Additionally, counselors can offer practical guidance for managing everyday situations that pose risks, such as social events where drugs may be present.

Medical treatment also plays an important role in the recovery process.

Although there are no medications specifically approved solely for treating cocaine addiction, some drugs can be helpful in managing withdrawal symptoms and related conditions such as depression, anxiety, or sleep disorders.

For example, antidepressants may help stabilize mood, while certain dopamine antagonists are being studied as promising options to reduce cravings.

Working with a physician specializing in addiction ensures that any pharmacological interventions are safe and tailored to the individual's specific needs.

13

**Seeking professional help:
Psychotherapy, counseling, and treatments.**

Cocaine profoundly affects the brain, altering dopamine levels and creating both physical and psychological dependence that requires specialized interventions.

Professional help includes psychotherapy, counseling, and medical treatments that not only assist in managing withdrawal symptoms but also address the underlying causes of use, thought patterns, and strategies for preventing relapse.

Psychotherapy, particularly cognitive-behavioral therapy (CBT), is a widely used and effective tool for treating cocaine addiction. It focuses on identifying and modifying the thought and behavior patterns that lead to drug use.

For example, someone might discover they turn to cocaine to cope with work-related stress.

In therapy, they would learn to replace this behavior with healthier strategies, such as relaxation techniques, exercise, or time management.

CBT also helps develop skills to handle triggers and manage cravings, providing a practical framework for maintaining sobriety.

Another helpful psychotherapy modality is acceptance and commitment therapy (ACT), which focuses on teaching individuals to accept their difficult thoughts and emotions without letting them dictate their behavior.

Finding and joining a support group is an act of courage and commitment to well-being, demonstrating that while the fight against addiction is challenging, it does not have to be faced alone.

The connection with others who share the same goal can transform the recovery process and open the door to a fuller and more meaningful life.

Groups like SMART Recovery offer a science-based approach, using cognitive-behavioral therapy techniques to help individuals identify and change thought and behavior patterns related to addiction.

Another key benefit of support groups is the regular structure they provide.

Meetings are often held weekly or even daily, helping to create a positive habit and routine.

For someone used to cocaine use dominating their time and energy, attending meetings can offer a healthy and constructive alternative.

For example, someone who used to use cocaine on weekends could replace that time with attending meetings and participating in group-related activities.

In the context of recovery, support groups also help individuals rebuild their self-esteem.

Sharing achievements, no matter how small, and receiving recognition from other members can boost self-confidence.

For instance, a member who managed to avoid a major trigger for a week might share their experience at a meeting and receive words of encouragement and congratulations from others.

While participating in support groups does not guarantee instant recovery, it forms a solid foundation for long-term change.

These spaces not only help address immediate challenges but also teach life skills, foster meaningful relationships, and provide a support network that can last for many years.

For example, someone who has relapsed multiple times might feel motivated after hearing how another person overcame numerous relapses and managed to stay sober.

Support groups also provide an environment of mutual accountability.

Participants share their progress and struggles, which fosters a commitment to sobriety.

Many find it helpful to have a sponsor, a more experienced member of the program who can offer guidance and personal support.

For instance, a new member facing a strong urge to use might contact their sponsor for practical advice or simply to talk, which can be enough to get through a critical moment.

Support groups are also an excellent source of practical tools and strategies for managing recovery challenges.

During meetings, participants share techniques they have found helpful for overcoming cravings, managing stress, or rebuilding relationships.

For example, someone might learn a breathing technique or a distraction strategy that another member found effective during moments of temptation.

In addition to NA, there are other support groups that may be helpful depending on individual needs and preferences.

Some focus on specific populations, such as women, youth, or LGBTQ+ individuals, providing an even more personalized environment.

12

**Finding support groups
(such as Narcotics Anonymous).**

Support groups provide a safe and confidential space where individuals can share their experiences, challenges, and achievements with others who deeply understand what it means to struggle with addiction.

The community and mutual support offered by these groups can be an invaluable source of motivation and strength during the recovery process.

Narcotics Anonymous (NA) is a nonprofit organization that follows the 12-step model originally designed for Alcoholics Anonymous.

This program is based on principles such as honesty, humility, and acceptance and promotes personal growth through self-reflection and collective support.

In NA, there are no financial requirements or specific affiliations, and the only condition for participation is the desire to stop using drugs.

This inclusive approach makes it accessible to people from all backgrounds and levels of drug use.

One of the main advantages of joining a support group like NA is the opportunity to connect with others who have faced similar challenges.

Addiction often generates feelings of isolation and shame, and hearing the stories of others who have gone through similar experiences can provide a sense of belonging and understanding.

For example, a mother attending a support group could learn to set healthy boundaries while maintaining a compassionate attitude toward her recovering child.

Open and regular communication is key to maintaining family and social support.

This involves discussing progress, struggles, and goals without fear of judgment.

It is also important to express gratitude and acknowledge the support received, reinforcing mutual commitment.

For instance, after a challenging week, someone might say to a friend: "Thank you for being there when I had that craving. Your support made a difference."

It is also essential to prepare family and friends for possible relapses.

While relapses are part of the recovery process, they can cause frustration or distrust among loved ones.

Explaining that a relapse is not a failure but an opportunity to learn and adjust the recovery plan helps maintain a constructive perspective.

For example, if someone relapses, they might talk with a close friend to analyze what happened and work together on strategies to avoid similar situations in the future.

Involving family and friends not only provides emotional support but also creates a safer and more motivating environment for recovery.

These relationships can offer a sense of purpose and belonging that counteracts the impulses to turn to cocaine.

Providing clear, evidence-based information about addiction as a medical condition can help reduce judgment and foster empathy.

For example, sharing resources like articles, educational videos, or even inviting a family member to a session with a specialized therapist can be helpful.

A practical way to involve loved ones is to include them in the recovery plan.

This might involve asking them to participate in activities that reinforce sobriety, such as engaging in sports together, attending family gatherings without alcohol or drugs, or accompanying the person to medical or therapy appointments.

For example, a sibling or close friend could commit to daily walks or runs with the recovering individual, providing a healthy activity and an opportunity to strengthen their bond.

Setting clear expectations and boundaries is essential to ensure that the involvement of family and friends is constructive.

This includes communicating how they can help and what types of behaviors or comments are most supportive.

For instance, someone might ask them to avoid bringing up past drug use in a reproachful tone and instead focus on offering encouragement and recognition for current achievements, no matter how small.

Support groups for families, such as Al-Anon or Nar-Anon, can be valuable resources to help loved ones understand how to provide effective support without falling into harmful dynamics, such as enabling drug use.

11

How to involve family and friends in the process.

Involving family and friends is essential for building a strong support network that facilitates recovery.

The role of close loved ones can be pivotal at every stage, from recognizing the problem to maintaining long-term sobriety.

Addiction often creates tension in relationships, leading to distrust, conflict, and distance.

However, with open communication, mutual commitment, and a focus on healing, these relationships can become an invaluable source of strength and motivation.

The first step to involving family and friends is being honest about the problem.

Acknowledging the addiction and sharing the desire to change can be difficult, but this openness is crucial for establishing a foundation of trust.

Explaining what addiction entails, how it affects the mind and body, and the reasons for seeking help can help loved ones understand the seriousness of the situation.

For example, someone might say: "I know my cocaine use has caused harm, and I want you to know that I'm working to change. I need your support on this journey."

It is also important to educate family and friends about addiction, as many people have misconceptions about drug use, viewing it as a matter of weak willpower or character.

THE POWER OF SUPPORT

A strong support system is also invaluable for managing cravings, as talking to a friend, family member, or therapist can provide immediate relief and prevent the urge from intensifying.

Support groups like Narcotics Anonymous offer a safe environment where individuals can share their experiences and learn from others.

For example, someone experiencing a strong desire to use could attend a meeting to hear stories of overcoming addiction, reinforcing their motivation to stay sober.

Physical exercise is another practical tool for overcoming cravings.

Activities such as running, swimming, or playing sports not only distract the mind but also release endorphins, neurotransmitters associated with pleasure and happiness.

For instance, someone facing a craving might decide to go for a run, which not only alleviates the urge but also improves mood and physical health.

Balanced nutrition and proper hydration also play an important role in managing cravings.

A nutritious diet stabilizes blood sugar levels, which can reduce irritability and anxiety—factors that often trigger cravings.

For example, someone might opt for a healthy snack, such as fruit or nuts, when they feel the urge to use.

It is important to remember that cravings are temporary and decrease in intensity over time, especially when a person is committed to their recovery process.

Another powerful tool is the use of deep breathing and relaxation techniques, as cravings are often accompanied by anxiety or physical tension.

Learning to control breathing can help calm both the mind and body.

A simple technique is the 4-7-8 breathing method: inhale deeply for four seconds, hold the breath for seven seconds, and exhale slowly for eight seconds.

Repeating this cycle several times can reduce the intensity of the craving and restore a sense of control.

The "stop, think, act" method is another effective technique.

When a craving arises, it's important to pause and reflect before taking any action.

Thinking about the consequences of using—such as the negative effects on health, relationships, or the progress made in recovery—can help curb the urge.

This approach provides time to choose a healthier response, such as calling a member of the support system or engaging in a stress-relieving activity.

Identifying and challenging the automatic thoughts that accompany cravings is also essential.

Cravings are often accompanied by irrational ideas, such as "Just once won't hurt" or "I need it to feel better."

Challenging these beliefs and replacing them with realistic thoughts can strengthen resistance.

For example, someone might remind themselves that using once could trigger a full relapse or that there are healthier ways to feel good, such as exercising or spending time with friends.

10

Overcoming cravings:
Practical tools and techniques.

Cravings are intense and often overwhelming urges that arise due to the chemical changes the drug causes in the brain, particularly in systems related to pleasure and reward.

While they are a normal part of the recovery process, cravings can be difficult to manage without practical tools and techniques.

Learning to overcome these urges is essential to prevent relapses and progress toward a cocaine-free life.

One of the most effective tools for managing cravings is distraction.

Shifting the mind's focus to a different activity can reduce the intensity of the urge.

For example, someone experiencing a craving might take a walk, listen to music, watch a movie, or call a friend.

The key is to engage in something that requires concentration and diverts attention from the desire to use.

Another useful technique is substitution, which involves replacing the behavior of using cocaine with a healthy activity.

For instance, if someone used cocaine to cope with stress, they might practice yoga or meditation to achieve a similar sense of calm and relaxation.

Another strategy is to use the "stop, think, act" method, which involves pausing to reflect on the consequences of using before taking any action.

This allows time and perspective to make a healthier decision.

Building a strong support system is also essential for managing triggers and avoiding risky situations.

Having trustworthy people, such as friends, family, or members of a support group, can provide invaluable emotional backing.

Avoiding risky situations may also involve making significant lifestyle changes.

This could include moving to a new location, changing jobs, or even ending relationships that encourage drug use.

Although these changes can be challenging, they are necessary to protect the recovery process.

For example, someone who lived in an environment where cocaine was easily accessible might decide to move to a different community to start fresh in a healthier setting.

Managing triggers and avoiding risky situations is an ongoing process that requires self-awareness, preparation, and practice.

It will not always be possible to avoid all triggers, but with the right strategies, individuals can develop the strength needed to face them without relapsing.

Every effort to manage a trigger or avoid a risky situation is a step forward toward a healthier, more stable life free from cocaine dependence.

For example, if someone feels anxious, instead of turning to cocaine, they could practice relaxation techniques such as deep breathing, meditation, or yoga.

Additionally, physical activities like running or swimming can release endorphins, naturally improving mood.

An effective approach to managing triggers is creating a personalized relapse prevention plan.

This plan should include a list of identified triggers and specific strategies to address them.

For instance, if contact with former drug-using peers is a trigger, the plan might include limiting interactions with those individuals and building new friendships in healthy environments.

If work-related stress is a factor, techniques such as time management, task delegation, or setting clear boundaries at work can be implemented.

It is important to note that avoiding risky situations is not always sufficient, as some triggers may be unavoidable.

In such cases, it is essential to develop skills to handle them effectively.

A useful technique is distraction, which involves redirecting attention to productive or enjoyable activities when a craving arises.

For example, someone who feels the urge to use cocaine could take a walk, call a trusted friend, listen to music, or engage in a hobby such as painting or cooking.

9

Managing triggers and avoiding risky situations.

Triggers can be external, such as places, people, or events associated with drug use, or internal, such as emotions, thoughts, or physical sensations.

Identifying and learning to manage them effectively is crucial for maintaining sobriety and preventing relapses.

External triggers are often related to the social or physical environment where cocaine was used.

For example, bars, parties, or gatherings with others who use drugs can be powerful reminders of past use.

Avoiding these places or situations is an effective strategy to reduce temptation.

A practical example might be someone who used to consume cocaine during social events and decides to temporarily limit their attendance at parties or seek healthier environments, such as gatherings with friends who do not use drugs or outdoor activities.

Internal triggers, on the other hand, are related to the person's emotional or mental state.

Many people turn to cocaine to cope with difficult emotions such as stress, sadness, loneliness, or even boredom.

Learning to manage these emotions without resorting to drugs is essential for long-term success.

The action plan should be reviewed and adjusted regularly to ensure it remains relevant and effective.

This involves evaluating progress, celebrating achievements, identifying areas for improvement, and being willing to make changes when necessary.

For example, if a strategy for managing stress does not work, an alternative could be explored, such as incorporating artistic activities or relaxation therapies.

Creating an action plan to quit cocaine is not only a practical step but also an act of empowerment.

It helps turn the intention to change into concrete actions and provides a clear path toward a healthier and more fulfilling life.

For example, someone experiencing a strong craving might call a close friend who understands their struggle and can offer words of encouragement or companionship.

Groups like Narcotics Anonymous also provide a safe environment to share experiences and receive emotional support.

The action plan should include measures to manage cravings and prevent relapses. Cravings are a natural part of the recovery process, but they can be overcome with effective strategies.

For example, someone experiencing a craving could use distraction techniques such as taking a walk, listening to music, or talking with a friend.

If a relapse occurs, the plan should include steps to address it constructively, such as analyzing its cause, seeking professional help, and adjusting the plan as necessary.

For instance, if a relapse occurred after attending a party, the plan might include avoiding similar social situations until sobriety is more firmly established.

A practical example is Paul, who decided to quit cocaine after realizing it was affecting his health and family relationships.

He worked with a therapist to create a plan that included attending weekly therapy sessions, identifying and avoiding places associated with drug use, and establishing a daily routine that involved morning runs, exploring new activities like learning to cook, and spending time with his family.

He also joined a support group where he found inspiration in the stories of others who had overcome addiction.

Once triggers are identified, it is important to develop strategies to avoid or manage them in a healthy way.

For example, if work stress is a trigger, the person could include stress-reducing activities in their plan, such as practicing yoga, meditation, or breathing techniques.

If certain friendships encourage drug use, the plan might include limiting contact with those individuals and seeking new social circles that support a healthy lifestyle.

Setting clear and realistic goals is also essential in the action plan.

These goals should be specific, measurable, and achievable, providing a sense of progress and accomplishment.

For instance, an immediate goal could be attending a Narcotics Anonymous meeting that week, while a long-term goal might be staying sober for six months and resuming a forgotten hobby, such as playing a musical instrument or participating in a sport.

An action plan should also include a detailed schedule to keep time productively occupied and avoid boredom, which can often trigger drug use.

This could involve activities such as exercising, learning something new, volunteering, or spending time with family.

For example, someone might plan daily gym sessions in the morning, attend cooking classes in the afternoon, and dedicate evenings to reading or engaging in a creative hobby.

A support system is another essential pillar of the plan.

Surrounding oneself with understanding and encouraging people can make a significant difference in the recovery process, including family, friends, therapists, and members of support groups.

8

Creating an action plan to quit cocaine.

An effective plan must address the physical, emotional, social, and practical needs of the individual, ensuring resources and strategies are available to face any challenges that may arise.

This process begins with acknowledging the problem and making a personal commitment to quit the drug, which involves being willing to make difficult decisions and prioritize long-term well-being over immediate gratification.

The first component of an action plan is seeking professional support.

Cocaine addiction is a complex condition that requires the intervention of addiction specialists, such as doctors, psychologists, and counselors.

These professionals can conduct a comprehensive assessment of the level of dependency and design a personalized treatment program.

For instance, someone experiencing severe withdrawal symptoms, such as extreme anxiety or depression, might benefit from supervised detoxification in a clinical setting and medications to stabilize their emotional state.

Another essential aspect of the plan is identifying the triggers that lead to drug use.

These could be situations, emotions, or people that provoke the desire to use cocaine.

HOW TO QUIT COCAINE:
STRATEGIES AND
APPROACHES

This approach strengthens resilience and reduces the risk of abandoning the process entirely.

Another key aspect of preparation is creating a support system, which includes identifying trusted individuals, such as friends, family, or members of support groups, who can offer encouragement and understanding during difficult times.

For instance, someone experiencing a craving might call a friend or attend a Narcotics Anonymous meeting instead of using.

Surrounding oneself with people who support the decision to quit cocaine also helps reinforce motivation and avoid environments that promote drug use.

Mental and emotional preparation also involves planning how to manage time and daily activities.

Cocaine often takes a central role in a person's life, so quitting can create a void.

Filling that space with positive activities—such as playing sports, learning a new skill, resuming hobbies, or doing volunteer work—not only distracts from drug use but also contributes to overall well-being.

For example, someone who used to spend their nights using cocaine might start attending art classes or joining a sports team, which not only provides a healthier routine but also helps build a new identity free from the drug.

This type of preparation also includes learning to tolerate uncomfortable emotions without resorting to the drug.

This can be achieved by working with a therapist who helps develop emotional skills, such as identifying and naming feelings and learning to manage them in a healthy way.

It is important to set clear and achievable goals as part of the mental preparation for change.

Visualizing what one wants to achieve by quitting cocaine - whether it's regaining health, rebuilding relationships, advancing professionally, or simply feeling free from dependency- can be a powerful source of motivation.

For example, a person who has lost contact with their family due to drug use might visualize reconnecting with loved ones, sharing meaningful moments, and restoring trust.

Having a clear vision of the future helps maintain focus on the long-term benefits of sobriety.

Emotional preparation also requires accepting that recovery is a process, not a single event.

There will be difficult days, intense cravings, and possibly relapses.

However, being emotionally prepared means understanding that these obstacles are not failures but part of the learning process.

For example, if someone relapses after a period of abstinence, they can analyze what happened, identify the triggers, and develop a plan to handle similar situations in the future.

7

Preparing mentally and emotionally for change.

This is a fundamental step in the recovery process, as it involves confronting not only physical dependence but also the thought patterns and emotions that fuel substance use.

This process requires deep personal commitment, self-awareness, and a willingness to work on the most vulnerable areas of life.

Mental preparation begins with recognizing that addiction is not a personal failure but a complex condition that affects the brain and emotions.

This recognition helps reduce guilt and shame, allowing the individual to focus on change with a more constructive mindset.

A positive and realistic attitude is essential, understanding that the path to recovery is not linear and that there will be challenges, but every small step represents significant progress.

Emotional preparation involves exploring the underlying reasons for cocaine use.

Many people turn to this drug to cope with difficult emotions such as stress, sadness, boredom, or social pressure.

Identifying these emotional triggers is crucial for developing healthier and more effective coping strategies.

For example, someone who uses cocaine to escape anxiety might begin practicing relaxation techniques such as meditation, deep breathing, or yoga.

Visualization also involves planning how to manage challenges without turning to cocaine.

This can include developing skills to handle stress, anxiety, or boredom in healthier and more constructive ways.

For example, a person who used cocaine to cope with long workdays might envision themselves engaging in physical exercise or meditation as a way to release tension.

This process not only strengthens emotional resilience but also helps identify which activities and practices contribute to overall well-being.

The key to visualizing a life without cocaine is focusing on what can be gained by quitting the drug rather than on what is being lost.

This shift in perspective helps create a narrative of hope and empowerment.

Although the path to sobriety may be challenging, each step represents progress toward a fuller and more authentic life.

Visualizing a life without cocaine also involves imagining a healthier social and emotional environment, as addiction often destroys relationships by creating distrust, isolation, and conflict.

Quitting the drug makes it possible to rebuild damaged bonds and establish relationships based on honesty and mutual support.

For example, someone who has become estranged from their family due to cocaine use might envision moments of reconciliation and connection, such as a family dinner free of tension and lies.

This new social perspective might also include creating a support network of people who share similar goals, such as recovery group members or friends who encourage a healthy lifestyle.

Another key aspect of visualizing a life without cocaine is imagining how to regain or discover personal purpose.

Addiction often diverts attention from individual goals and passions, replacing them with a constant pursuit of the drug.

By quitting cocaine, individuals can focus on pursuing objectives that bring satisfaction and a sense of accomplishment.

For instance, someone who left their studies due to cocaine use might envision returning to education, earning a degree, and building a career they are passionate about.

Another example could be a parent striving to reclaim an active role in their children's lives, imagining themselves participating in school activities, sharing quality time, and being a positive role model.

6

Visualizing a life without cocaine.

Visualizing a life without cocaine is an essential step in the recovery process, as it allows individuals to imagine and build a future full of possibilities, free from the limitations and harm caused by this addiction.

This mental exercise not only helps establish clear goals but also strengthens the motivation to stay on the path to sobriety.

Cocaine often creates a dependence that clouds the ability to dream of a different life, but visualization can serve as a guiding light toward positive and meaningful change.

A life without cocaine means regaining physical and mental health.

Without the use of this substance, the body begins to heal from the damage caused, such as cardiovascular harm, respiratory difficulties, nervous system deterioration, and sleep problems.

For instance, someone who has experienced palpitations and high blood pressure due to cocaine use may begin to notice how their heart stabilizes and their energy returns to healthier levels after quitting.

It also means being free from the extreme emotional highs and lows caused by the drug, such as momentary euphoria followed by anxiety, paranoia, or depression.

Instead of relying on a substance to feel pleasure or relief, individuals can rediscover the ability to enjoy simple and meaningful activities, such as spending time with loved ones, playing sports, or pursuing a hobby.

support, people can overcome this addiction and rebuild their lives.

It is essential to remember that no one is alone in this process and that resources are available for every stage of the journey toward recovery.

Saying "enough" is not the end but the beginning of a new opportunity to live fully and find peace within oneself.

to make significant changes in their lives.

This might include avoiding certain friendships, places, or activities that encourage cocaine use.

For example, someone who used to consume cocaine at parties might decide to distance themselves from that social environment.

Instead, they could focus on healthier activities, such as sports or learning a new skill.

It can also mean addressing the underlying issues that led to drug use in the first place, such as stress, low self-esteem, or emotional pain.

A therapist can help explore these areas and provide tools to manage them in a healthy way.

It is important to acknowledge that saying "enough" does not mean the journey will be easy or linear.

Relapses are a common part of the recovery process, but they should not be seen as failures.

Each relapse offers an opportunity to learn about triggers and strengthen the commitment to sobriety.

For instance, if someone relapses after facing intense stress, they can work with a therapist to develop more effective coping strategies for the future.

Deciding to quit cocaine is an act of self-love and a commitment to a better future.

Although it may seem overwhelming at first, with the right

Acknowledging the issue does not always happen spontaneously.

Some people require a "wake-up call" through interventions by family or friends who express concern about their drug use.

These moments can be challenging but also provide important opportunities for reflection.

For instance, someone might realize their relationship with a loved one is at risk due to the lies associated with their drug use, prompting them to consider seeking help.

Another example could be a person who, after experiencing alarming physical symptoms such as chest pains or severe insomnia, begins to question whether the drug is worth the risk.

The process of saying "enough" involves not only recognizing the problem but also accepting that help is necessary.

This requires humility and courage, as many people feel shame or fear in admitting their addiction.

However, it is crucial to remember that addiction is a medical condition, not a moral failing.

Seeking professional help—such as from doctors, addiction specialists, or support groups—is an act of strength, not weakness.

For example, someone who joins a group like Narcotics Anonymous may find comfort and motivation by listening to the stories of others who have overcome similar challenges.

For many people, the moment to say "enough" also involves identifying the triggers that lead to drug use and being willing

5

Recognizing the problem
and the moment to say "Enough".

This moment can be different for each person and often comes after facing significant consequences related to drug use.

Acknowledging that there is a problem involves confronting the reality of how cocaine has impacted not only personal life but also physical health, mental well-being, relationships, and responsibilities.

Many people struggling with this addiction go through a phase of denial, where they try to justify their use as controlled or minimize its impact on their lives.

However, recognizing the harm is the first step toward change and finding a solution.

The moment to say "enough" often arises when the consequences of use become too obvious to ignore.

This might include physical deterioration, such as respiratory problems, nasal septum damage, or frequent panic attacks.

It could also manifest emotionally, with constant anxiety, paranoia, or deep depression when the drug's effects wear off.

Socially, drug use can lead to isolation, as personal and family relationships are strained by erratic behavior, lies, or broken promises.

In many cases, legal or work-related consequences, such as losing a job or facing legal troubles, also serve as catalysts for recognizing the severity of the problem.

THE DECISION TO CHANGE

For example, a person who associates cocaine with success may end up losing their job, damaging personal relationships, and facing legal problems due to their addiction.

There is also a common misconception that pure cocaine is less harmful than adulterated cocaine.

While it is true that adulterants increase the risks associated with use, cocaine in any form is dangerous.

It directly impacts the cardiovascular and nervous systems, and its purity does not reduce the risk of addiction, overdose, or severe side effects.

An example of this is someone who believes the drug they use is of high quality but still experiences panic attacks, chronic insomnia, and irreversible heart damage.

Additionally, occasional use can quickly turn into a habit, as the addictive nature of the drug causes users to develop tolerance, requiring higher doses to achieve the same effect.

A third myth is that cocaine enhances physical or mental performance.

Some people believe the drug helps them work longer hours, concentrate better, or perform better in sports.

In reality, while cocaine may temporarily provide a sense of energy and confidence, its long-term effects are devastating.

Physically, prolonged use can lead to heart, respiratory, and neurological problems.

Mentally, it can cause anxiety, paranoia, and a decline in cognitive abilities.

For example, a college student using cocaine to study for extended hours might notice an initial improvement in performance, but over time they will experience memory problems, difficulty concentrating, and severe exhaustion that negatively affects their studies.

A particularly dangerous myth is that cocaine is safe because some consider it a "luxury" or "glamorous" drug.

This perception stems from its association with certain social and cultural circles but completely disregards the harm it causes.

Cocaine does not discriminate; it affects all users, regardless of their economic or social status.

The physical, mental, and social consequences of its use are equally devastating.

4

Myths and realities about cocaine.

Cocaine is one of the most well-known and controversial drugs, surrounded by numerous myths that often distort the perception of its effects and risks.

Understanding the reality behind these myths is crucial for those seeking to quit cocaine, as these misconceptions can influence the decision to use it or the reluctance to seek help.

One of the most common myths is that cocaine does not cause physical addiction because it does not produce the obvious withdrawal symptoms seen with opioids or alcohol.

The reality is that while physical symptoms may be subtler, cocaine is highly addictive due to its impact on the central nervous system, creating intense psychological dependence.

People who use it experience a compulsive desire to replicate the feeling of euphoria, and the absence of the drug can lead to extreme fatigue, depression, irritability, and strong cravings, perpetuating the cycle of use.

Another widespread myth is that occasional cocaine use is not dangerous.

Many people believe they can control their use, limiting it to recreational settings such as parties or social gatherings.

However, cocaine is unpredictable and can cause severe adverse effects even in occasional users.

For example, its use can trigger a sudden increase in blood pressure or an irregular heartbeat, which could lead to a heart attack or stroke, even in young and healthy individuals.

Additionally, depending on how it is consumed, other specific physical symptoms may appear: users who inhale cocaine may experience frequent nosebleeds or damage to the nasal septum, while those who smoke or inject it may develop respiratory problems or infections at injection sites.

From a psychological and emotional perspective, cocaine addiction manifests in extreme mood swings.

During use, a person may appear excessively confident, sociable, or hyperactive.

However, these episodes are often followed by periods of irritability, paranoia, and extreme anxiety.

In severe cases, prolonged use can trigger episodes of psychosis, including hallucinations and delusions, causing the individual to lose touch with reality.

The obsession with obtaining and using cocaine can also lead to impulsive or risky behaviors, such as spending large amounts of money, neglecting work or family responsibilities, or even engaging in illegal activities.

Changes in social behavior are another clear sign of addiction.

The person may begin avoiding family and friends who do not use drugs, seek out companions who facilitate access to cocaine, or isolate themselves entirely.

It is also common for individuals with addiction to lie or be secretive about their activities, attempting to conceal their drug use.

3

Signs and symptoms of cocaine addiction.

Cocaine addiction is a complex disorder that affects both the body and mind and can be identified through a variety of signs and symptoms.

Cocaine acts directly on the central nervous system, altering brain chemistry and causing behavioral and physical changes that may be noticeable to the affected person and those around them.

Recognizing these signs is essential for identifying the problem and seeking help.

One of the most characteristic signs of cocaine addiction is the repeated and compulsive use of the drug, even when the person is aware of its negative consequences.

Psychological dependence is intense due to the pleasurable effects of the substance, such as momentary euphoria and increased energy, followed by a "crash" that leaves the person anxious, depressed, and with a strong urge to use more.

Common physical symptoms include loss of appetite, weight loss, and insomnia, as cocaine suppresses hunger and disrupts sleep patterns.

Frequent users may also develop tolerance, meaning they require higher doses to achieve the same effects, increasing the risk of overdose.

Other physical signs include dilated pupils, increased heart rate, and elevated blood pressure, which can lead to severe cardiovascular complications.

can be with alcohol or opioids, the psychological symptoms can be very intense and overwhelming.

For this reason, it is crucial to seek professional support during this process.

Addiction specialists can help design a personalized treatment plan that includes supervised detoxification, psychological therapy, and, in some cases, medications to manage specific symptoms.

damage, reducing the brain's ability to respond even to natural positive stimuli.

This perpetuates a state of anhedonia, or the inability to feel pleasure.

In the body, cocaine has devastating effects.

As a powerful stimulant, it increases heart rate, blood pressure, and body temperature, significantly raising the risk of heart attacks, strokes, and arrhythmias.

Frequent use can cause permanent damage to the heart and blood vessels.

For example, someone who regularly consumes cocaine may experience severe hypertension that, if left untreated, can lead to fatal complications.

Moreover, the method of cocaine consumption has distinct physical consequences.

Inhalation can damage nasal membranes and cause perforations in the nasal septum.

Smoking can harm the lungs and lead to severe respiratory diseases.

Injection significantly increases the risk of infections, including hepatitis and HIV, particularly when needles are shared.

Quitting cocaine involves confronting not only the psychological addiction but also the physical effects of withdrawal, which may include extreme fatigue, insomnia or hypersomnia, severe depression, irritability, and intense cravings.

While withdrawal is not typically physically dangerous as it

2

How it affects the brain and body.

Cocaine is an extremely addictive drug that has a profound impact on the brain and body, causing effects ranging from intense pleasure to severe physical and psychological harm.

This substance acts as a stimulant to the central nervous system by blocking the reuptake of dopamine in nerve cells.

Dopamine is a neurotransmitter that plays a key role in the sensation of reward and pleasure.

When cocaine is consumed, dopamine levels in the brain increase dramatically, producing an intense but short-lived euphoria.

However, this rapid and abnormal release depletes the brain's natural dopamine reserves, leaving the user feeling depressed, irritable, and anxious once the drug's effects wear off.

This cycle of euphoria and depression drives the compulsive urge to use the drug again, forming the foundation of psychological addiction.

In the brain, prolonged cocaine use can alter the structure and function of regions responsible for decision-making, impulse control, and emotional regulation.

This can lead to impulsive behaviors, difficulty experiencing pleasure without the drug, and problems with memory and concentration.

In the long term, chronic use of cocaine can cause neuronal

Additionally, the social and economic consequences can be devastating, impacting employment, personal relationships, and overall quality of life.

1

What is cocaine?

Cocaine is a highly powerful psychoactive substance that acts as a stimulant to the central nervous system.

It is derived from the leaves of the coca plant, native to South America, and typically appears as a white, crystalline powder.

Its primary mechanism of action involves blocking the reuptake of dopamine in the brain, leading to an abnormal accumulation of this chemical.

Dopamine is associated with feelings of pleasure and reward, so this buildup produces intense but short-lived euphoria.

Cocaine can be consumed in various ways: inhaled through the nostrils, smoked as "crack" (a solid form of the drug), or injected in liquid form.

These methods produce almost immediate effects but also significantly increase the risks of addiction and physical harm.

Cocaine has a high addictive potential because it directly affects the brain's reward systems, causing users to develop both physical and psychological dependence.

In the long term, its use can lead to a range of serious problems, including mood disorders and damage to nasal tissues (in the case of inhalation).

It can also cause cardiovascular issues such as heart attacks and cognitive impairment.

UNDERSTANDING
COCAINE ADDICTION

Important notice.

This book is designed as a tool for support and inspiration for those who wish to quit cocaine and build a healthier, more meaningful life.

However, it is important to note that each person faces their own unique journey and challenges in the recovery process.

This content does not replace the advice, diagnosis, or treatment of a healthcare professional.

If you are struggling with cocaine addiction, it is essential to seek professional help.

Doctors, therapists, support groups, and specialized recovery programs can provide you with the guidance and support you need.

It is important to remember that quitting cocaine can involve both emotional and physical challenges.

Some individuals may experience withdrawal symptoms requiring medical attention, such as extreme fatigue, depression, irritability, or intense cravings.

Your health and safety should always be the top priority.

This book is intended to be a motivational guide and a source of hope, but the most courageous and significant step is recognizing the need for help and turning to the appropriate resources.

You are not alone in this process. There are tools, people, and communities ready to support you at every stage of this journey.

Change is possible, and it is worth every effort because your well-being and happiness deserve it!

Recovering physical and mental health

15. Nutrition and exercise for recovery

16. Improving sleep and managing stress without drugs

Overcoming obstacles

17. How to handle a relapse

18. Facing guilt and shame

19. Resisting social pressure

Rebuilding your life

20. Reestablishing personal and family relationships

21. Regaining self-confidence

22. Rediscovering your passions and goals

Stories of transformation

23. Robert Downey Jr.

24. Demi Lovato

25. Eminem

26. Jamie Lee Curtis

27. Elton John

28. Eric Clapton

29. Angelina Jolie

30. Samuel L. Jackson